The Hidden History of Bletch

# The Hidden History of Bletchley Park

## A Social and Organisational History, 1939–1945

Christopher Smith
*Aberystwyth University, UK*

palgrave
macmillan

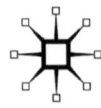

© Christopher Smith 2015

All rights reserved. No reproduction, copy or transmission of this publication may be made without written permission.

No portion of this publication may be reproduced, copied or transmitted save with written permission or in accordance with the provisions of the Copyright, Designs and Patents Act 1988, or under the terms of any licence permitting limited copying issued by the Copyright Licensing Agency, Saffron House, 6–10 Kirby Street, London EC1N 8TS.

Any person who does any unauthorised act in relation to this publication may be liable to criminal prosecution and civil claims for damages.

The author has asserted his right to be identified as the author of this work in accordance with the Copyright, Designs and Patents Act 1988.

First published 2015 by
PALGRAVE MACMILLAN

Palgrave Macmillan in the UK is an imprint of Macmillan Publishers Limited, registered in England, company number 785998, of Houndmills, Basingstoke, Hampshire RG21 6XS.

Palgrave Macmillan in the US is a division of St Martin's Press LLC, 175 Fifth Avenue, New York, NY 10010.

Palgrave Macmillan is the global academic imprint of the above companies and has companies and representatives throughout the world.

Palgrave® and Macmillan® are registered trademarks in the United States, the United Kingdom, Europe and other countries.

ISBN 978-1-349-69489-1    ISBN 978-1-137-48493-2 (eBook)
DOI 10.1057/9781137484932

This book is printed on paper suitable for recycling and made from fully managed and sustained forest sources. Logging, pulping and manufacturing processes are expected to conform to the environmental regulations of the country of origin.

A catalogue record for this book is available from the British Library.

Library of Congress Cataloging-in-Publication Data

Smith, Christopher, 1986–
   The hidden history of Bletchley Park : a social and organisational history, 1939–1945 / Christopher Smith, Aberystwyth University, UK.
      pages cm

   1. Great Britain. Government Communications Headquarters – History. 2. World War, 1939–1945 – Cryptography. 3. World War, 1939–1945 – Secret service – Great Britain. 4. World War, 1939–1945 – Electronic intelligence – Great Britain. 5. World War, 1939–1945 – England – Bletchley (Buckinghamshire) 6. World War, 1939–1945 – Women – Great Britain. 7. Intelligence service – Social aspects – Great Britain – History – 20th century. 8. Great Britain. Government Communications Headquarters – Personnel management. 9. Corporate culture – England – Bletchley (Buckinghamshire) – History – 20th century. 10. Bletchley (Buckinghamshire, England) – Social conditions – 20th century. I. Title.

D810.C88C653 2015
940.54'8641—dc23                                                2015015176

# Contents

| | |
|---|---|
| *Acknowledgements* | vi |
| Introduction | 1 |
| 1  The Organisation of the Government Code and Cypher School | 15 |
| 2  Recruitment at GC&CS: 1919–1945 | 40 |
| 3  On-Duty Life at the Government Code and Cypher School | 70 |
| 4  The Administration of Off-Duty Life and Staff Welfare | 99 |
| 5  Off-Duty Life: Staff Experience | 118 |
| 6  Bletchley Park and Its Impact on the Local Community | 140 |
| Conclusion | 158 |
| *Appendices* | 174 |
| *Glossary* | 188 |
| *Notes* | 191 |
| *Bibliography* | 220 |
| *Index* | 231 |

# Acknowledgements

Over the course of writing this book I have incurred a great many debts. First and foremost, I owe a huge debt of gratitude to Dr Siân Nicholas who read through several drafts of this work – without her extraordinary efforts, endless patience, meticulous attention to detail and insightful comments this book could not have been written. I would also like to take the opportunity to thank Professor Iwan Morus and Professor Christopher Grey, both of whom also commented extensively on this work. I am also extremely grateful to Jimmy Thirsk, Professor Joan Thirsk, Barbara Moor, Ruth Bourne, Alice Wolynskj, Gwendoline Page and Ron Hellier, who all generously invited me into their homes and shared their wartime memories. I have also received invaluable help from the staff at the Imperial War Museum Archive, the National Archives, The Centre for Buckinghamshire Studies in Aylesbury, the Milton Keynes Library, and all my friends and former colleagues at the Bletchley Park Trust.

I would also like to thank Richard Lewis of the Bletchley Park Trust Archive for his help. I also owe thanks to the Bletchley Park Trust, the Milton Keynes Council, and the Centre for Buckinghamshire Studies for allowing liberal quotation from their records and archives. M&M Baldwin also granted kind permission to reproduce extracts from their books, both of which remain in print: *Bletchley Park: An Inmate's Story* by James Thirsk and *My Road to Bletchley Park* by Doreen Luke. Similarly, I also owe thanks to Peter Lewis-Smith for allowing me to quote a large extract from his late wife's, Anne Lewis-Smith, book *Off Duty! Bletchley Park Outstation Gayhurst Manor WW2*; Michael Smith for extracts from his book *Station X*; and Christopher Grey for extracts from *Decoding Organisation*.

I have also been helped along the way by the support of all the staff of the Department of History and Welsh History at Aberystwyth University. In particular I would like to thank Dr David Ceri Jones, Dr Peter Lambert and Professor Björn Weiler, as well as the department's administrative staff, whose doors are always open. Similarly, the friendship of the post-graduate community within the department has been a great support. I have also received help from Dr R. Gerald Hughes, Kimberly Cosgrove, Kris Lovell, Yvonne Harries and my mother, Susan Smith, who all read through parts of the book and offered invaluable advice. It is necessary to thank my mother again for all her love and support, not just over the course of this project. I would like to thank all my friends from Aberystwyth and the University of Worcester for putting up with me while this book was being written.

Finally, I would like to thank Dr Corinna Peniston-Bird and Dr Richard Coopey for all their help, feedback and suggestions. Similarly, I owe thanks to staff of Palgrave Macmillan, as well as the publishers' anonymous reader who inspected the proposal for this book and made useful and constructive suggestions. Any errors within this book are all entirely my own and have occurred in spite of all the efforts of the people named above.

# Introduction

Few aspects of the Second World War have captured the imagination of the British public like the story of Bletchley Park. The main wartime station of the Government Code and Cypher School (GC&CS), Bletchley Park was the home of Britain's codebreakers. Over the course of the war, the agency broke vast quantities of Axis messages which had a profound influence on the Allies' prosecution of the war. In order to achieve this, the denizens of Bletchley Park designed entirely new technologies which helped usher in the computer age. Adding still further intrigue to the mix, all this work was conducted with the utmost emphasis on secrecy – indeed, it took until the 1970s for that blanket of secrecy to be lifted. It is little wonder, therefore, that Bletchley Park has taken centre stage in British popular memory of the Second World War. In testament to this insatiable popular interest, at the time of writing this book, Bletchley Park has been the subject of television dramas, a bestselling novel, a radio sitcom, countless television documentaries, and no less than two major movies.[1]

In addition to being of significant popular interest, the agency has, because of its successes in the arenas of both espionage and scientific endeavour, a major place within the history of computer science, military history and intelligence history.[2] GC&CS was tasked with reading the intercepted messages of foreign powers and turning that traffic into a source of useful intelligence. Situated in Bletchley, a small town in north Buckinghamshire, the Bletchley Park estate, a Victorian-era mansion surrounded by a number of smaller buildings and around 60 acres of grounds, expanded over the course of the war into a sprawling complex of prefabricated huts and concrete blocks teeming with the activity of the hundreds, and later thousands, of men and women employed in an industrialised effort to read Axis wireless transmissions. This effort was conducted on a scale hitherto unprecedented in the history of intelligence.

The success of GC&CS's cryptanalysts in reading vast quantities of enciphered Axis radio traffic has alone guaranteed the agency a unique legacy. The influence this intelligence had on the Second World War, and the technologies invented to generate that success, have added immeasurably to that legacy. The official historian of British intelligence in the Second World War, F. H. Hinsley, contends that Bletchley Park's contribution reduced the length of the war by two years.[3] In terms of GC&CS's technological legacy, Bletchley Park was the home of the Colossus machine – a landmark development in the history of computer science. These achievements remained a closely guarded secret until 1974, further adding to the more recent popular interest in the agency's activities.

The impact of signals intelligence (SIGINT), in particular the wartime intelligence which the British codenamed Ultra and comprised material derived from the reading of high-level Axis messages, has been examined at length by historians. However, relatively little scholarly attention has been paid to the day-to-day running of Bletchley Park or the wartime experiences of the vast majority of its staff members. The aim of this book is thus to examine the hidden social history of Bletchley Park during the Second World War. Specifically, I examine the development of GC&CS from its arrival at Bletchley Park in 1939 as a small agency of around 200 individuals with an amateur ethos and collegiate approach to its work, into a mechanised, professionalised and regimented bureaucracy with nearly 9000 staff members at Bletchley Park. This book narrates the story of this transformation.

Secrecy was key to Bletchley Park; so sensitive was its wartime role deemed to be that it remained shrouded by shadow until the 1970s. Those thousands of members of staff who worked for the agency during the war years were all bound to strict secrecy, which coloured both their wartime experiences and then their post-war lives, unable to tell their friends and families of their contribution to the British war effort. The remarkable degree of secrecy which surrounded the agency, and its longevity, places the agency into its own unique category. Where the secrecy surrounding other vast scientific projects of the war, such as development of the atomic bomb which was revealed to the world in the devastation of both Hiroshima and Nagasaki, did not survive the war, Bletchley Park remained largely hidden from public view for nearly three decades. This was in spite of the fact that Bletchley's work was of the utmost importance, providing vital intelligence to Allied commanders and in unprecedented quantities. The utility of a weapon like the atomic bomb was dependent on its ability to shock, awe and strike fear into an enemy; Bletchley's product, which gave Allied commanders key insights into the minds of their opponents, in its peculiar way was just as powerful, but was effective only as long as it remained secret.

To fully appreciate the enormity of this secret, it is necessary to emphasise the scale of GC&CS's wartime operation. By the height of Bletchley's war, in the winter of 1944, the agency employed over 12,000 people. The majority of them, approaching 9000 staff members, were posted to Bletchley Park. However, hundreds more were employed in various offices and small stations, known as 'outstations', in the neighbouring region. The agency formed the epicentre of a vast hub of information gathering and distribution, as wireless transmissions were intercepted across Britain, the Empire, and the front lines of the Second World War. This information was fed to Bletchley Park, processed and subsequently distributed to military commands and government ministries.

Another remarkable feature of GC&CS was that over the course of the Second World War the agency brought together some of the finest minds to facilitate its mission. This was to include a diverse range of individuals: scientists, literary scholars, historians, engineers, international chess players and businessmen. Many of these men and (in some instances) women were recruited directly from the universities, and would go on to play important roles in post-war intellectual, cultural, scientific and political life. For instance, the famous mathematicians Alan Turing and Max Newman became pioneering figures in the world of computer science at Manchester University. The famous poet Vernon Watkins and the novelist Angus Wilson also found employment at Bletchley Park. Meanwhile, some of Britain's most eminent historians of the post-war period served at Bletchley Park. These include, but by no means were limited to, Lord Asa Briggs the official historian of the BBC, and the eighteenth-century historian Sir J. 'Jack' H. Plumb. To the legal profession went Telford Taylor, in the war a wartime US liaison officer to Bletchley Park, who found fame for his role in the Council for the Prosecution at the Nuremberg Trials. Peter Calvocoressi (himself an eminent historian, scholar of international affairs, and memoirist) also played a role at Nuremberg as a member of the British prosecution team. Some of Bletchley's veterans found a political calling. Jean Campbell-Harris (later Baroness Trumpington) among other distinctions became the Mayor of Cambridge before being created a Conservative life peer in the House of Lords. On the other side of the political spectrum, Roy Jenkins went on to become a Labour MP and served in a variety of ministerial posts, including Home Secretary and Chancellor of the Exchequer, under Harold Wilson.

Yet also at Bletchley Park were thousands of others, mainly young women, who provided the logistical and mechanical backbone which supported the cryptanalysts and translators. This side of the Bletchley Park story is often overlooked because of a natural emphasis on the agency's achievements in the arena of cryptanalysis, technology and security. Yet the vast growth of the agency and its ability to adapt to the pressures of total war were of vital importance. Behind, and directly facilitating, the codebreaking efforts and technological developments was the construction of a vast and complex bureaucracy.

The growth of Bletchley Park, which expanded from 200 individuals in September 1939 to nearly 700 by December 1940, over 5000 by the summer of 1942, and over 8000 by June 1944, was extraordinarily rapid.[4] Even the mundane morale-boosting act of providing a hard-pressed employee with a cup of tea became an extraordinary logistical and organisational feat. This was all the more impressive given that the agency had no history of employing staff in such huge numbers, and therefore no institutional memory or infrastructure upon which to draw. The agency's supporting structures had to grow, and adapt, like the cryptanalytic sections which have built its legacy, to make the agency a success. In addition to catering, the agency also had to address the mammoth task of housing and transporting its workers, whose numbers at Bletchley Park rose to well in excess of the total population of the town of Bletchley by 1944. Without these behind-the-scenes logistical and bureaucratic successes the agency would surely have collapsed. Yet, the agency's managers initially had little grasp of how to provide these services, and as we shall see with its cryptanalytic victories, often remained only a step ahead of disaster.

I also consider the impact that the above changes had, not only on the agency, but upon the wartime lives of the staff members employed by GC&CS and the local population of Bletchley. Particular attention is paid to social class and gender in the operational and administrative decision-making processes within the agency. Despite frequent allusions within the literature on GC&CS to the existence of wider social influences, no sustained analysis of these factors has been conducted. The interplay between secrecy and attitudes towards social class and gender had a profound influence on the culture of the agency. Notions of integrity and trust, governed by dominant perceptions of class and gender, influenced agency recruitment policy, the allocation of work, and the distribution of information within GC&CS. Each of these factors had a profound impact on how the agency developed, how it functioned, and how individual members of staff experienced the Second World War.

My central argument is that the changes to Bletchley Park were far from inevitable, and that processes of mechanisation, industrialisation and professionalisation were fiercely contested within the agency. Moreover, those senior figures tasked with directing the progression of the agency were not working to a clearly defined plan – they were caught in the ebb and flow of events beyond their control. The information factory, among the most technologically advanced and effective intelligence agencies in the world by 1945, emerged as a result of cumulative *ad hoc* decisions taken to address specific short-term problems.

This book, therefore, is both a social history of Bletchley Park and GC&CS as well as an organisational and administrative history. Some of the other themes explored in this book focus on the development of bureaucratic apparatus within the agency. This includes efforts to provide drained wartime staff with a restorative cup of tea, to the mechanisms in place to avoid important secrets leaking to the local people of Bletchley. The logistical and administrative structures which allowed Bletchley Park to keep ticking over on a day-to-day basis have rarely been given any thought by historians of the agency.

## The origins of the Government Code and Cypher School

The key development which directly led to the birth of industrialised cryptanalysis was a revolution in communications technology: the invention of radio by the Italian physicist Guglielmo Marconi in 1896. The obvious military benefit of radio was that it allowed commanders to communicate with troops, regardless of their position and without the need for telegraphy cables. However, radio posed a major problem. The medium was inherently insecure; any message sent over the airwaves could just as easily be received by an enemy as the intended recipient. The insecurity of radio, or wireless telegraphy (W/T), proved an important source of intelligence to Britain during the First World War. Numerous intercept and direction finding stations were built across the country to listen into the wireless traffic of the Central Powers. Intercept stations were used to listen in to enemy transmissions and record messages, while direction finding (D/F) stations triangulated the location signals were transmitted from; collectively these stations were known as 'Y stations'. Extending the interception net, mobile stations followed armies behind the battlefields of continental Europe.

During the First World War, Britain had two main bureaus dedicated to cryptanalysis: the War Office ran Military Intelligence 1b (MI1b), and the Admiralty ran Naval Intelligence Division 25, also known as Room 40.[5] By the end of the First World War, Room 40 alone had approximately 100 staff members,[6] while the War Office arrangements were more complex. Individual commands had their own interception and cryptanalysis staff who liaised with MI1b. Meanwhile, MI1b had acquired 85 staff members, comprising 34 officers, 11 civilians and 40 women in supporting roles.[7] The most notable cryptanalytic success story came when Room 40 'broke' the Zimmerman Telegram, which outlined a German proposal suggesting that Mexico invade the US. The message was passed onto the United States and played an important role in bringing the US into the war against the Central Powers.[8]

At the end of the First World War both MI1b and Room 40 were disbanded. In their place a single cryptanalysis department was proposed, drawing staff from both bureaus. The two organisations had rarely interacted with each other, resulting in departmental jealousy.[9] Alastair Denniston, who led Room 40, the Admiralty's codebreaking department, complained that the result of this friction between departments led to inefficiency. After the war, in 1919, a conference was held at the Admiralty to discuss the future of British codebreaking efforts. The Admiralty and the War Office disputed which service should provide the head of a combined services codebreaking effort. The Admiralty gained the upper hand, and Denniston became the head of the new Government Code and Cypher School.[10] Its task was two-fold. First, and overtly, it was charged with ensuring the security of the cipher systems of the British government and to train personnel from the various ministries and commands in cipher security. Its second clandestine purpose was to act as the British government's cryptanalysis bureau – the organisation in which Britain conducted its codebreaking.[11]

Despite the successes of the codebreakers in the First World War, for much of the interwar period GC&CS was essentially a minor institution and enjoyed only limited success. GC&CS had 56 employees, only half of whom were codebreakers.[12] The primary subjects of the new agency's focus were the communications of Britain's former allies, namely those of the French, Japanese, Americans and the Russians (and the latter in particular).[13] During the interwar period British cryptanalytic efforts largely ignored German traffic. Germany was a defeated power and had been accorded a diminished status. By the mid-1930s, British intelligence chiefs had targeted the resurgent Nazi Germany as the most likely potential threat to British interests.[14] However, in the intervening period, when British cryptanalysts had been otherwise occupied by her former allies, Germany had upgraded its cipher systems. As early as 1926 the German military services began introducing the Enigma machine cipher system – a system which, by the standards of the day, was extremely secure. As a result, when the British cryptanalysts turned their attention towards the problem of German ciphers in the 1930s their efforts proved futile.[15]

Enigma was a cipher system developed by the German electrical engineer Arthur Scherbius at the end of the First World War and made commercially available in the early 1920s. The machine resembled a typewriter with 26 small lamps above the keyboard, each corresponding to a letter of the alphabet. Inside the machine were three rotors, each with 26 contacts, which were used to scramble the message; when a letter was pressed on the keyboard a different letter on the lamp-board would light. The operator would read out the letters illuminated on the lamp-board to a wireless operator who would transmit the message in Morse code. From 1930, variants of the machine adopted by the German military also included a 'plugboard'. A plugboard allowed the operator to plug a cable corresponding to a specific letter into the plug for a different letter, so 'A' could be altered to light 'B' on the lamp-board, adding an extra layer of scrambling and vastly increasing the system's security. Enigma, by the standard of the day, offered unrivalled security. The military Enigma system could be configured to any one of 159 quintillion (159 followed by 18 zeros) possible settings – which were known as 'keys' – that made finding the correct key highly unlikely.[16] The keys employed were also changed each day, so even if the improbable did occur and the day's key was broken, the cryptanalyst would be back to square one the following day. To further heighten security, each branch of the German military and diplomatic services employed a different setting; thus breaking one key would compromise only a small part of Germany's wireless network. British cryptanalysts deemed the system impregnable at that time and predicted that successful efforts to break Enigma would probably require the invention of an 'elaborate apparatus' which did not yet exist.[17]

However, British cryptanalysts were not the only group examining German traffic. Poland, in particular, which faced the Soviet Union on the one side and an aggrieved Germany on the other, maintained a singularly watchful eye upon German traffic and employed a highly competent staff of cryptanalysts in an attempt to read it. In 1929, 20 mathematics students from the University of Poznań were sent on cryptanalysis courses. Those courses produced three exceptional cryptanalysts;

these were Jerzy Różycki, Henryk Zygalski and Marian Rejewski, who made a concerted effort to break Enigma.[18] With the aid of French intelligence, the Poles were able to acquire key information regarding Enigma's operation and two months' worth of German keys. Armed with this knowledge the Poles were, by 1938, able to build machines to speed up the process of calculating rotor and plugboard settings, which they dubbed the Bomba. The success of the Polish cryptographers was short lived: in 1938, the Germans altered the system, greatly increasing the time it took for the Poles to read German traffic. In 1939, as the invasion of Poland became an increasingly likely prospect, Polish intelligence made the decision to share their knowledge of the German cipher systems with their counterparts in Britain and France before Poland was invaded. Two of the Polish mathematicians who had pioneered the efforts to break the Enigma cipher, Rejewski and Zygalski, escaped to France, and then to Britain, where they continued working.[19]

As a result of the Polish efforts British cryptanalysts gained a significant boost in their understanding of the Enigma system from the outset of the Second World War. GC&CS employed the knowledge gained from the Poles to construct its own methods and machines to read German traffic. The intelligence was deemed extremely sensitive; if the Axis powers realised that their cipher security had been compromised all that was required to immediately plug the leak was to adopt a different system or improve the one in place. At that time the highest level of classification in the British security lexicon was 'Most Secret'. Given the potential value of this intelligence, a new and higher level of classification was created, designated 'Most Secret Ultra', or 'Ultra'.

## Ultra and the Second World War

At the outbreak of the Second World War, GC&CS evacuated from London to the Bletchley Park estate. Once the war began in earnest, GC&CS took on an increasingly important role as both the amount and value of Ultra intelligence grew.[20] At first Ultra intelligence was undervalued, particularly in the Battle of France; by late 1940 GC&CS regularly broke the *Luftwaffe* Enigma ciphers. This provided information suggesting that preparations for Operation Sea Lion (the German plan for the invasion of Britain) were under way.[21] Despite these successes the breaks into German traffic were patchy and incomplete. As a result, it took some time, and a greater degree of sustained success, until the true value of Ultra came to be realised. Peter Calvocoressi has suggested that this point came in 1941 when Germany began to annex South-Eastern Europe.[22]

Perhaps most famously, Ultra was extremely valuable during the Battle of the Atlantic and helped the Allies to utilise the U-boat wolf-pack tactic against the German submariners. The basis of the wolf-pack tactic was for a group of U-boats to patrol convoy routes in a thinly spread line. When one U-boat detected a convoy it would radio to the other U-boats within the pack which would then converge on the convoy at night, thus forcing the convoy to have to deal with multiple U-boats. Utilising this method, U-boat packs sank a great deal of shipping, starving Britain of vital supplies and placing her ability to continue the war in jeopardy. The ability to read German naval messages allowed the Allies to begin to reroute convoys when those convoys were discovered by U-boats. The first breaks into the naval Enigma system occurred in March 1941; by the end of the year GC&CS had read 25,000 naval messages. By reading U-boat signals the Royal Navy was able to reduce the loss of shipping from 282,000 tons between March and June 1941, to 120,000 tons in July to December. This success was short lived.[23] In February 1942 the U-boat cipher was changed, effectively locking GC&CS out of U-boat traffic. The agency's failure to read German U-boat messages at least partially contributed to a significant increase in Allied convoy losses, until December 1942 when GC&CS broke the new system. With access to this vital source of intelligence restored the Allies once again had the upper hand.[24]

As noted, the official historian Sir Harry Hinsley argued that the Ultra intelligence generated at Bletchley Park reduced the length of the war by at least two years. Others, including the eminent Cambridge historian and Bletchley Park veteran Ralph Bennett, have dismissed such claims and concluded that it is impossible to measure the extent to which Ultra reduced the length of the war.[25] Attempts to quantify the influence of Ultra are inherently counterfactual. Commanders behaved in particular ways precisely because they *did* have access to Ultra. Had Ultra never existed it is impossible to know whether different strategies and methods might have been adopted in its stead. Nevertheless, leaving aside unanswerable counterfactual scenarios, we can at least say with assurance that Ultra did provide the Allies with a key advantage.

## Historians, Bletchley Park and wartime Britain

In 1974, Group Captain Frederick Winterbotham, who from 1930 to 1945 was the head of the Air Department of the Secret Intelligence Service, received permission to publish his wartime memoirs.[26] The publication of Winterbotham's memoir marked the end of the policy of secrecy surrounding Ultra and the agency adopted by successive post-war British governments. There had been a number of books and press articles making mention of British codebreaking efforts, which had largely passed without notice from the British government and the British public.[27] However, Winterbotham's memoir became a bestseller and went on to sell over four million copies worldwide, and instantly rendered much of the considerable historical scholarship examining the course of the Second World War if not obsolete, then incomplete.[28]

## The histories of the agency

With the publication of Winterbotham's memoir, the floodgates opened. In the years that followed in the 1970s and 1980s, a stream of memoirs emerged, not least including the important *Beyond Top Secret U* (1977) by Ewen Montagu and Peter Calvocoressi's *Top Secret Ultra* (1980), detailing the successes of GC&CS and seeking to correct errors in Winterbotham's memoir. By the late 1970s academic historians also began to focus their attentions on the agency, and the British government commissioned an official history of intelligence in the Second World War, the first volume of which was published in 1979. Largely the primary theme of these various works, until the early 1990s, was to reflect on the influence of Ultra in the various campaigns of the war and to examine the cryptanalytic technologies and methods devised by the agency.[29]

In the 1990s and beyond, junior members of GC&CS's staff began to produce accounts of their wartime lives.[30] These memoirs provide an insight into themes largely left unconsidered in earlier works. The emphasis shifted to GC&CS's role as an employer and to the experience of wartime life in the agency. They provide what one memoirist, Irene Young, described as a 'worm's eye view' of Britain's largest wartime intelligence agency.[31] Unsurprisingly, as increased attention began to be paid to Bletchley Park, and accounts from across the agency's hierarchy entered the public domain, journalists and popular historians began to take an interest in the agency.[32] Such histories have endeavoured to provide accessible narratives detailing Ultra's contribution to the Second World War and to capture something of the flavour of wartime life within the agency. Some, including two recent works by Michael Smith and Tessa Dunlop, have overtly focused on the work of the agency's female staff.[33] They have not, however, sought to contextualise that history or analyse it through the prisms of gender and social class, nor were they interested in the influence of these factors on the mechanics of the organisation; rather they aimed to produce popular narratives for a non-academic audience. Thus, no sustained historical examination of GC&CS has placed the agency into the wider context of British society during the Second World War.

## Social class and gender in the Second World War

The class structure of the bulk of GC&CS's workforce has not been examined in any significant detail. By extension, consideration of the role of class on recruitment practices and how work was both undertaken and distributed in the agency is notable for its absence. While the gender breakdown of staff is better understood, again comparatively little scholarly research has been conducted into how gender influenced recruitment and how it also affected the type of work allocated to staff members.[34] Yet these issues are vital in understanding how and why GC&CS developed as it did. By the height of the agency's wartime activity, in the winter of 1944, it had recruited over 9000 staff members, more than 70% of whom were female.[35] Social class and gender were key elements in the decision-making process in the hiring of those staff members and allocating the work they performed. However, within the wider historiography considering Britain during the Second World War the issues of gender and social class have provoked considerable interest. Historians have been concerned with the question of whether the Second World War altered perceptions of social class and gender in Britain, and in turn how these changes in perception, if any, influenced life both during and after the war.

Richard Titmuss argues that the Second World War had a profound influence on British society resulting, not least, in the introduction of egalitarian social reforms and legislation.[36] In the 1960s, Arthur Marwick advanced a similar thesis, arguing that participation in the war benefited the working classes, women and children.[37] The working classes, Marwick argues, benefited because of their essential role in the front lines of the war's battlefields as well as in wartime production. As such, the government was to grant major concessions to these workers in order to ensure their continued support and cooperation.[38] Given their role in the wartime economy, this also ensured that the war had a lasting impact upon the lives of women in both social and economic terms.[39] The wartime demand for female labour led women to be engaged in spheres of work that were previously male dominated – particularly factory work and employment in the civil service.[40]

The 1980s saw a sea change in the historiography: the thesis that the war was a catalyst for lasting social change was subjected to increased criticism and qualification.[41] For instance, Penny Summerfield, pointing to three different gauges with which to judge the levelling of class (was it across the board, was it permanent, did it extend beyond income to property ownership and saving patterns?) argues that change was, at most, limited.[42] Similarly, Summerfield has also argued that despite the apparent gains made by women moving into previously male-dominated sections of the workplace, divisions continued to prevail, and that women often encountered considerable difficulties integrating into a male-dominated working environment. Rather, work previously classified as 'men's work' was reclassified as 'women's work' for the duration of the labour crisis created by the war. Moreover, women were employed in work which was not deemed to be skilled, or the position was downgraded to unskilled or semi-skilled. For instance, Summerfield points to the fact that the Ministry of Labour and National Service found it difficult to employ women in work that befitted the level of training that the Ministry had provided them, and training courses were reduced to general training in 'machine minding'.[43] This issue is particularly relevant to GC&CS because, as we shall see, comparatively few women were employed in what might be described as 'skilled work', while an abundance of 'machine minding' was conducted by women.

In summary, these trends within the wider social history of Britain during the Second World War, particularly those of social class and gender, raise important questions in regard to a history of GC&CS. GC&CS was, after all, an agency that contained a considerable female staff contingent; it drew heavily from both the civilian and military workforce, and necessarily included a wide range of jobs from the relatively unskilled task of machine minding to work that required very precise skills such as cryptography. Furthermore, these workers had to be considered trustworthy enough to be inducted (or in the parlance of the agency, 'indoctrinated'), even if in many cases to only a limited degree, into one of Britain's most heavily protected secrets. As a result, GC&CS is an ideal laboratory to examine the various historiographical arguments regarding the employment of women in the Second World War.

Fortunately, if the subject of GC&CS's social history is less developed, then its organisation and administrative evolution is rather better documented; being the subject of important scholarly studies. For instance, Jon Agar argues that GC&CS's transformation into an industrialised information 'machine' was part of a wider trend within British government circles, in which middle-ranking technocratic experts led the way in a sustained effort to mechanise the apparatus of government.[44] R. A. Ratcliff also emphasises the importance of mechanisation to GC&CS in the creation of an information 'production line'.[45] For Ratcliff, these factors, among others, were defining features in the success of Allied signals intelligence.[46] The organisational theorist Christopher Grey has also examined the organisational and staff makeup of GC&CS. In addition to Ratcliff, Grey explores the organisation and administration of GC&CS, but in considerably greater detail, placing emphasis on the importance of staff recruitment, section organisation and development, internal lines of communication, and the influence of outside forces, to explain the agency's development. The central aim of Grey's important study is to utilise Bletchley Park as a case study to test various axioms in the field of organization studies and highlight 'problems and possibilities' within that discipline.[47] However, Grey examines the broader development of the agency as a whole and tends to place emphasis on the senior and managerial strata of the agency. I focus on the problems faced by GC&CS's administrators at ground level and how they influenced the wartime experiences of staff within the wider context of British wartime social history.

## Conclusion

Seventy years have now passed since the Allied victory in the Second World War and a little over 40 since the revelation of the Ultra secret. Since the opening of the Bletchley Park Trust Museum in 1991 on the Bletchley Park estate, Bletchley Park has achieved a public profile that has continued to grow unabated; the agency now enjoys a hitherto unprecedented degree of acclaim and popular interest. As such it seems an appropriate juncture to reconsider the agency. Questions regarding the wartime mechanisms of the British state, secret work, and wartime socio-cultural attitudes and values have become increasingly prescient in discussion of Britain's role and British experience in the Second World War. The position of Bletchley Park, a now much-admired British wartime institution pivotal in the conduct of the war and a hub of scientific research and technologies which have come to dominate modern society, lends itself to such enquiry.

The key paradox of Bletchley Park is that it was simultaneously 'normal' yet also extraordinary. On the one hand, the very existence of the agency was a closely guarded national secret, as it would remain for nearly three decades. Yet, on the other hand, GC&CS and its staff faced the same bureaucratic day-to-day problems, and operated in much the same way, as many other British institutions in wartime. The social and cultural norms of wartime British society played a significant and hitherto largely ignored role in the development of the agency.

The aim of this book, then, is to provide a hitherto missing social and administrative history of Bletchley Park. It will examine how Bletchley Park developed, how it worked on a day-to-day nuts-and-bolts level, how it interacted with its staff members and the local community, the experiences of those staff members while at work and while off duty, and consider, within the context of this highly secret quasi-military setting, the extent to which the organisation was typical of, or diverged in any remarkable fashion from, the 'norms' of British society during the Second World War. These are 'hidden' aspects of the Bletchley Park story.

# 1
# The Organisation of the Government Code and Cypher School

## Introduction

The Government Code and Cypher School underwent considerable change during the Second World War. The agency left the interwar period built on a collegiate model, but over the course of the war GC&CS mechanised and bureaucratised its processes and increasingly came to resemble a factory operated on production-line principles. The problem of attacking mechanised cipher systems required a mechanised cryptanalytic approach. The wholesale incorporation of machines fundamentally altered the agency. The machine sections operated on factory principles, far removed in both organisational and operational terms from the cryptanalysis sections which operated on collegiate principles. Mechanisation allowed GC&CS to process vast numbers of Axis wireless transmissions. The scale of the agency's success necessitated the incorporation of a vast index and catalogue of information derived from those transmissions, which itself demanded a dedicated mechanised section. The addition of these sections, and with them numerous new staff members, increased the administrative and clerical demands on the agency and new sections emerged to address these problems. The result was that numerous new sections were incorporated into the agency over the course of the war and that the mandate of pre-existing sections changed.

The aim of this chapter is to outline the evolving organisational and administrative structure of GC&CS from its foundation as a small cryptanalysis bureau in 1919 to a large intelligence factory with nearly 9,000 staff members at the height of the Second World War. Not only did the organisational structure of the agency change, but so too did its physical geography. The *ad hoc* nature of these changes left the agency with an often bewildering array of sections arranged with little apparent order. This was also reflected by the construction of new buildings to house these emerging sections. As sections expanded beyond the confines of the physical buildings they inhabited, new buildings were constructed and sections migrated across the estate. However, because sections typically took the name of the original building in which they were housed, the relationship between the name of the section and the name of the building in which it was housed often did not correlate. Thus, like the expansion of the agency's organisational structure, the changes to the physical geography of the agency was an organic process.

This chapter will identify key sections which emerged within the agency and explain their function. It will navigate the transformation of the agency organisationally and map its spread across the Bletchley Park estate and beyond. The other main aim of this chapter is to outline a running theme throughout this book: the response of the agency to the administrative problems created by a rapid expansion in size and scale of its operations.

## Institutional evacuation in wartime

GC&CS was by no means the only organisation to be evacuated during the war. Numerous institutions, including arms of government and private businesses, were evacuated – some in whole, others in part – from urban areas. To offer several examples, the Air Ministry evacuated significant elements of its staff to Harrogate while the Admiralty moved 4,000 of its staff to Bath.[1] Similarly, buildings were requisitioned in the Thames Valley and Hampshire to accommodate Vickers and Supermarine, both involved in aircraft production, following the first daylight bombing raids directed at their respective factories in Weybridge and Southampton.[2] This policy of evacuating key industry and the machinery of government from areas deemed to be at risk dated from 1936 when the government began examining the problem of defence planning.[3]

The mass movement of such institutions brought with it considerable administrative and organisational issues. Among the most pressing, when it came to evacuating industry, was selecting a region with a suitable infrastructure and workforce already in place to accommodate new factories. The economic depression during the interwar period partially solved these problems, as the southward migration of industry had left many industrial areas with empty or underutilised factories and high unemployment. For example, the War Office employed a number of textile manufacturing firms in Lancashire for shell production.[4] Nevertheless, finding suitable locations for new factories proved problematic, particularly by 1940, when widespread unemployment had ceased.[5] This resulted in persistent problems, such as: locating suitable sites for factories; acquiring enough labour; and providing billets and transport for workers. Most of these problems were also shared by GC&CS following its departure from London to Bletchley.

## Organisational problems, evacuation and growth

To discuss the organisation of Bletchley Park is perhaps misleading, because Bletchley Park was only one war station within a larger agency. Bletchley Park was the headquarters of GC&CS and its largest station, but the organisation actually extended beyond the gates of Bletchley Park. GC&CS had a number of outstations, including nearby sites at Gayhurst Manor, Wavendon House and Adstock. Indeed, GC&CS spread still further, retaining offices in London and – when the 'Y Service' stations are considered – more widely still. The Y Service was Britain's wireless intercept service and was run by a number of different agencies; its role during the war was to intercept radio traffic and despatch the messages to GC&CS for analysis. While not actually a part of GC&CS, the Y Service was an integral part of the work in which GC&CS was engaged, and in a discussion of GC&CS's organisation can not be discounted. As a result, it is difficult to establish the true size of Britain's codebreaking establishment as the operation was spread over multiple locations and handled by different agencies, not just GC&CS at Bletchley Park itself.

When GC&CS was first established in 1919 it numbered 53 individuals, half of whom were actively engaged in the business of cryptanalysis.[6] The organisation was headed by Commander Alistair Denniston beneath whom were 24 officers.[7] To support this establishment a clerical staff of less than 30 was employed. Over time the organisation grew and by 1925 a further six officers were added to the establishment. GC&CS was noted during the Second World War as having a comparatively loose hierarchy, with junior staff working alongside senior officers, a fact that was true of its earliest days. As Denniston wrote in December 1944, 'there was little or no difference in the work of good juniors and seniors'.[8]

In 1937 the head of the Secret Intelligence Service (SIS), Admiral Hugh Sinclair (also known as 'C' – the title given to the head of the SIS), concluded that contingency plans needed to be formed to increase the size of the establishment in wartime. He instructed GC&CS to earmark and train potential recruits from the universities to join the agency should Britain find herself involved in another major war. The Treasury sanctioned the proposal, which was to increase GC&CS by a further 56 officers and 30 female linguists in the eventuality of a war.[9] Over the course of the interwar period the clerical staff increased in number to in excess of 50.[10] The result was that when Britain declared war on Germany in 1939, the agency had a staff of 200 individuals.[11]

In 1938 Bletchley Park was acquired for GC&CS, and its sister organisations SIS and SOE, as home for the two agencies in the event that war should necessitate evacuation. By August 1939, with war on the horizon, the decision was taken to carry out those plans.[12] Bletchley Park was a logical choice for a war station for a number of reasons. While only 50 miles from London, Bletchley was sufficiently distant from large urban areas to be deemed safe from the threat of German bombers. Moreover, it contained several large buildings that could accommodate staff. These included the mansion as well as a number of cottages.[13] The estate also had grounds of approximately 60 acres, which, though unanticipated at the time of purchase, would later facilitate considerable building work.[14]

The town of Bletchley also provided some advantages of its own. For example, Bletchley had significant rail links, being located on the West Coast Main Line as well as the Oxford–Cambridge Varsity Line. These links allowed easy travel between Bletchley and London, as well as the key recruitment grounds of Oxford and Cambridge. The town also had the added benefit of granting easy road to London, being located on the A5 section of Watling Street. These reasons are often cited as key factors in the choice of Bletchley Park as the wartime location for GC&CS.[15] Useful though these connections proved, recent research suggests that the key advantage Bletchley offered was its position on a major artery of the telephone network.[16] Proximity to Britain's north–south telephone lines provided ready teleprinter access to government ministries in London as well as the Y Services listening stations dotted around the country.[17]

Despite the considerable room for expansion offered by the estate, in 1938 nobody had envisioned the scale of the agency's eventual growth. The organisation actually extended well beyond the gates of Bletchley Park. Not only did it retain offices in London, but over the course of the war acquired its outstations. The internal organisation and administration of Bletchley Park at various stages throughout the war became heavily strained, as competing demands on the agency's resources became increasingly pronounced, limiting efficiency. Client ministries, such as the War Office, Foreign Office, Admiralty and Air Ministry, attempted to exert control over GC&CS. These competing organisational pressures led to the foundation of multiple new sections to tackle problems as they arose and a major reorganisation of the agency took place in 1942. Additionally, the pressures of increasing demand and rapid growth resulted in physical geographical changes to Bletchley Park. As sections grew in size they required more workspace. The demand for workspace led to the construction of multiple wooden huts and concrete blocks across the Bletchley Park estate.

Once at Bletchley Park, GC&CS continued to grow in size and its internal structure became increasingly complex. This was because GC&CS was the joint venture of several different agencies: the Foreign Office, and the three military services. These various ministries and services all provided personnel and resources to GC&CS, and in exchange expected GC&CS to work for them. As such, GC&CS had varying demands upon it from these different agencies, yet it lacked the resources to adequately meet those competing demands. As a result, the agency had to prioritise some work for some ministries at the expense of others. In a memorandum circulated in March 1943, Bletchley Park's then second-in-command, Nigel de Grey, described the organisation.[18]

> I suppose that if you were to put forward a scheme of organizations for any service which laid down as its basis that it would take a lot of men and women from civil life and dress some of them in one kind of clothes and some in another, and told all those dressed in black that they came under one set of rules and all those in white under another and so on and then told them that they had a double allegiance, firstly to the ruler of their black or white motley party and secondly to a man who would partly rule over all of them, but only partly, any ordinary tribunal would order you to take rest in an asylum.[19]

Clearly, the organisation had a peculiar and extremely confused structure; a result of dual allegiances of various sections and section heads, both to their home service or agency, but also to GC&CS. Establishing a clear overview of the organisational structure of the agency is made more complicated by the compartmentalisation of the organisation. From the point of view of maintaining security this measure was essential as it limited the amount of information available to any single person. As a result, very few individuals within GC&CS knew the work being performed outside their sections, and nor were they aware of the full extent of the agency's activities.[20] Matters were complicated further by major administrative reorganisation in 1942. This reorganisation saw both major administrative restructuring and the emergence of new leadership both within individual sections and at the highest level: the most notable casualty of the reorganisation was the replacement of Commander Alistair Denniston by Commander Edward Travis as the head of GC&CS in February 1942. The mounting organisational problems within GC&CS had become acute and GC&CS's client ministries lost confidence in the agency's leadership.

## The role and function of sections within GC&CS

Identifying sections and painting a broad geographical picture of how GC&CS functioned is necessary, not only to understand how GC&CS was structured and operated but also to understand how it developed over the course of the war. In doing so it also becomes increasingly clear that this process of development was distinctly *ad hoc* in nature. Sections were formed, expanded, gained responsibilities, lost responsibilities and moved location fairly regularly. These changes occurred as and when the situation changed, in many cases with little reference to the agency's wider organisation or structure. As Frank Birch wrote in GCHQ's internal history of its wartime activities, the agency was like 'a rudderless vessel buffeted about at the mercy of every wave of circumstance'.[21]

By 1934, and throughout the duration of the Second World War, there were three main service sections within GC&CS. A service section was dedicated to the extraction of intelligence from enciphered traffic from military sources: the *Luftwaffe*, the Imperial Japanese Navy, and so forth. It is also necessary to note that during the interwar period there was no division of labour between cryptanalysis and translation of intercepted messages as there would be during the Second World War. Thus, when the Military Section was formed in 1930, cryptanalysis, translation, and the distribution of the material was all done together.[22] During the war this system altered and cryptanalysis was divided from the work of translation and distribution. This division of labour held two main advantages. First, the wartime system facilitated staff specialisation, and second, it compartmentalised the work, which was an invaluable benefit to security because it limited an individual's knowledge of GC&CS's activities to one specific area.

### The service sections

The peace of the interwar years had significantly influenced the priorities of GC&CS. Service traffic (the traffic created by the military branches of foreign powers) was extremely low and ceased to be relevant, while diplomatic traffic steadily increased in volume, and, as such, GC&CS's chief customer became the Foreign Office. As a result, the Foreign Secretary, Lord Curzon, arranged for GC&CS to be transferred from the Admiralty to the Foreign Office vote.[23] The lack of service traffic and the emphasis on diplomatic traffic meant that during the early stages of the interwar years the agency did not even have a section dedicated to service traffic.

The first service section to be established was the Naval Section in 1924.[24] Like the Military Section, during the interwar period, it was tasked with the job of cryptanalysis – in this instance the cryptanalysis of foreign naval wireless traffic. The section was founded under the direction of William F. 'Nobby' Clarke, under whose control it would remain until the end of 1940.[25] By the 'phoney war' the Naval Section started to become increasingly compartmentalised, to the extent that the section was effectively disintegrated. Clarke was moved sideways to head the Italian Naval Section and cryptanalyst and historian Frank Birch took his place. The work on Japanese material was placed under the control of the Diplomatic Sections, and Spanish and German naval work became increasingly autonomous to the point of virtual independence.[26] These sections were unusual because they were directly under the control of GC&CS without Admiralty control.[27] This differed substantially from the other service sections, which shared dual loyalty to both GC&CS and to their client ministries. These changes were also marked by the geographical decentralisation of the section across Bletchley Park. For example, the physical and geographical division of naval cryptanalysis and the work of translating and analysing the content of messages was made in June 1940 when the cryptanalysts moved into their own separate building.[28]

The second service section to be established was the Military Section. This section initially dealt with the cryptanalysis, translation and production of intelligence that was of primary relevance to the War Office. It was founded in 1930 under the leadership of the cryptanalyst John Tiltman.[29] In the opening years of the Second World War the section was under the control of the War Office, and unlike the Naval Sections, while compartmentalised it retained its status as an individual section. However, in 1940 there was comparatively little traffic to work on. This was because it did not, unlike GC&CS's naval contingent, work on Enigma traffic. Furthermore, it had relinquished responsibility for Italian and Japanese work to the Combined Bureau Middle East and the Far East Combined Bureau respectively. As a result there was comparatively little cryptanalysis work for the Military Section to do. Instead, it aided other groups in their cryptanalysis efforts, and trained new recruits in cryptanalysis for other sections within GC&CS.[30] Tiltman, as its head, was in the increasingly typical position of being responsible to two different organisations. On the one hand his section was controlled by (and reported to) Commander Denniston, the head of GC&CS; on the other it also was controlled by the Director of Military Intelligence at the War Office.[31]

The third major service section to be founded during the interwar period was the Air Section. This section was founded in 1934 under the leadership of J. E. S. 'Josh' Cooper. As in the case of the previous two sections, the wartime task of the Air Section was to attack the enciphered traffic from foreign air services, such as the *Luftwaffe*, and produce relevant intelligence from that source.[32] This section dealt with the decryption and exploitation of low-grade material: that is, non-Enigma traffic.[33] The section was under the direct control of, and reported to, the Air Ministry, and was not under the control of Denniston.[34]

The main reason that the Military and Air Sections were restricted from work on Enigma traffic, and instead worked on low-grade material, appears to have been the paranoia surrounding the potential loss of Enigma as a source. By April 1940, with the exception of officers from within GC&CS and SIS, only 30 individuals had been informed regarding the existence of Ultra. To maintain that degree of secrecy, initially all intelligence derived from Enigma traffic destined for the various commands of the War Office and the Air Ministry was transmitted via the SIS for distribution until at least 1942.[35] This created the impression to those individuals within the ministries not inducted into the Ultra secret that the source of information was from a fictitious secret agent, codenamed Boniface, working within the German High Command.[36] Enigma work was conducted within GC&CS, without the knowledge of the Military and Air Sections, by two separate but closely related sections. One section, Hut 6, dealt with the cryptanalysis of Enigma traffic relevant to the War Office and Air Ministry, while the other, Hut 3, dealt with the translation and distribution of intelligence from that source. The cryptanalysis section was formed by Gordon Welchman in early 1940; Welchman was eventually promoted to head of machine coordination in 1943 and control of the section passed to the Chess Master, Stuart Milner-Barry. The translation, analysis and distribution section was formed in late 1939, initially as part of the SIS, under the command of Wing Commander F. W. Winterbotham. In January 1940 control of the section passed to Commander Malcolm Saunders before eventually being placed under the leadership of Wing Commander Eric Jones.[37]

The work on the German naval Enigma was also split across two separate sections. Again, one section would work on the cryptanalysis side of the process while the other worked on the translation and prioritisation of the material for eventual distribution. However, unlike the case of the Military and Air Sections, no attempts were made to disguise the true origin of the source. Unlike Military and Air material, Naval Enigma intelligence from ships and U-boats at sea could not, for obvious reasons, be disguised as the report of an SIS agent.[38]

As a final note, alongside to the service sections there were a number of other sections which worked on the traffic of the German intelligence service, the *Abwehr*. These included the Illicit Service Knox (ISK), founded in late 1939 to deal with the *Abwehr* Enigma system, and the Illicit Signals Oliver Strachey (ISOS), formed in 1940 to address manual cipher systems used by the *Abwehr*.[39] Both sections were named after their respective leaders, Dillwyn Knox and Oliver Strachey.

## Machine sections and 'Fish'

In order to facilitate the process of swift cryptanalysis the agency developed a number of machines, perhaps the most notable being the 'Bombe' machine which was used to aid the cracking of Enigma systems. The Bombe was named after a Polish cryptanalysis machine called the 'Bomba'. With the threat of the German invasion of Poland looming in 1939, a conference between Polish, British and French cryptanalysts was organised to pass on the findings of the Polish cryptanalysts before it was too late. Up to that point, British cryptanalysts had achieved very little success in cracking Enigma. That was not the case in Poland, where breaks into German service Enigma traffic had already been achieved. Furthermore, the Polish cryptanalysts had also produced a mechanical device – the Bomba – to aid cryptanalysis. In the wake of the conference, the British cryptanalysts returned to England with the details of the research the Poles had conducted on Enigma, including the plans for their machine.[40] The British logician, mathematician and cryptanalyst Alan Turing went about the ultimately successful process of designing a more advanced machine – the Bombe machine – which in turn was again improved by fellow mathematician Gordon Welchman. The machines were built by the British Tabulating Machine Company (BTM) in Letchworth.[41] The first of these machines began operating at Bletchley Park in March 1940 and was used in the process of discovering daily Enigma key settings.[42] Once a key had been discovered, the enciphered messages could be passed through a modified British Type-x machine, which operated on similar principles to the Enigma system, to restore the message into plain text. The operation of these machines was split into various sections and subsections. Bombe operation, in particular, was not conducted in Bletchley Park alone. The outstations, discussed earlier, primarily housed Bombe machines.

As the war progressed, other forms of cipher machine began to be implemented by the Axis powers. The most notable of these was the development by the Germans of a means of sending teleprinter signals via radio. This led to the development of cipher machines for these teleprinter systems – the most famous were the Lorenz SZ-40 and SZ-42 machines, developed in 1940 and 1942 respectively. Material from teleprinters was codenamed 'Fish' by the British codebreakers. There were three different systems employed by the German High Command, including the Lorenz machines. The traffic using Lorenz machines was codenamed 'Tunny' and the British codebreakers were highly successful in reading this material. The other two systems were codenamed 'Sturgeon' and 'Thrasher'. Sturgeon was material enciphered by the Siemens and Halske T52 machine, while Thrasher was enciphered by the Siemans T42 machine. Solutions to Sturgeon and Thrasher proved difficult, and only a few Sturgeon messages were broken and Thrasher remained entirely impenetrable.[43] The highly advanced cipher systems generated by these machines required the development of new cryptanalysis machines; for example, the 'Colossus' machine.[44] These various new cipher systems also required new sections to decipher the messages. The section which operated the machines necessary to break the daily keys being used was known as the Newmanry, named after its chief, Dr Max Newman, and it was this section that employed machines such as Colossus. The second of these sections was the Testry, named after its chief Major Ralf Tester. The Testry employed the keys discovered in the Newmanry to turn the raw enciphered messages into plain text. This process also required machinery such as the Tunny machine, a device that replicated the logic and functions of the Lorenz machines, and that was used to turn the enciphered messages back into plain text.[45]

However, in order to find ways into this complex traffic, considerable research had to be conducted. The need for dedicated research resulted in the formation of the Research Section. The Research Section had its roots in a small team of researchers from the interwar period, headed by Dillwyn Knox, who pioneered British research on the Enigma problem.[46] The formal Research Section was formed in September 1941 under the command of John Tiltman. The section was formed to investigate new and unbroken cryptanalytic problems, as well as to devise improved methods of attacking systems already receiving attention.[47]

## Diplomatic and commercial sections

GC&CS also operated Diplomatic and Commercial Sections to deal with the messages derived from Axis diplomatic traffic and the traffic of private commercial companies within the Axis powers (civil traffic). These sections reported directly to Commander Denniston, who in addition to heading the agency as a whole, also directed the civil sections.[48] The agency's preparations for war in the late 1930s marked an inevitable shift towards an emphasis on service traffic, and the new recruits who began working for the agency at the outbreak of war were largely assigned to that traffic at the expense of civil material.[49]

The result was that these sections did not grow as quickly as the service sections. The 1942 reorganisation of GC&CS split the Diplomatic and Commercial Sections from the main war station at Bletchley Park and returned them to London. They remained under the leadership of Commander Denniston, who moved with them, while Edward Travis took command of Bletchley Park.

## Other cryptanalysis sections

GC&CS also ran sections that analysed traffic from auxiliary branches of the Axis states. GC&CS invested resources and formed sections and subsections to deal with messages on a wide variety of topics. This was because messages containing even seemingly mundane information with only tangential relevance to Axis military operations could prove invaluable. For example, the German Police employed cipher systems (including Enigma from 1944) to secure their wireless communications. This led to the creation, in 1939, of a separate German Police Section in GC&CS.[50] German meteorological data was also transmitted using Enigma; as result this material was also examined by GC&CS and a subsection of the Air Section was formed to deal with it. Once deciphered the messages were sent to a Meteorological Office facility in Dunstable in Bedfordshire to be exploited. This subsection of GC&CS was, in terms of staff numbers, relatively small, comprising around 30 staff members from June 1941 onwards.[51] The German weather messages, in particular, proved highly useful. This was because the various different arms of the German military provided weather reports on a regular basis in a typically uniform style and included the same information. Thus, weather reports provided an invaluable source of cribs.[52] The agency chose to invest resources and personnel into the messages of every element of Axis traffic, on the basis that it might prove useful. As R. A. Ratcliff notes, this form of centralised, thematic approach to every aspect of the Axis wireless net, and the preservation of information for future reference was a key factor in allowing GC&CS to correlate information and discover connecting patterns for exploitation.[53]

**Administrative and auxiliary sections**

The agency also included a variety of other sections formed to support the main work being conducted by GC&CS. Three of the larger sections were the Communications Sections, a Tabulating Section, and a typing pool. The Communications Sections handled incoming and outgoing traffic to and from the agency. The Tabulating Section was used to store information derived from decrypts. This section used an array of Hollerith tabulating machinery to sort and search the punch cards upon request. The Typing Pool dealt with the general secretarial and administrative duties of the agency.[54]

## The physical geography of the Bletchley Park war station

SIS acquired 58 acres of the estate, including the Victorian mansion and surrounding cottages, in 1937 from a local property developer.[55] Once GC&CS had arrived at Bletchley Park its numbers began to expand rapidly. These staff were divided into various sections dedicated to analysing the messages of different arms of the Axis powers: army, air force, navy, diplomatic, and so forth.

At this stage, the operation was conducted from the pre-existing buildings on the site, primarily the mansion and the cottages located adjacent to it. The bulk of GC&CS's operation was conducted from the ground floor of the mansion, while the first floor housed the SIS. Restrictions on space soon forced expansion into the outlying buildings. The cottages that had previously housed servants became the temporary home of the Army and Air Section, and the Diplomatic Section moved to Elmer's School – a private boys' boarding school neighbouring the park.[56] Later in the war the school building would house the Japanese Naval Section. Wooden huts in the grounds of the Bletchley Park estate immediately surrounding the mansion were constructed to house the expanding sections.

The tasks performed in the huts soon became synonymous with the name, or rather the number, of the hut itself. For example, a message from a German U-boat would originally be decrypted in Hut 8, and the decrypted message would then be sent to Hut 4 for analysis. But even after the staff of the various sections were rehoused in concrete blocks later in the war, they were still known by the name of the hut in which they had been initially housed: thus the section that decoded the

German naval Enigma retained the title 'Hut 8' even after the home of the operation had moved to different parts of the park. Eventually there were a sizable number of buildings, huts and concrete blocks dotted around the site. At this stage it is worth mapping some of the major buildings on the estate and identifying the sections which occupied them at various points.

## The huts of Bletchley Park

Hut 1 began construction in 1939 under the direction of the former estate owner and local property developer Captain Faulkner. The hut contained equipment used by the diplomatic wireless service and was linked by a cable to the radio room located in a small tower in the mansion which contained an SIS radio station.[57] As a result Hut 1 temporarily became the Bletchley Park wireless station.[58] Soon the section was moved to Old Whaddon Hall, some six miles from Bletchley.[59] The hut was 40ft by 16ft, making it a relatively small building compared to many of the other huts and blocks that would be constructed during the war. Following the departure of the wireless service the building had a number of purposes, including acting as the test site for the first Bombe machine in 1940. The hut was also the home of a first aid post until March 1943, after which it was occupied by the Transport Office until 1945.[60]

Hut 2, like Hut 1, was also constructed in August 1939. The primary purpose of the building throughout the war was the welfare of Bletchley Park's staff members. The building was used as a communal building and NAAFI.[61] It also contained a lending library, and was the home of the Bletchley Park Recreation Club until May 1942 when SIS departed the site for London, freeing rooms in the mansion.[62]

Hut 3, as well as being the location for some of the earliest cryptanalysis undertaken at the Park,[63] was used to sort and prioritise the intelligence from the Army and Navy Section that had been gathered from Hut 6. William Millward, a veteran of Hut 3, described how he and his colleagues task was to evaluate the raw decrypts provided by Hut 6, 'and put the intelligence they contained into a form suitable for passing to the competent authorities, be they ministries or commands.'[64] When the section, named Hut 3 after the building, moved to D Block in 1943 the physical building was renamed Hut 23. Hut 23 then, among other purposes, housed a battery room. Senior staff from the Bombe Section also had offices in the building.[65]

Hut 4 was 145 feet in length and 30 feet in width. This section worked in parallel with Hut 8, and had a similar purpose to that of Hut 3, in that it was tasked with the translation of messages and organising the distribution of intelligence gathered, in this case, from German naval traffic. As with the bulk of the major sections within GC&CS, Hut 4 moved to the spacious blocks opening in 1942. In the case of Hut 4 it actually went on to occupy parts of both A and B Blocks. The then empty hut was occupied by a number of different sections.[66] Initially it housed two Tunny machines, which were used to decipher teleprinter messages, until these machines were moved again to Hut 15A in February 1943. At that point the building became home to a number of smaller sections for the remainder of the war.[67]

Hut 5, also constructed in August 1939, was a relatively small building, between 60 and 70 feet in length. It was initially built to house overflow from the Military Section housed in the mansion. However, the Military Section eventually moved to Hut 9, and instead Hut 5 was used by part of the Naval Section until 1942. In 1942 the building was briefly used to train Type-x operators until early 1943, and by June 1943 part of Hut 5 was being used for staff welfare. The Senior Medical Officer, Major Melrose, had an office in the building, and a sunray clinic also occupied several rooms.[68] Several small sections, such as Balkan military subsections, occupied the remaining rooms until the end of the war.[69]

Hut 6 was the section that dealt with the breaking of German army and air messages and was constructed in early 1940.[70] Frank Birch's internal history of British signals intelligence (commissioned by GCHQ at the end of the war) describes the origins of Hut 6:

> Apart from general research of the [Steckered (armed forces) Enigma] problem, therefore, it seemed opportune to create a production section to exploit these weaknesses [careless use by operators]. Since priority had been accorded to army traffic [...], it was on the army and air Enigma that a party of young and exceptionally able university men were set to work at GC&CS. Therefore, huts were erected in the grounds to accommodate part of the overflow. Hut 6 remained a convenient cover-name for this section throughout the war.[71]

The work of Hut 6 was brought to light with the publication of Gordon Welchman's *The Hut Six Story* in 1982.[72] Welchman was the initial commander of Hut 6, a post in which he remained until he was promoted to Assistant Director for Mechinization in 1943. Welchman was replaced as head of Hut 6 in September 1943 by his deputy, the famous chess player and post-war civil servant Stuart Milner-Barry. Following the departure of Hut 6 to D Block in February 1943, the building was renumbered Hut 16, and housed the Illicit Service Knox Section until September 1943, when that section moved into G Block.[73] The building was then used as office space by the Communications Section and also provided a home for the Wireless Telegraphy Co-ordination Section, which coordinated with the Y Service and the agency's traffic analysts to prioritise message interception.[74]

Hut 7, when it was first built in May 1940, housed Bletchley Park's early card index system and its Hollerith punch card machines. The Hollerith machines, named after their American inventor Hermann Hollerith, tabulated and sorted punch cards, allowing data to be complied automatically. The machines were used at Bletchley Park to create an 'index' recording vital information regarding Axis messages that was used as a reference source for Bletchley Park's cryptographers.[75] As GC&CS become more successful and the number of decrypted messages increased, so did the work of, and the physical space required by, the Tabulating Section. The section was forced to move to a more spacious home, and by November 1942 the section had moved to C Block.[76] This left Hut 7 unused, so the building was soon reallocated to a new section, the Japanese Naval Code Section, until it eventually relocated to B Block in 1943.[77]

Hut 8 was used primarily for the breaking of German naval traffic. The hut was built in early 1940 and was the longest hut, being some 155 feet in length. Its original leader was the Cambridge mathematician Alan Turing, later replaced as head of section by the British chess player Hugh Alexander, followed in December 1944 by A. P. Mahon. In February 1943 the naval cryptanalysts relocated to D Block and the building was renamed Hut 18. The ISOS Section then moved into the building until October 1943, after which it housed part of the Japanese Naval Section until July 1944. The building was then used by a number of different sections, such as the Naval Section which occupied a number of rooms for training purposes.[78]

Hut 9, after an initial period of use by other sections, including overflow from the Japanese and Italian Naval Sections, eventually became in 1942 the centre of pay and administration within Bletchley Park. The building was thought to originally have been numbered Hut 3, but was allocated the number '9' when the Army and Air Force Enigma Translation Section hut took the number '3' early in the war.[79]

Hut 10 was GC&CS's Meteorological Section. The section, headed by George C. McVittie, was limited in size, initially numbering fewer than a dozen individuals, though, as noted above, it did increase in size to around 30 individuals by 1941. It was created with the intention of providing Allied air and sea forces with useful meteorological information around Europe.[80]

Hut 11 was the home of the Bombe machines. The machines were first placed in Hut 11 in 1940.[81] During the war some two hundred of these machines were built, far outstripping the physical capacity of Hut 11. Two further huts were constructed, Hut 11A and Hut 11B, to increase capacity. Yet even then considerably more space was required. As a result, Bombe machines were also used at Bletchley Park's outstations, Adstock, Gayhurst, Wavendon, Stanmore and Eastcote.[82]

Hut 14 primarily housed Bletchley Park's Communications Centre, and Traffic and Cypher Office. The Communications Centre dealt with British cipher security, ensuring that British traffic was secure. The section also dealt with GC&CS's complement of Type-x machines which were used to secure GC&CS's own traffic and in the decryption process of Enigma traffic. The hut was constructed in late 1941 and continued to be used by the Traffic and Cypher Office until 1943 when those sections moved into A Block. However, subsections of the Communications Section still continued using the hut until September 1945.[83]

### Blocks at Bletchley Park

As the various sections expanded, their location typically overflowed into other buildings, in particular, from the huts into the various purpose-built concrete blocks that were built on the site as the war progressed. These blocks were listed alphabetically from A through to G. The space in the blocks was also allocated by demand, meaning that as a result some of the individual blocks would house several different sections within their various wings. D Block, for example, provided space for Hut 3, Hut 6 and Hut 8. The same was the case of E Block and G Block. The latter, however, also housed a training section for Canadian and American staff who formed special liaison units to work in the field.[84]

A Block's primary use was to house Bletchley Park's teleprinters. Teleprinters were electromechanical typewriters used for swift transmission of information into (and out of) the park. As a result, A Block was a primary point of communication with the outside world. A Block also provided room for the expanding Naval Section. The primary use of B Block was to house sections dealing with Fish messages. C Block housed the expanding Tabulating Section and its rapidly growing library of punch cards. F Block, along with H Block, also housed overflow from the expanding sections dealing with Fish traffic, and housed several of the ten Colossus computers produced to break the messages produced by the Lorenz SZ machines. F Block also housed the expanding Japanese Section that had formerly been in the school building and Hut 7.[85]

## Internal section structures

Having established a number of the sections at Bletchley Park, it is worth considering how they were typically organised. In fact the short answer is that there was no 'typical' organisation: different sections were run according to principles that the section heads believed would produce the greatest output from their staff. As Christopher Grey notes, different organisational models and managerial systems were utilised.[86] For example, in Hut 3 a considerable degree of scope was provided to allow people to work in their own way in the hope of acquiring the most from them; as the anonymous author of the internal history of Hut 3 noted, 'Those who did their work well were left, within the inevitable limits, to do it their own way.'[87] If an individual produced good results they were left to continue with their own methods, providing they continued to deliver the goods. Continuing in this fashion, which prioritised results over managerial structures, the hierarchy of these sections became very loose and rank often became largely irrelevant. As Bill Bundy, an American intelligence officer posted to Bletchley Park, recalled, the 'structure was one where you might readily find a Major working under a Lieutenant or under a civilian, somewhat younger. Whoever was in charge was the person who had been judged to be more effective at doing it.'[88]

This practice was actually supported and championed from the highest levels within GC&CS when it came to sections such as Hut 3. For example, in October 1939 Alistair Denniston criticized in no uncertain terms the then commander of Hut 3, Commander Malcolm Saunders, for interfering in the work of his staff, and informed him 'not to butt in on the jobs of others who are obviously better qualified to carry them out'.[89] As a result, sections such as Hut 3 functioned essentially as meritocracies, where ability substituted for rank and downward interference was deliberately limited. However, that is not to say that Hut 3 had no organisation or internal structure or that everyone agreed with a lax policy. As stated, the head of Hut 3, Malcolm Saunders, had been rebuked for attempting to interfere with the work of his staff. Later, in late 1941 and again in early 1942, the issue rose to the fore again. The internal dispute within Hut 3 led to a memo being sent to Denniston describing Saunders as 'interfering, intriguing, creating and magnifying difficulties and misunderstandings, causing friction, undermining confidence and, incidentally, making proper liaison impossible'.[90] The dispute also resulted in Saunders' replacement by Eric Jones in 1942.

However, it would be a mistake to imply that sections such as Hut 3 and Hut 6 were without a fixed internal structure. Gordon Welchman, the senior figure within the Hut 6 hierarchy until 1943, formed a core group of five individuals each of whom headed a subsection. Each man, and they were all male, was responsible for managing a key process within the section.[91] Welchman noted that these leaders were tasked with drawing up weekly reports and, particularly during the early Bombe phase, attending regular meetings providing feedback, and providing a forum to discuss problems and potential solutions. The reports provided by the heads of these subsections were posted on the walls within Hut 6 in order to keep staff in the various other subsections informed, but also to provide proof that their efforts were contributing to the war, and to improve morale.[92]

Hut 6 was not alone in maintaining a distinct internal structure with its own leadership; Hut 8 had a similar internal structure. Hugh Alexander, who Welchman refers to as a leader in the Machine Room in Hut 6, joined Hut 8 in 1941. At this time Hut 8 was under the command of Alan Turing. According to Alexander, Turing shared a similar view on seniority as other section heads, that is, that the only sound basis for allocating authority and responsibility to an individual was if that person had demonstrated the most superior mastery of the problems at hand.[93]

However, the professionalisation of the agency led to an added requirement for senior section management, beyond cryptanalytical ability – skilled section management. Turing was not an adept manager and was replaced by Alexander as head of Hut 8 in 1943. In his internal history of the agency, Frank Birch damningly noted that when Alexander replaced Turing, relations between Hut 8 and the Naval Section, while 'always close and cordial, were henceforward business-like as well'.[94] This was not the first time that Birch had taken issue with Turing's managerial capabilities. In August 1940 he sent Alistair Denniston a memo highlighting Turing's general lack of organisation, noting that while Turing was 'brilliant' he was not a practical man, and was prone to being both untidy and 'losing things'.[95] Thus, Turing moved on to working in research, while the abler manager Alexander formally took command of the section, a task he had already been performing on an unofficial and informal basis for some time.[96] Similarly, when Malcolm Saunders could not solve the internal disputes of Hut 3 he was replaced by Eric Jones. Jones, unlike some other senior figures within GC&CS, did not have an academic background or any particular cryptanalytic or linguistic skill, nor was he a trained intelligence officer. Rather, he was a manager, brought to GC&CS from the Air Ministry because of the management crisis in Hut 3. Jones, prior to the war, had run a large textile agency.[97] Clearly, managerialism and efficient leadership had won priority.

Sections such as Hut 3, 6 and 8 paint a picture of GC&CS in which staff members were provided a considerable degree of latitude if it allowed them to produce superior results. The picture also suggests that seniority depended not upon formal rank but on ability. However, other sections were run on very different principles. The Type-x office, for example, employed a far greater degree of control over its staff. The Type-x was the British adaptation of the Enigma machine. 'Labour was "directed" and the interest nil. It became necessary to intervene and institute factory methods. This was done chiefly by keeping careful records of output per watch, per machine and per girl.'[98]

The Indexing Section in C Block was run on a similar basis. The punch card operators were under regular supervision from senior members of the section, not least its commander Mr Freeborn. Phyllis Coles, a veteran from C Block, when describing the section stated:

> We would see quite a lot of Mr. Freeborn, he was always about. There was Mr. Whelan, Ronnie and Norman they were like the chief ones. And there was a Mr. Smith, a very elegant man, always walking about making sure everything was being done right. ...
>
> We were all divided up but we always had a young man, our one had been brought up from Hollerith, as he knew the working of the punch card thing. We also had a girl who was very highly qualified. But we just did what they told us to do ...[99]

Clearly this type of section, those tasked with operating machines, such as the Type-x and Hollerith machines, were administrated both strictly and with considerable degrees of supervision. Staff members in these sections were also provided with far less information regarding how their exertions contributed to the wider war effort. In Hut 6, Gordon Welchman attempted to inform all of his staff of the purpose of their work, and the successes that had been achieved, but in the machine sections, individuals knew very little about their work. For example, one worker, who operated Colossus machines, stated that she and her coworkers were initially unaware even of the name of the machine they were working on, and 'knew nothing about it'.[100] Thus, the internal management structure of different sections reflected the type of work being conducted.

## The reorganisations of GC&CS

Over the course of the war GC&CS underwent two major reorganisations. The most profound of these reorganisations occurred in February 1942 and saw Commander Alistair Denniston replaced by Commander Edward Travis as the head of GC&CS at Bletchley Park. Under this reorganisation GC&CS was split in two, the military wing of GC&CS remaining at Bletchley under Travis, and the civil wing returning to London under Denniston. Both men were provided the same rank (Deputy Director) within the organisation, which made Denniston's shift of position technically a step sideways. In reality it was a significant demotion and reduction of responsibility for Denniston, and a promotion for Travis.

The reasons for the reorganisation lie in the growth of a number of severe administrative problems, internal disagreement within GC&CS's management, and dissatisfaction from GC&CS's client organisations. The main problems were administrative issues directly related to GC&CS's substantial growth, from 200 individuals to nearly 9,000, during the Second World War. The agency failed to acquire enough support staff, such as typists and clerks, to cater for its growing operations. Similarly, when the agency did acquire additional staff it proved difficult to provide satisfactory billets, meals and recreational facilities.[101] Denniston also found it difficult to quell internal divisions with the increasingly sizable agency and repeatedly found himself battling GC&CS's 'Old Guard' – those staff members who had been with the agency prior to the Second World War. In particular, Denniston had repeated arguments with Dillwyn Knox, one of the longest-serving members of GC&CS and head of the attempt to break German *Abwehr* Enigma traffic. Knox objected to the division of labour within the wartime agency, and disliked his relegation to a research position as opposed to continuing his former control over the entirety of the Enigma problem.[102] He also complained about the division of cryptanalysis and translation into separate sections, despite the obvious benefits of dividing the work. Knox saw this as a loss of control over 'his' work, resenting having worked on the decipherment process only to have then to release his findings onto other staff along the production line. He announced his distaste for the new wartime structure in a particularly angry letter of complaint to Denniston.

> [T]o concede your monstrous theory of collecting material for others is impossible. By profession and in all his contracts a scholar is bound to see his research through from the raw material to the final text.

From 1920 to 1936, I was always able to proceed as a scholar. I simply cannot understand, nor I imagine can the many other scholars at BP understand, your grocer's theories of 'window dressing'.[103]

Knox went on to add that if the methods being adopted by the agency had been applied to the development of human civilisation the world would never had left the 'dark ages'. Clearly, Knox viewed his own work as a scholarly exercise, and he resented the interference of bean-counting others micromanaging his work and selling its products to client ministries. Knox's attack on Denniston also holds clear class-based overtones; Knox was engaged in the scholarly pursuits of the gentleman amateur, while he associated Denniston's behaviour, despite his having attended the same kinds of elite schooling and university education as Knox, with that of a lower-middle class professional shop keeper.

Knox's complaint highlights two key related issues which will be returned to throughout this book. First, he outlined the kind of individual and ethos employed by GC&CS's upper echelons throughout the bulk of the interwar period. These individuals were, as Knox describes them, 'scholars'. However, soon into the Second World War the amateur scholars were not deemed adequate by either their younger colleagues or Bletchley's senior managers in an age of machine ciphers – and nor were their methods. Second, Knox rejected the agency's overall trajectory towards specialisation and professionalism. This transition was alien to Knox's near three-decade career as a cryptanalyst.

Symptomatic of this transition was the arrival of the new, young, mathematicians brought into GC&CS at the beginning of the Second World War. These recruits brought with them their own ideas and methods and began to supplant the 'Old Guard' of cryptanalysts and translators – many of whom had been together since the days of Room 40. Christopher Grey's oral history interview with an anonymous GC&CS cryptanalyst includes a highly revealing statement on this issue.

> We regarded anyone over 40 as very unlikely to be of any use and quite a lot of the Room 40 people were moved into undemanding jobs, for example Clarke [William 'Nobby' Clarke, whose relationship to GC&CS dated back to his days in Room 40], Head of German Naval Section before Birch, [was] moved but was very unhappy about it.[104]

Of course, this comment generalises the situation. While individuals such as Clarke, and eventually Denniston, were side-lined, that was not universally the case. A number of Room 40 cryptanalysts working for

GC&CS during the Second World War continued to have highly distinguished careers. John Tiltman, for example, was the first individual to make a break in Tunny and from 1942 was head cryptanalyst, replacing Knox who was, by then, terminally ill.

Nevertheless, the arrival of these new, young staff members marked a transfer within GC&CS from the old way of approaching its business to meeting the new challenges posed by the Second World War, which involved new cryptographic technologies, an increasing appreciation of signals intelligence by GC&CS's client ministries, and a far larger amount of wireless traffic to process. In many ways Denniston, a member of that 'Old Guard', paved the way for change by initiating changes in recruitment policy and altered the manner in which GC&CS functioned.[105]

Much of this change was conducted in an *ad hoc* fashion when the existing configuration of GC&CS required alteration in order to efficiently do its job. Ultimately, however, the rapid growth in demand, and with it the growth and organisational changes within GC&CS, produced considerable organisational and logistical problems that eventually saw Denniston's own downfall. Under Denniston's command, Bletchley Park had grown from an organisation of 200 staff members to one that exceeded 1,500 individuals.[106] Yet even after this considerable growth major bottlenecks persisted because of a lack of staff and machines. As Stephen Budiansky notes, these problems came to a head when four of Denniston's chief cryptographers went behind his back and wrote a letter to the Prime Minister requesting more resources. The letter, which offered lavish praise on the ability of Commander Travis, completely failed to make mention of Denniston – an assassination by omission.[107] Certainly by 1942 Denniston was the scapegoat of two competing factions. On the one hand the cryptanalysts, the 'Old Guard' such as Knox in particular, resented the imposition of structure, oversight and management in their work, while on the other the new younger generation of cryptanalysts complained when these new administrative structures were not implemented quickly enough or lacked the efficiency to provide the resources they required.

Where Budiansky emphasises the pressures of expansion, this perhaps fails to acknowledge with sufficient emphasis the growing dissatisfaction of the military services with Denniston and GC&CS. GC&CS had a history of controversy with the services themselves dating back at least as far as 1940. The complaint of the War Office was that it had invested a considerable amount of resources to the Enigma problem and had seen relatively little return on that investment: in particular

*Luftwaffe* messages were being broken regularly, yet military decryption was 'sparse and spasmodic'.[108]

As a result, the army in particular wanted to invest a greater degree of control over the operations of GC&CS. The War Office argued, at the Directors' level, that control of signals intelligence organisations should not have been held in the hands of cryptographers but by the Services. The Director of Military Intelligence argued, 'With distribution governed by "C" [by then Major General Stuart Menzies] and direct control from GC&CS to the (Wireless Telegraphy) Stations, the Services have little or no responsibility to administer their stations.'[109] As a result, he and those who shared his views argued that the Services should hold a greater degree of control of both GC&CS and also the Y stations (intercept and direction-finding stations).

Inevitably Denniston disagreed with this argument, and responded that 'It is now urged that cryptography shall be subservient to interception. It is quite obvious that cryptographers will always know more of interception than the interceptors can possibly know of cryptography.'[110] On this issue, Denniston got his way and the Y Board, the inter-service body responsible for coordinating Y, decided that the Y Services should be responsible for interception but 'not cryptography and its fruits'.[111] However, the dissatisfaction of the Services, the War Office in particular, still remained, and similar disputes continued to be a feature of GC&CS's relationship with the Services. The most notable of these was a controversy surrounding control of Hut 3. Given that Hut 3 was tasked with the translating and analysing of German air force and army messages, both the army and the RAF provided officers to act as liaisons between the section and their service. However, the two officers and their respective services expected to be the senior officials within the Hut and to control their respective branches. At the heart of their demands were that Hut 3 be subordinated to their command and that GC&CS act in a purely administrative role.[112] In this they were supported by MI6 and AI 1(e) (the Signals and Wireless Intelligence Section of the Air Ministry).[113] Hut 3's commanding officer, Malcolm Saunders, was unable to adequately control these officers and respond to the challenge to his authority. The escalating crisis within the hut, which had partially precipitated the removal of Denniston, still continued unabated under Travis. Eventually, the crisis eased when the senior RAF intelligence officer was temporarily sent on a mission to Egypt, and Eric Jones was sent by the Air Ministry to act in his stead for the duration of the mission. Jones was a skilled manager and tensions eased. Travis, who had consistently advocated individual leadership of Hut 3 free from responsibility to any single ministry (as opposed to joint control of the hut by the three senior officers involved in the dispute), finally got his way and Jones was placed in sole command of the hut.

The struggle for control of Hut 3 was symptomatic of the wider disputes that existed within GC&CS. As the agency became increasingly successful it was met with escalating demands on its sparse resources by its client ministries. Thus GC&CS's administrators and managers had two problems: first, the growth in demand outpaced the acquisition of resources; second, when the service ministries did provide GC&CS with resources, they expected a return on that investment without appreciating the scale of the agency's commitments. When, eventually, GC&CS's management proved incapable of meeting these duel challenges, the client ministries began to step in. The eventual solution, to improve efficiency and appease the ministries, was to replace the existing leadership with skilled managers capable of addressing the increasingly pronounced administrative and personnel problems. Jones replaced Saunders in Hut 3, Alexander replaced Turing in Hut 8, and Travis replaced Denniston as head of Bletchley Park. Following the departure of Denniston in 1942, Bletchley Park continued to rapidly expand and by January 1945 nearly 9,000 staff members were employed there.[114] It is clear that GC&CS's rate of growth could not be sustained without major organisational changes and a shift towards professionalisation.[115]

## Conclusion

GC&CS began life in 1919 as a form of information-processing workshop with an ethos that revolved around gentlemanly scholarship; the war transformed it into an industrialised and mechanised information-processing factory. Signals intercepted by the Y Service arrived at Bletchley Park, where they were logged, converted from an unintelligible group of letters into plain text, translated and indexed, before being forwarded to relevant ministries and commands so their intelligence could be put to use. This led to the expansion of existing specialist sections and the creation of numerous new sections and subsections as new demands were placed on the agency. Initially it had been a small organisation, of less than 60 individuals, and remained small throughout the interwar period. The threat of war saw plans made to increase the size of the organisation and move the operation from London to the safety of Bletchley. Plans were also made to increase staff numbers to meet the demands of war. This rise in staff numbers, which would continue throughout the war until GC&CS numbered nearly 9,000 individuals at Bletchley Park alone, resulted in the widescale construction work that radically altered the physical appearance of the Bletchley Park estate.

Yet the creation of new sections, the acquisition of new staff and the construction of new buildings was all conducted in a distinctly *ad hoc* fashion. As quoted earlier, Frank Birch described the development of GC&CS as like 'a rudderless vessel buffeted about at the mercy of every wave of circumstance'.[116] As sections outgrew their accommodation they would move to new larger huts, and eventually blocks, on the site. Those empty buildings were soon filled by smaller sections or the overflow from other sections that had also outgrown their accommodation. However, because the sections in some cases took the names of the buildings they were initially provided, buildings were regularly renamed and sections took with them the number of their old building. For example, the specific section Hut 3 did not occupy the original Hut 3 and nor did it remain in the building eventually named Hut 3. The section, Hut 3, migrated around the estate as did most other sections, but the section name of Hut 3 remained attributed to that section for the duration of the war. The sections also produced multiple subsections which in many cases were not housed in the same building as the rest of the section. Indeed, the expansion was not even confined within the estate of Bletchley Park; the agency acquired a number of outstations to house and operate a considerable portion of its machinery. The result of these expansions and internal geographical migration resulted in a highly complex organisation that was extremely difficult to map or chart, geographically or administratively.

These processes of change and growth were not without their casualties. The development of GC&CS created a perennial tension between a partially scholarly workforce with an amateur ethos and the need to bureaucratise, compartmentalise and professionalise the agency. The inability to resolve these tensions or meet the expectations of client ministries led to the replacement of several senior figures within GC&CS and a major reorganisation of the agency. In the following chapters the internal processes of the agency will be examined in greater depth to explore how it evolved as an agency, why it evolved in the manner it did, and the impact this growth and change had upon the wartime lives of staff members.

# 2
# Recruitment at GC&CS: 1919–1945

## Introduction

During the interwar period the British armed forces were scaled back and military spending was cut to the extent that when calls for rearmament were made in the 1930s the beleaguered armaments industry was not capable of adequately responding.[1] Britain's newly formed cryptanalytic unit was not spared these cuts. The Admiralty's cryptanalysis department, Room 40, ended the First World War with a staff of around a hundred individuals, while the War Office's military cryptanalysis section comprised some 85 individuals at the armistice.[2] The newly formed GC&CS was formed with a staff contingent of 53 individuals, less than 30% of the wartime staff numbers.[3] In the late 1930s, as the international situation changed, it became increasingly important for the agency to rebuild its ranks of specialist cryptanalysts and linguists and reverse the rot of post-war retrenchment. This chapter explores GC&CS's efforts to recruit staff at all levels of the agency.

As in the First World War, the cryptanalysts turned to Britain's elite universities as the primary pool of recruitment, selecting the brightest academics and students available. Over time, the agency began to deplete this resource, and the net was cast further afield, moreover the nature of the agency had changed. The rise of managerialism necessitated a different type of recruit to take positions of leadership at various levels of the agency. Nevertheless, at its core GC&CS remained wedded to the university common room culture it had inherited from the First World War. The primary difference lay in the type of academic recruited, and there was a clear step away from an emphasis on the arts and classics towards the sciences and mathematics.

Of course, recruitment from these kinds of elite institutions of education produced a certain type of individual, largely drawn from similar class backgrounds and typically male, the result being that the agency's top tiers were dominated by men drawn from the upper-middle classes. On a superficial level, this policy can be explained by the agency's need to fill its ranks with the most able and educated specialists available. However, more complex factors, involving wider social attitudes towards gender, social class and status, heavily tied to notions of good character and integrity, were vitally important in shaping the agency's recruitment policies.

## 'Chiefs and Indians': cryptanalysts, linguists and management

In his book *Top Secret Ultra* (1980), Peter Calvocoressi, historian, publisher and former senior Bletchley Park employee, divided Bletchley Park's employees into two categories, 'Chiefs' and 'Indians'.[4] Calvocoressi's two tiers are broken down into those individuals who orchestrated cryptanalytic and translation work – Chiefs – and those individuals who carried out cryptanalysis and translation of messages – Indians. Calvocoressi was located firmly within these two tiers as an intelligence officer in Hut 3, eventually rising to the head of its Air Section. Absent from his two tiers are the many thousands of auxiliary and support staff within GC&CS: with the exception of very brief references this majority portion of GC&CS staff are entirely omitted from his account. This is unsurprising given that the work of GC&CS was compartmentalised – both in terms of physical geography and in terms of social class. Calvocoressi's contact with individuals below his immediate station within GC&CS was, at most, limited. As a result, they exist only on the extreme peripheries of his account. Despite the inadequacy of Calvocoressi's model in examining the full range of GC&CS's staff it does remain a detailed and useful examination of the top two tiers, identifying a number of key similarities and differences between the 'Chiefs' and 'Indians'.

The 'Chiefs' were, according to Calvocoressi, predominantly male, but in terms of education and background little different from the 'Indians' serving under them. Calvocoressi noted that Bletchley Park was in this respect different from the armed forces, in that the staff at every level – at least those two levels he acknowledges – came from a broadly similar background and held similar intellectual traits.[5] They had attended, or resided in, the same universities – notably the ancient universities; held a common class background; and were highly intelligent, having attained a considerable grasp of key academic fields, such as languages and mathematics. In his words, these recruits belonged to 'a restricted middleclass professional world where it was comparatively easy to get trustworthy reports about individuals'.[6] In terms of education and ability they were required to have a 'well-trained mind, a considerable knowledge of the subject matter with which they were dealing, their wits about them, and a measure of resourcefulness. So, like their Chiefs, most of them came from universities and had honours degrees.'[7]

As Calvocoressi suggested, his own privileged background was relatively typical of Bletchley Park's 'Chiefs' and 'Indians'. Calvocoressi won a scholarship to Eton College.[8] While at Eton he studied, among other subjects, classics, history and languages. In terms of languages, he did well at both Latin and Greek and he already had French from childhood. In an effort to expand his already broad range of languages, he chose to study German. In addition to his lessons, he spent a summer with a German professor near Cologne to improve his command of the language.[9] From Eton Calvocoressi then attended university at Balliol College, Oxford, where he studied history, graduating with a First in 1934.[10] He opted for a career in law and was called to the Bar in 1935.[11] On the outbreak of war he was recruited to the Ministry of Economic Warfare.[12] In 1940 he volunteered for the army where he hoped to be an officer. However, at the end of various aptitude and fitness tests he was deemed of insufficient quality to even be posted to intelligence work.[13] Instead, he used the connections he had forged within the Ministry of Economic Warfare to arrange an interview for a position within the intelligence community of the Air Ministry. After a series of interviews he found himself working at Bletchley Park in Hut 3, and as noted above, he eventually rose to chief of its Air subsection.[14]

## 'Chiefs': senior staff members

In 2006 the Bletchley Park Trust produced a pamphlet offering brief biographical details of what the author believed to be 15 of the most outstanding individuals who had shaped the course of GC&CS's development,[15] all of whom held some form of senior administrative position at one point in their career within GC&CS and all of whom had, at one stage, also worked directly either as intelligence analysts and translators or as cryptanalysts.[16] These included Alistair Denniston, the first head of GC&CS, and his successor as head, Edward Travis. Of the 15 individuals, 11 had attended a prestigious private school; only four had a state school education and, of those four, three had attended a grammar school. Of those four who had a state education, two went on to study at Cambridge University, another went on to Oxford, and the fourth joined his family's textile business. Of the universities, Cambridge was the major contributor supplying 10 of the university educated men. The individual colleges these men attended are also revealing. Four had attended King's College, three Trinity College, two St John's College and one Christ's College. Of the remaining two both had also attended elite universities, one attending both Bonn University and Paris University, while the other had attended Brasenose College, Oxford.[17]

Thus, of the 15 individuals included, only two had neither attended an independent school or an ancient university, and nor had they, as in a majority of these individuals, attended both. The two individuals not to have attended either were Edward Travis and Eric Jones. Travis, the head of GC&CS from 1942, found his way into intelligence work through a naval career.[18] Jones had attended King's School, Macclesfield, but left at the age of 15 to join his family's textile firm. After a successful career in business he joined the RAF in 1940 and became an intelligence officer, before being seconded to GC&CS in 1942 to manage Hut 3.

This survey of 15 of the more senior figures, or as Calvocoressi described them 'Chiefs', within GC&CS produces some interesting commonalities. As noted, the vast majority of them came from similar educational backgrounds. Of the three who did not, two of them held military careers prior to the outbreak of the Second World War which brought them to GC&CS. Further analysis shows that they nearly all had a considerable knowledge of mathematics, languages or, again, both.

## 'Indians': cryptanalysts, translators and analysts

With regards to the Indians, that is, the individuals employed as translators, analysts, cryptanalysts or research scientists, but not in an obvious managerial position leading a section or subsection, it is possible to produce a similar list of 20 individuals.[19]

As with the 'chiefs', the biographical information of the 'Indians' reveals numerous common features. Of the 20, all had a university education, typically from a highly prestigious university. Indeed, four individuals had attended two or more universities – John Cairncross, for example, had attended Glasgow University; the Sorbonne, Paris; and Trinity College, Cambridge. Similarly, Asa Briggs had attended Trinity College, Cambridge as well as holding an external degree from the University of London. As in the case of the Chiefs, the university that had provided the largest number of individuals was, again, Cambridge – contributing nine. Other significant contributors included London colleges, which provided five (including Briggs), and Oxford University, providing four. Cryptanalysts, in particular, tended to have been educated at Cambridge, though there were representatives from Oxford University, the London colleges and Edinburgh University. Translators and analysts came from the same group of universities, though with slightly less emphasis on Cambridge University. The final two individuals in the sample, while both working in Hut 6, were involved in non-cryptanalytic work. Joan Thirsk worked in a subsection known as the Fusion Room, whose purpose was to compare Hut 6's decrypts with data produced by Hut 6's traffic analysts. Irene Young worked in Hut 6's Registration Room, in which incoming messages to Hut 6 were sorted by frequency and call-sign – she had however briefly worked in the main Decoding Room when she first arrived. Both women had non-Oxbridge university educations, Thirsk having attended Westfield College, London, and Irene, Edinburgh University.

However, one major difference between the Chiefs and the Indians emerging from these samples is school education. The number of Indians who had a state education, primarily in grammar schools, was significantly higher than that of the 'chiefs' who tended to have a public school education. The school education of 15 Indians within the sample has been ascertained; of that figure, ten attended grammar schools while four attended independent schools and the funding status of one school is unclear.

These two staff samples of veterans suggests that those at the highest levels within the GC&CS wartime structure came from a highly select background. They typically enjoyed the most prestigious, and often most expensive, school educations Britain had to offer. They then progressed to obtain degrees from, again, among the most prestigious university institutions in Britain or abroad. Their immediate subordinates, on the other hand, tended to have slightly less prestigious educations. Many attended grammar schools prior to progressing to university. Linguists and intelligence analysts in particular tended to have attended a wide variety of institutions, unlike their superiors who largely attended a range of Cambridge colleges, including, but not limited to, King's College, Magdalene College, Trinity College and (the ladies only) Newnham College.

The domination of university-educated staff members in the technical roles in GC&CS is not surprising, given that GC&CS was a scientific and administrative information-processing institution. In fact, GC&CS's policy conformed to the wider trends within the British state at the time. As David Edgerton notes, prestigious universities dominated recruitment to the scientific contingent of the civil service. Oxbridge graduates contributed approximately 31% of the scientific officers recruited to government laboratories, London colleges contributed a further 24%, and Scottish universities 13%. Still more pronounced was the Oxbridge domination of recruitment to the administrative class of the civil service, which filled 85% of its places from the two universities. Former pupils of secondary moderns were also singularly underrepresented among scientific officers, comprising only 6%. Public/fee paying schools, on the other hand, produced 23% of scientific officers, while direct grant schools produced 21% and the remaining 50% came from LEA grammar schools. Meanwhile, 50% of the administrative class of the civil service was drawn from public/fee paying schools, while only 28% came from LEA grammar schools, 20% from directed grant schools and just 2% from secondary modern schools.[20] School education and university education were also linked, as pupils of public schools also dominated the ancient universities. Approximately 75% of scholarships awarded by Oxford and Cambridge went to individuals who had attended public schools.[21]

### The recruitment of Chiefs and Indians

The domination of university-educated staff also lay partly in GC&CS's own history. One of GC&CS's two predecessor organisations, Room 40, had employed a number of civilian academics during the First World War. This was in no small part because the head of Room 40 was the naval officer and scientist Sir Alfred Ewing,[22] a Cambridge graduate, who retained close links with his old college, King's, and who used his connection to find recruits for Room 40.[23] This policy was continued by GC&CS when it formulated contingency plans for war in the late 1930s, using former colleagues who had moved on to an academic career to act as recruiters. Thus when, in 1937, Hugh Sinclair (head of the SIS) ordered Denniston to start taking note of potentially suitable candidates for the agency's work, he suggested they approach 'men of the professor type.'[24] Specifically, that consisted of young, intelligent, well-educated individuals, experts in a range of academic subjects including mathematics, languages, history and classics, and products of Britain's ancient universities. In 1944, Denniston explained GC&CS's 1937 recruitment policy as follows: 'At certain universities, however, there were men now in senior positions who had worked in our ranks during 1914–18. These men knew the type required. Thus it fell out that our most successful recruiting occurred from these universities.'[25] Continuing in the tradition set by Ewing, particular among those universities was Cambridge.[26]

The dominance of Cambridge was natural given that recruitment was built on the exploitation of social networks; Ewing had a longstanding connection with the university, having held posts at both Trinity College and King's College.[27] Thus, Cambridge had stood at the epicentre of those social networks since the First World War.

In 1937, GC&CS selected 56 men 'with the right background and training' as potential cryptanalysts on a salary of £600, and 30 'girls' with knowledge (to a university graduate's standard) of two of the languages prized by the agency, who would earn three pounds a week.[28] The latter group were to be engaged in the process of translating deciphered messages.[29] Significantly this suggests that not only was there an allocation of labour type by gender, but also that the agency demanded highly qualified women even in relatively low-level administrative posts.

However, the need for recruits soon exceeded the numbers the 'professor type' could provide, and the agency set about drafting undergraduate students, an example being (later Sir) Harry Hinsley. In 1939 Hinsley was a 20-year-old undergraduate student at St John's College,[30] and among the first of GC&CS's annual drafts of recruits from the universities. He described his interview, which was conducted in the rooms of the President of St John's College by Alistair Denniston and John Tiltman, the chief cryptanalyst, as being both brief and informal.[31] The manner in which Hinsley was recruited is important because his arrival in GC&CS was in many ways typical of recruits from his elite academic background. Specifically, he was recruited via the informal network GC&CS had established at Cambridge University. Precisely which member of the Cambridge faculty informed GC&CS that Hinsley was a suitable candidate is unclear. However, the fact that both Denniston and Tiltman interviewed him, informally and briefly, in the rooms of the President of his college is highly revealing, suggestive that both recruiters were known to the university and indeed the college and that Hinsley's suitability had already been assessed in advance of their arrival.

Hinsley's experience was by no means unique. One of GC&CS's chief talent scouts at Cambridge was F. E. Adcock, a specialist in ancient history who had worked for Room 40 during World War I.[32] In 1938, Adcock introduced Lancelot Patrick Wilkinson, of King's College, Cambridge, to Alistair Denniston. Wilkinson, like Hinsley, was one of the first new recruits to GC&CS upon the outbreak of war in 1939.[33] Though informal there clearly was a crude vetting system in place. In 1937 Denniston wrote to a member of the University of London appointments board stating that,

I know the [GC&CS] selection Board appreciates any details which you could let them have about these men. You may be in a position to know yourself or through their tutors or professors further details as to the merits of these candidates, and I know from experience that the Board set great importance on the views of schoolmasters and tutors.[34]

An earlier letter from 1932 revealed that part of the process was to ensure that GC&CS could be assured that the candidates put forward were individuals of 'sound character in whom we can place implicit faith'.[35] These sentiments were echoed in 1935 when Denniston wrote to Oxford University requesting individuals not only with a 'thorough knowledge of Italian', but were 'trustworthy'.[36] This policy of vetting through examination of a candidate's past was expanded during wartime and candidates became subject to a formal period of vetting. Gil Hayward, despite having been an intelligence officer since 1940, still had to undergo a period of vetting after being transferred to work on the development of Colossus in 1944.[37] Once within the intelligence services, young academics in turn began recruiting from their own social circles, inviting their peers in academia to join them in their war work. For instance, Walter Eytan, also at Oxford, believed he was first probed for recruitment by the Egyptologist, and Bletchley Park translator, Alec Dakin.[38]

The heavy recruitment from the universities soon began to exhaust those pools of their most suitable candidates. Frank Birch noted in the internal agency history, commissioned by GCHQ immediately after the war, that 'The continuous expansion [of GC&CS] was made possible only by lowering the standard of education required and throwing the net of recruitment over a larger area.'[39] This meant that GC&CS began recruiting students and graduates with less prestigious educational achievements as well as individuals from non-Oxbridge colleges. For instance, Irene Young, a Hut 6 veteran, who had been educated at Edinburgh University, was recruited to GC&CS in 1942.[40]

As a result of the demands of expansion GC&CS was not in the habit of missing the opportunity to recruit talented individuals from other areas of Britain's elite circles as and when the opportunity arose. Among Bletchley Park's staff were Egyptologists, distinguished chess players including Conel Hugh O'Donel Alexander, Harry Golombek and Stuart Milner-Barry, and members of the British business world as showcased by the example of Squadron Leader Eric Jones.[41] These individuals were recruited because it was believed that they had talent that GC&CS

could exploit. This was not necessarily for cryptanalysis or translation: Jones was recruited to GC&CS because of his managerial experience. Even with the widening of the recruitment net cast by GC&CS into the civilian employment market, be it the universities or further afield, by 1942 supply was again becoming scarce, in no small part due to full adult male conscription. As a result, GC&CS 'became dependent upon the seconding of officers from the Services and the earmarking of men appearing before Service selection boards prior to their call-up'.[42]

Yet despite the difficulty in retaining such exclusive requirements for recruits alluded to by Birch, GC&CS's records still show that even in August 1942 recruits for senior positions were required to have 'first-class' skills. In correspondence regarding filling three positions of the civil service's Temporary Senior Assistant grade, the following guidelines were produced: 'Age 25–40. They must have first-class Italian and, perhaps more importantly still, first-class intelligence. They are required for positions of responsibility, each of them to be in charge of a watch. The work requires leadership, accuracy and speed.'[43]

## Academic specialism

Specific academic skills were considered to rest at the heart of cryptanalysis, in particular those which required the use of lateral thinking and the ability to spot patterns, to tease meaning from complex, garbled and alien sources of information. Therefore, GC&CS's first cryptanalysts tended to be specialists in languages and classicists in particular. Prior to the rise to primacy of Enigma as the system of choice for Germany's armed forces and with it the dominance of machine ciphers, this focus on language had been met with proven success particularly during the First World War. This was because the deductive and inductive elements of cryptanalysis both primarily revolve around a detailed understanding of how languages work, in particular which letters, words and phrases are most likely to appear, and where they are likely to appear.[44]

Of the initial draft of 16 recruits to GC&CS on the outbreak of war, only two were mathematicians.[45] The reason for this, other than the fact that cryptanalysis was only part of the task performed at Bletchley Park, was that it was believed that while mathematicians tended to be good at cryptanalysis, the work 'did not really need mathematics'.[46] This was because prior to the emergence of machine cipher systems, such as Enigma, Britain's cryptanalysts had not required mathematicians in order to find solutions. The skills derived from the study of languages and complex texts had provided the necessary tools to tackle cryptanalytic problems up to that point. For example, one of the most celebrated

British cryptanalysts of the First and Second World Wars, Dillwyn Knox, was a Cambridge scholar not of mathematics but of classics.[47] This was because, as the wartime cryptanalyst Mavis Batey suggests, translation work and the repair of corrupted texts require both similar 'attitudes' and 'thought processes' to that of cryptanalysis.[48]

Christopher Andrew has also suggested that the agency was reticent to hire mathematicians because the Admiralty's Room 40 had been largely made up of arts graduates who were 'suspicious of mathematicians'.[49] In a letter to Andrew, Peter Twinn, an Oxford mathematician recruited to GC&CS in 1938, wrote that there had been doubts that mathematicians were suitable for the task because they were 'strange fellows, notoriously unpractical'.[50] Twinn suggested that he was recruited because his postgraduate work had been in physics, and the prevailing view was that if a scientist were to be recruited it should be a physicist because, presumably unlike mathematicians, physicists might have some 'appreciation of the real world'.[51] Andrew suggests that the two mathematicians recruited on the outbreak of war in 1939, Turing and Twinn, were chosen not because of their work in mathematics but because of their mastery of chess.[52] According to the GC&CS cryptanalyst E. R. P. Vincent, chess players were selected because cryptanalysis required 'patient consideration of endless permutations' and therefore, 'chess players filled the bill'.[53] However, according to Peter Twinn, Turing was not a strong chess player; he noted that despite his brilliance he was 'absolutely no good at chess at all'.[54]

Whatever the reason for Turing's selection by GC&CS, the inclusion of mathematicians within its ranks, along with others such as Twinn and Gordon Welchman, broke the general trend GC&CS had maintained of largely eschewing mathematicians. This shift was practical because the emergence of increasingly complex machine ciphers in the 1930s required a considerable grasp of mathematics and logic in order to analyse and understand how these cipher systems functioned and to create solutions to them. Once that trend began to change, the opportunity existed for GC&CS's mathematicians to emulate their colleagues in the arts, and increase their numbers by recruiting from within their own professional social networks.

While it was the case that GC&CS considerably expanded its roster of mathematicians immediately prior to and during the war, the extent of this trend has been overstated and is in need of qualification. For instance, Alan Turing's biographer, Andrew Hodges, notes that the introduction of mathematicians to the agency in the opening months of the Second World War profoundly altered the manner in which the agency operated, the underlying assumption being that the agency had not recruited mathematicians prior to that point.[55] Similarly, Christopher Andrew suggests that GC&CS turned to mathematicians in 1938 only when faced with Enigma, a problem that had proven stubbornly resilient to the efforts made by GC&CS's 'old guard' of classics- and linguistics-trained cryptanalysts. Thus, GC&CS employed mathematicians when repeated efforts to break Enigma using 'orthodox' methods had failed, and fresh insight and new methods were required.[56] However, there is ample evidence to suggest that earlier in the interwar period GC&CS had recruited mathematicians. In 1932 Denniston wrote to a contact at Oxford University noting that, 'Of the men we have had during the last six years, I think two took classical degrees, two mathematics and two English'.[57] Clearly, while GC&CS certainly favoured classicists and linguists to perform its cryptanalytic work, and increasingly turned towards mathematicians in the late 1930s to tackle the Enigma problem, mathematicians had already begun to infiltrate the organisation from at least the early 1930s.

Even after the agency had begun actively targeting mathematicians for recruitment as cryptanalysts, the belief in the tried and tested skill of languages remained important. For instance, in 1938, Denniston signalled GC&CS's interest in finding gifted recruits and emphasised the fact that the specific degree of the applicant was not really relevant, though an aptitude for both mathematics and languages would be a benefit.[58] The attitude continued into the war: when recruiting in 1943 for six mathematicians, it was requested that the candidates have both mathematical training and grounding in classics: 'The ideal type of candidate is the one who is good at Classics and has further specialised in Mathematics.'[59] So, even though mathematical training had achieved recognition the skills imparted through training in classics and linguistics remained important.

### Gender and the recruitment of 'Indians'

In spite of the highly specialised nature of much of the work conducted by GC&CS, and the high standard of competency – be it mathematics, languages or any other academic specialisation – required of candidates, the agency was always uncomfortable with the prospect of hiring women into senior positions, or even those positions thought to be intellectually exacting. By 1944 not a single section head was female;[60] this is not surprising because very few women were employed even as cryptanalysts. Though no definitive breakdown of numbers has emerged, women were seemingly employed more frequently as translators than in cryptanalysis, a policy that dated back to the agency's foundation, but nevertheless they tended to occupy junior roles.[61]

While the employment of women in any senior role in 1930s Britain would be unlikely, there are several reasons why male domination at GC&CS was particularly entrenched. First, the chief recruiting ground employed by GC&CS for cryptanalysts was the universities. During this period it is a truism to suggest that university attendance was male dominated, and all the more so in subjects such as mathematics. For example, between 1935 and 1939, Cambridge University produced 484 mathematics graduates, of whom only 16% were female.[62] As a result the exacting standards of GC&CS, to employ primarily graduates for these positions, automatically ensured that women would be in the minority of recruits.

Second, at the highest levels there was a deliberate preference, dating back to the interwar period, for maintaining male domination of high-level work within GC&CS and ensuring that women were in a numerical minority in these roles. For example, in 1938 Commander Denniston wrote to a colleague in the Foreign Office on the subject of recruitment and made a telling statement.

> I did not get in touch with any of the ladies' colleges because there is a very strong candidate, a Miss Egan, who has actually worked here for three years and will receive the strong backing of the heads of the sections in which she has worked, and I could not face the prospect of having our vacancies filled 100 per cent by women.[63]

Thus, not only did women make up a smaller portion of the recruitment pool that was the universities, their gender disadvantaged them. Certainly a list of some 28 junior and senior assistants within the agency in late interwar years lists a total of just four female employees, all but one of whom were junior assistants.[64]

This policy was by no means restricted to the interwar period. Even in late 1942, when the number of recruits with the highest of qualifications were growing fewer, GC&CS policy was to ensure that women were employed only when there were not enough suitable male recruits to fill the same position. When recruiting for 11 senior assistant posts to work as linguists in November 1942, recruiters were instructed that: 'Of these 5 must be men. The remainder could be women, if these were really first class people, but the age for women candidates would have to be a young forty.'[65] The men were to be placed into a more exacting role and thus required additional qualities: '[they] should have excellent German, be a clear thinking type, with health and eyesight strong enough to stand up to hard work and the night shift, etc. They should be rather more the academic type than the commercial.' On the other hand, the positions which were open to women only required 'a first class knowledge of the language at least up to University standard and the ability to work hard under trying conditions'.[66] While the potential female candidates were still required to have a high level of competency regarding their grasp of the relevant language and an ability to work hard, the depiction of the male candidates required suggests that the men were to be placed both into roles with more demanding work and leadership roles. The obvious underlying assumption was that that men were suitable for those five roles and women simply were not.

On occasion very different standards were also demanded of female candidates than male candidates. One set of recruitment guidelines produced in 1943 for the recruitment of temporary junior administrative officers suggested that male recruits be drawn directly from the universities without any particular work experience. Female applicants, on the other hand, were required to have obtained 'first class' business experience and no educational requirements were specified.[67]

Of course, GC&CS was far from unique in this regard. Nesca Robb, while discussing the wastage of women's labour in a 1940 article for *The Spectator*, argued that the misuse of the labour of professional women with highly specialised qualifications was 'infinitely depressing'. She also noted that 'The central register of the Ministry of Labour contains the names of some 96,000 specialists. Since the outbreak of war it has placed between 200 and 300 women. The others who lie buried in this august mausoleum of all the talents see little hope of resurrection.'[68]

Ultimately, despite the preference for male candidates, GC&CS did have to eventually accept female candidates and advertise positions to them. One revealing letter from Commander Bradshaw, GC&CS's paymaster and Assistant Director (Administration), in 1943 illustrates the mindset:

> We still have three vacancies which we are anxious to fill and I would be grateful for any likely men to be submitted quickly. I realise that most of the students have been placed and there is not much material left, but if it is any help to you we should be willing to take women, providing they have first class qualifications.[69]

The women employed by GC&CS could also expect lower pay than their male counterparts even for precisely the same position advertised.

When recruiting for junior assistants to work on drawing up maps, charts, diagrams and other materials at Bletchley Park, the Foreign Office recruiters were instructed to offer male recruits a salary of between £250 to £400, but female recruits £200 to £320.[70] Similarly, when the War Bonus was provided in December 1944, the bonus received by women was invariably less than that received by men in the same grade.[71] Again, GC&CS was hardly unusual in this regard and nor was it necessarily to blame. The majority of GC&CS's civilian workforce were on the Foreign Office books and thus paid on the civil service pay rates, which explicitly differentiated between male and female pay rates at the same grade.[72]

**Recruitment and the issue of 'character'**

Aside from specific intellectual or academic expertise, the correct 'character' was also a necessary qualification for employment within GC&CS. Denniston's interwar correspondence shows that candidates could be rejected, regardless of qualifications, based on perceived 'character' flaws. Such character flaws included a 'tendency for nerves'; for instance, one of GC&CS's recruiters described a 'nervous breakdown' as a direct reflection on the candidate's limited 'strength of character', and Denniston replied that he 'would hesitate to support a candidate, however good his qualifications, who showed signs of nerve weakness'.[73] As such, GC&CS's recruiters put considerable store by character references to weed out unsuitable candidates. As noted above, GC&CS actively sought the opinions of university professors and schoolmasters to determine the quality of candidates.[74] Another method of ensuring that an individual was of the correct 'character' was an examination of their social background, where good 'character' was bred. As established, an individual's education was of paramount importance to GC&CS from its creation. Christopher Grey notes that it was felt that the middle classes, both educationally and socially, produced a certain 'type' of individual who had 'integrity'.[75] In Peter Calvocoressi's view, employees shared a common, middle-class-educated background, and that background generated the kind of character traits GC&CS were looking for. Employees made 'unwittingly for the most part, the same assumptions about life and work and discipline and values'. By implication, these produced character traits which, in his view, were partially responsible for the maintenance of the Ultra secret for nearly 30 years.[76]

These assumptions regarding the type of educational and social backgrounds that bred the best intelligence officers were common across the intelligence services. Sir Paul Dukes of the SIS wrote in 1938 that the qualities that made a good member of the secret services were not 'acquired in any secret service training establishment. They are bred first in school and university life, in form room and lecture room, on the cricket and football grounds, in the boxing ring, at the chess table, in debating clubs'.[77] Thomas J. Price has suggested that the intelligence community was 'staffed with people who saw the secret service as a gentlemen's club', and, quoting Phillip Knightley, stated that they were 'amateurs – and proud of it'.[78] Summing up the attitude of amateurism as opposed to professionalism, Dukes also wrote that young men joining the intelligence services 'must not imagine it as a "career"'.[79]

As a 'gentlemen's club', the British intelligence community was willing to recruit individuals based on the recommendation of those already within the 'club'. This policy came back to haunt the intelligence community some years later, as it facilitated the recruitment of the Cambridge Five.[80] Fredrick Winterbotham, an RAF intelligence officer during the Second World War, suggested that one of the Soviet moles, Kim Philby, was recruited to MI6 without question or sufficient vetting because he had social connections to a senior figure within the agency.[81] Of course, as far as Philby's contemporaries within the intelligence services were concerned he, and other individuals later revealed to be on the Soviet payroll, were gentlemen and that alone was considered evidence of their patriotism.[82] Even the fact that another Soviet mole, Anthony Blunt, was well known to have had communist associations in his past, and was removed from an intelligence training course in 1939, did not prevent his recruitment to MI5 a few months later.[83] As Christopher Andrew notes, had the Cambridge spy-ring's members 'come from humbler backgrounds their doubtful early records would scarcely have been so easily dismissed as youthful indiscretions'.[84]

The preference for employing individuals with exclusive educational backgrounds, linked to the idea of character, was not restricted to the state and its intelligence agencies. As Peter Mandler suggests, a common belief was that 'gentlemanly spirit' was diffused to the social elites through the public schools.[85]

## Junior staff – the third tier

Peter Calvocoressi's 'Chiefs' and 'Indians', those two groups within GC&CS that worked in breaking codes and translating messages, do not include junior staff members. Thus, although Calvocoressi details at length the processes performed in his own section, Hut 3, his depiction of the work performed by Bombe operators comprised a single sentence and is not considered at all in Calvocoressi's 'Chiefs and Indians' model.[86] Calvocoressi's two-tier picture is clearly misleading because the vast majority of the agency's workforce were actually young women, often recruited into war work directly from school. These women operated machinery like the Bombes, teleprinters or punch card machines which documented the vast library of data recovered from deciphered messages, and performed the clerical work of the agency. These individuals add a third layer to the employment model constructed by Calvocoressi, one differentiated from the other two not just by the work done, but by both social class and gender.

The support staff, whose numbers were in the thousands, often came from different backgrounds to their colleagues from academia – though still tended to be distinctly middle class. To a large degree, GC&CS recruited its ancillary workforce from the armed services and the civil service, who in turn during the war had recruited or conscripted many hundreds of thousands of young women. Bletchley Park's chief pools of recruitment were the relatively socially exclusive women's branches of the Royal Navy and the RAF, both of which tended to recruit from the middle classes.[87] The agency also recruited young men with professional and trade skills to perform essential technical and mechanical work. For example, Mr H. L. Swatton, who was recruited from the Post Office Engineering Department, was employed to maintain Type-x machines.[88] Mr Swatton was a civilian and employed on the recommendation of another individual formerly employed by the Post Office, but others with technical skills that were utilised at Bletchley Park were drawn from the military. Don Smith, for instance, who prior to the war had been employed as a telephone engineer after rejection by the Royal Corps of Signals, was posted to Bletchley Park where he was employed in the maintenance of Bombes.[89]

Workers from the third tier of GC&CS's staff also found themselves recruited in a very different manner from the most senior staff. While students at the top universities found themselves approached by senior colleagues with an association with GC&CS, with perhaps an informal interview to follow, those in the third tier could expect very different treatment, including lengthy periods of waiting without contact from the agency. For example, Don Smith, after being called up and subsequently rejected by the Royal Corps of Signals, was told to report back to his previous job, but a month later out of the blue he received a letter from the Foreign Office calling him for an interview. After the interview he heard nothing again for a further six weeks, at which point he was told to report to Bletchley Park for a second interview.[90]

Don Smith's experience, characterised by its mystery and lengthy periods of silence on the part of the agency, represents one manner in which relatively junior staff members were interviewed. Others were met with intimidating interviews. For example, James 'Jimmy' Thirsk initially had a friendly and informal interview with an officer from the Intelligence Corps, where his suitability as a potential candidate for signals intelligence work was noted. After several weeks of silence a letter was sent requesting that he report to London for a second interview. This interview, carried out by a panel of seven staff officers, was far more 'intimidating'. Jimmy recalled volleys of questions: his pre-war occupation, his current role in the army, and whether he played chess or was skilled in solving crossword puzzles.[91] As with Don Smith, Jimmy was not told anything further for some time, and only some six weeks later was he told of his transfer. Other candidates were tested during their interview to ensure a degree of technical proficiency. Mr Swatton, in his capacity as a Post Office engineer, was not only interviewed but undertook a test on a variety of mechanical equipment, prior to being posted to Bletchley Park as a Type-x technician.[92]

These experiences stand in stark contrast to the recruitment practice for many of those in more senior positions. William Millward, a translator in Hut 3, underwent two interviews (one for the position he eventually received in Hut 3 and the other for similar work abroad), both of which he described as 'friendly' and 'encouraging', and was contacted within two weeks.[93] John Cairncross was subjected to even less: 'I suppose my position as Private Secretary to Lord Hankey had been sufficient guarantee of reliability, and I was taken on by the GC&CS and not even subjected to any interrogation.'[94]

Of course, the increase in staff to maintain GC&CS's operations required an increase in support staff, who occupied a lower fourth tier, to maintain the key operations. These staff members have left very little trace in the agency's archives and we know little about them. Nevertheless, these individuals played a vital role in the continued operation of GC&CS. For example, drivers were required in increasing numbers to transport staff members to and from Bletchley Park to their billets, to collect senior staff, and to perform numerous other transportation duties. In March 1942 this team of drivers was not insignificant, numbering some 50 individuals; however, by the time GC&CS was at its largest in 1944, there were over 130 drivers employed.[95] Similarly, Bletchley Park's staff required feeding, and in early 1943 SIS was supplying Bletchley Park with 100 caterers.[96]

The need for support staff also manifested itself in other ways. Bletchley Park now contained not only the mansion house but an ever-increasing number of wooden huts, followed by a series of larger steel and brick blocks. The blocks and huts had not only to be built, but also maintained, as did the house and grounds. This meant that Bletchley Park also required tradesmen, such as carpenters, joiners, gardeners, bricklayers and electricians, to build and maintain the site. Bletchley Park actually had a section of 25 builders and four gardeners to manage the necessary maintenance work. At least one of those employed in the maintenance of the site was a local man, Bob Watson, who worked on the site before, during and after the war.[97] While the majority of the staff at Bletchley Park were not locals, Bob was not unique. Mimi Gallilee, a school girl evacuated to the area, found work at the agency as a messenger runner.[98] Not only were staff members required for the maintenance of the buildings, but staff were also necessary to keep the building clean. As with the caterers, cleaners were largely employed by SIS, and by 1943 SIS was employing over 80 cleaners at Bletchley Park.[99]

## Gender and the third tier

At the height of the war a large portion of Bletchley Park's staff contingent consisted of women, who mostly filled many of the supporting positions necessary for the operations being carried out. Most of these women were assigned to Bletchley Park via the armed forces, and as with their male colleagues recruited to third-tier roles in GC&CS from the forces, they also were subjected to a formal interview process.[100] Only a few of these women were employed outside of the lower level positions, despite many having a specialised and even an exclusive education. The agency itself recorded in its post-war review that an 'unusually high percentage of supporting staff were i) university trained ii) Higher School certificate standard'.[101]

While the bulk of the women recruited to Bletchley Park were from the armed services or had relevant employment experience, the majority were typically drawn from the middle classes. Many were young women who had recently finished their school education and still lived with their parents. Others acquired their position at Bletchley Park through social connections. The bulk, however, had specific skills or qualifications, suggesting that recruiters for Bletchley Park had a particular brief. The fact that women engaged in low-grade work required relatively high qualifications is suggestive that the agency wanted relatively well-educated women not merely to ensure that they had a high calibre of recruit in terms of ability but also of relatively high social standing.[102] The GC&CS veteran James Hogarth recollects that these women came from both 'good families and good schools'.[103] As Christopher Grey argues, there was a belief that well-educated, middle-class individuals were likely to have the 'integrity' necessary for highly confidential work.[104] This link between social class and integrity among third-tier staff reflects the similar assumptions made by GC&CS's recruiters regarding 'character' outlined earlier in relation to high-grade staff members.

The most popular source for recruiters of women for lower-grade positions such as machine operators were the armed forces. Early in the war, the agency's deficit of employees to deal with the mundane tasks of machine and equipment operation was a major bottleneck demanding the attentions of high-grade staff who could otherwise have been employed in their primary function within the agency.[105] The solution to this was to draw female staff from the armed forces. The primary task of these female workers was to operate machinery, including Bombe machine operation, but later included machines constructed to deal with other forms of cipher.[106] Members of the Women's Royal Naval Service (WRNS) typically filled these positions, which numbered nearly 2,600 by the winter of 1944. The other major task that servicewomen fulfilled was the operation of the agency's communications devices such as teleprinters. This task was typically filled by members of the Women's Auxiliary Air Force (WAAF), and by the end of 1944 nearly 1,100 were employed.[107]

In the majority of cases the Wrens were young women in their late teens or early twenties and without any obvious qualifications for their role as Bombe operators. One Bombe operator noted that she believed she had no specific qualifications that gave her an advantage in the selection process other than a taste for crossword puzzles.[108] Other Wrens working on the Bombes also noted a lack of relevant, if any, qualifications for the work they were doing,[109] though some noted that they found themselves working on the Bombes after a series of choices made during the recruitment process.

> When we started talking about what one could do, there appeared to be only three categories available, and that was: steward, cook or what they called P5. So my friend and I asked what P5 was, and they said, 'Sorry, but we can't tell you.' So, being foolish and 17 ½ thought, that sounds exciting, let's go for P5. Actually it stood for HMS Pembroke 5. Then we went for the interview for that they asked if we wanted to be clerical or technical – we both said technical.[110]

The actual work which the Wrens would be engaged in was also a secret, and as a result those who were drafted to work on the Bombes had to accept the position without any idea of what it might entaile. All they were officially told was that it was shift work, had limited opportunity for promotion, and necessarily involved complete secrecy. Based on this limited information alone Wrens were asked to decide their future.[111]

As a result, it appears that GC&CS had no specific recruitment policy in place for Bombe operators that demanded a specific set of qualifications. Rather, operators were recruited to work on the Bombes because the work vaguely matched the preferences of those who applied to the WRNS and because the Wrens themselves held a basic standard of education. This suggests that the work was considered relatively unskilled – certainly, it did not require either the elite social or educational qualification that was considered essential in finding suitable cryptanalysts. However, the work was considered to require 'a high standard of mental agility', and as a result it was typical that those Wrens employed had passed their General School Certificate.[112] The operators were not, however, expected to begin work without formal introduction to and instruction on the work in question. Quite the reverse was the case: the machinery was considered to be complex and formal training was necessary before the Wrens were employed on the machines.[113] Wrens operating the Colossus machines had a similarly high standard of education, as well as appropriate social background. According to the *General Report on Tunny*,[114] '[T]wenty-one per cent had Higher Certificate, 9 per cent had been to a University, 22 per cent had some after school training and 28 per cent had previous paid employment. None had studied mathematics at the university.'[115]

The backgrounds of the bulk of the women employed by the agency were a reflection of the service they had joined. Gerard DeGroot suggests that both the WRNS and the WAAF tended to recruit women from middle-class backgrounds, while the Auxiliary Territorial Service (ATS) tended to recruit working-class women.[116] The contribution of the ATS to GC&CS's overall staff contingent was relatively minor: even when the figure was at its highest in January 1945, the number of ATS personnel was only 414, less than 5% of the agency's staff members.[117] The result of this suggests that the bulk of the women employed by GC&CS came from broadly similar backgrounds, because it was women from those backgrounds that these particular armed services tended to recruit. For instance, Bess Farrow, née Cooper, a member of the WRNS who had volunteered in 1942 immediately after completing school, was the daughter of Sir Stanford Cooper, a successful businessman.[118]

Similarly, Barbara Moor, a Wren employed by the agency to operate Bombe machines, recalled that she had attended grammar school and then college in Chelsea, studying child welfare and mother-craft. Following her education Barbara held a number of jobs working with children, but volunteered for the WRNS following the evacuation from Dunkirk. Her father had been in the Navy himself prior to finding employment in the insurance industry.[119] Her education and her father's employment in white-collar work are suggestive of a relatively middle-class background. Gwendoline Page, also a Wren, had attended grammar school and her father owned a 'reasonable shop with a number of assistants'. Gwendoline recalled that she had been relatively successful in school and had taken a second language, a privilege afforded only to the more gifted students (those less able had to forgo a second language and study sewing and domestic science).[120] Ruth Bourne, again a WRNS Bombe operator, had been schooled in both Switzerland and Wales prior to returning to her home city of Birmingham. Prior to her war service Ruth had taken the university matriculation exam and had begun the process of taking a university degree in German, French and Spanish. Her father was a doctor and her mother had, prior to marriage, been a violinist.[121] These factors again are indicative of a middle-class, even privileged, background. Alice Wolynskyj, prior to joining the WRNS, had a scholarship to a grammar school. Of the other five women selected for 'Special Duties' with whom Alice was grouped, three had also been scholarship girls and the other two had attended boarding school. Alice described her immediate colleagues as 'a social mix. Some girls were titled, tho' they never flaunted this. One could tell by their manicured hands and groomed hair.'[122] However, clearly that mix was within the upper and middle classes.

These examples suggest that while there was some diversity among the servicewomen employed at Bletchley, those within the WRNS did fit the general stereotype of a middle-class background. This stands in contrast with Joan Thirsk, a former member of the ATS and Bletchley Park veteran.[123] Unusually, Joan had come from a relatively working-class background in London and from the ATS. However, she was academically gifted, and had planned to attend university to study modern European languages. Though Joan did not mention her schooling, beyond to note that it was in London, her eventual departure to university suggests that it is likely that she too had attended a grammar school. However, women like Joan buck the general trend.

## The numerical expansion of GC&CS

At the beginning of the war, Bletchley Park employed approximately 200 staff members.[124] By January 1945 that number had increased to in excess of 8,000 individuals. Figure 2.1 and Table 2.1 illustrate that increase.[125]

However, until March 1942 full details of staff numbers were not kept by the agency or, if they were kept, have proved elusive. As the only full study of GC&CS's staff numbers, produced by Kerry Johnson and John Gallehawk, notes, the available evidence is 'fragmentary'. That said, Gallehawk and Johnson have shown that by December 1940 GC&CS's personnel had risen to at least 674.[126] This change, from 200

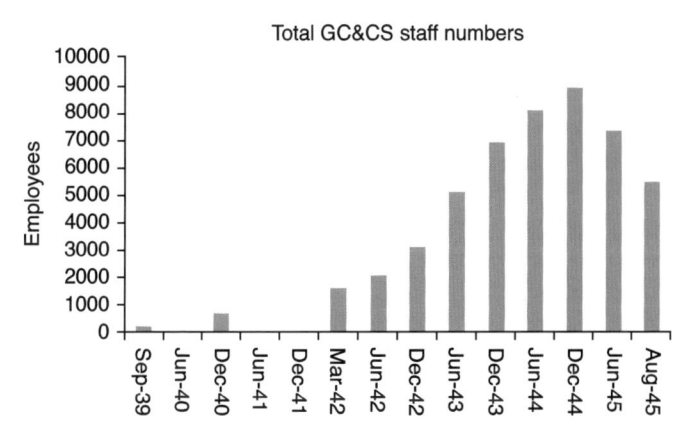

*Figure 2.1* Total GC&CS staff numbers

*Table 2.1* GC&CS staff numbers at Bletchley Park, 1939–1945

| Date | Staff numbers |
| --- | --- |
| September 1939 | 186 |
| December 1940 | 674 |
| March 1942 | 1,584 |
| June 1942 | 2,040 |
| December 1942 | 3,116 |
| June 1943 | 5,052 |
| December 1943 | 6,864 |
| June 1944 | 8,054 |
| December 1944 | 8,854 |
| June 1945 | 7,312 |
| August 1945 | 5,485 |

to nearly 700 individuals, is a remarkable increase in staff numbers over just 16 months, a staff expansion of some 262%. At no other stage during the expansion of the agency is there such a marked growth, in percentage terms.

Over the course of the war, the increases in staff levels slowed considerably. Between June 1942 and December of that year the staff contingent increased by some 52%; during the same months in 1944 that increase had slowed to just 10%. The bulk of this growth was in the form of auxiliary staff facilitating the expanding operations performed by the agency. The reason for the rapid expansion in the early phase of the war was the rapid rate in which Axis wireless traffic was being intercepted. During 1940 the cryptanalysts at GC&CS received some 100,000 messages,[127] by September 1941 the number of messages being intercepted each month exceeded 30,000 from the UK alone and within a further five months that figure exceeded 50,000.[128]

However, the declining rate of staff increases in percentile terms hides the numerical size of staff increases over the course of the war. While the increase of nearly 500 individuals between the outbreak of war in 1939 and the winter of 1940/41 represented an increase of over 260%, an increase in terms of percent which was not achieved again, in numerical terms it was far outshadowed. For example, between June 1942 and December 1943 GC&CSs staff numbers increased from 2,040 to 6,864; an increase of 227% but a numerical increase of 4,824.

The most striking feature regarding the enormous influx of staff into the agency is that of changing numerical gender domination. From the early years of GC&CS up until March 1942 this is very difficult, if not impossible, to establish as fact rather than assumption because of the fragmentary nature of the evidence available. That said, Alistair Denniston, writing after the war, contended that on GC&CS's formation in 1919 the staff contingent was made up of 25 'pensionable officers' and a further 28 'clerical staff'.[129] Given the recruitment practices outlined earlier of senior figures within GC&CS it seems likely that the vast majority of the 'pensionable officers' would have been male and the majority of the clerical staff would have been female. Later Denniston provided some further illumination regarding the gender breakdown of the clerical staff of the agency, when he noted that after discussion with the Treasury following the 1929 Tomlin Civil Service Commission,

> we did obtain sanction for the establishment of two higher clerical, [sic] some six to ten clerical officers, about a dozen clerical assistants and half a dozen typists.

By this means we were able to retain with prospects of pension some of those girls and women who had proved their value to us in both our functions.[130]

While not explicit, the implication of Denniston's statement is that the bulk of the clerical staff were female. As a result it seems likely that at its formation in 1919 approximately half the agency's employees were female, and that these women largely conducted the clerical work produced by the agency, while the men primarily dealt with the tasks of cryptanalysis and translation. However, as Denniston's statement also pointed out, when referring to 'both our functions', it is clear that men did not hold an absolute monopoly on this work – particularly in the case of translation.

During the interwar years it is clear that women also worked as translators. Denniston pointed out that in 1937 the agency persuaded the Treasury to recruit '56 seniors, men or women' as well as '30 girls with a graduate's knowledge of at least two of the languages required'.[131] These factors considered it is again reasonable to assume that of the approximately 200 employees of GC&CS at least half were female. Of these women, a small minority worked as a cryptanalysts, a larger proportion worked as linguists and a more significant number were employed in clerical and secretarial roles.

By March 1942 the introduction of new administrative policies created regularly produced documentation listing the agency's staff statistics. The newly instituted weekly returns provide not only the gender of employees but their service or ministry affiliation. By May the situation had become very different from the blurred image of the early war years. Numerically speaking, women had come to dominate GC&CS, comprising over two thirds of the staff. Over the course of the war this ratio increased. In the final week of March 1942 the agency had a total of 1,584 employees, 451 of whom were male and 1,133 female.[132] By the same point in 1944 there were, excluding the SIS contingent, some 7,456 individuals working at Bletchley Park, only 1,775 of whom were male and 5,681 female. Figure 2.2 shows the increase of staff members by gender from 1942 to 1945.[133] The rapid growth in the number of female staff numbers was a direct result of the changing policies of the agency following the 1942 reorganisation.

One of the chief causes of this reorganisation was serious issues with recruitment. While the agency had rapidly grown in size from the outbreak of the war to the end of 1940, GC&CS was still suffering severe labour shortages as, over the course of 1941, allied military efforts grew to

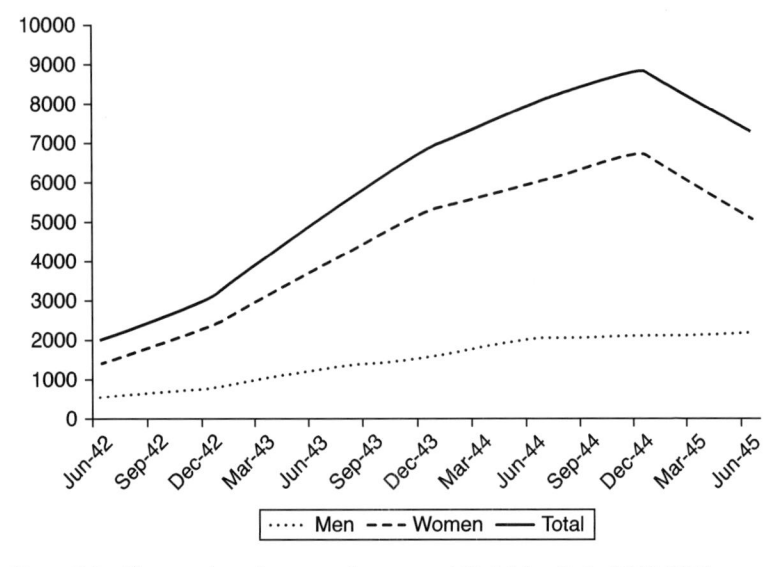

[Chart showing men, women, and total personnel at Bletchley Park from Jun-42 to Jun-45. Total rises from about 2000 in Jun-42 to a peak near 8800 in Dec-44, declining to about 7300 by Jun-45. Women rise from about 1500 to a peak around 6700 in Dec-44. Men remain relatively flat, rising slowly from about 500 to about 2100.]

*Figure 2.2* The number of men and women at Bletchley Park, 1942–1945

encompass many more theatres of war, ranging from the Mediterranean and North Africa to the Far East. Frank Birch, in GCHQ's own history of its predecessor organisation, noted that one of the key causes of the revision of the SIGINT services was the shortage of both equipment and personnel, both for GC&CS and the Y Service.[134]

The solution proposed by the agency to the latter problem was to employ members of the WRNS to operate the Bombe machines, which were both labour intensive and steadily growing in numbers. Wrens had already been employed by the Y Service as wireless operators as early as March 1940. The mass employment of female members of the armed services to ease the workload demanded by the process of generating SIGINT was soon to spread across the existing infrastructure. For the March following the February 1942 reorganisation of GC&CS, Frank Birch listed some 159 female members of the Royal Navy as having been employed by the agency. By 27 December 1942 this figure had risen to 613 and by December 1943 to 1,874. At the peak of GC&CS's growth in the winter of 1944/45 Birch listed the service branch of GC&CS as employing some 2,546 women from the Royal Navy.[135]

A similar trend can be observed in the recruitment of members of the Women's Auxiliary Air Force. GC&CS turned, as it had done to the Royal Navy when looking for machine operators, to the RAF for women recruits to operate its communications equipment. The result was that, as with the number of Wrens recruited, the number of members of the WAAF seconded by the agency rose steadily during the second half of the war. In March 1942 the agency had 158 WAAFs on its books. By the end of the year that figure had increased to 400, and by December 1944 there were 1,553.[136]

The winter of 1944 saw the peak of growth in GC&CS's staff numbers and marked the end of recruitment by GC&CS. Between 7 January 1945 and 20 May 1945 the staff numbers began to decline, though only by 129 individuals, from 8,982 to 8,853, a decline of only 1.4%. However, from 20 May 1945 the agency's numbers began to fall rapidly as military operations in Europe wound down following the German surrender on 8 May. Despite the ongoing conflict against Japan until August 1945 the agency very rapidly wound down and over the three months between May and August 1945 the number of individuals on GC&CS's books dropped from 8,853 to 5,485, an average decline of over 1,000 staff members each month.[137]

## GC&CS and staff pay

Staff payment at GC&CS was a major issue throughout the Second World War, part of the problem being that rates of pay were often determined by how staff members were recruited, and their status upon recruitment. While the disparity of pay between genders has been briefly discussed earlier in this chapter, the issue of pay disparity was a major administrative headache for GC&CS's management and requires further discussion. GC&CS itself largely did not provide the funds to pay its staff; instead, those staff members were paid by the service or ministry from which they had been drawn. As the civil service and armed services employed different pay scales, individuals employed in identical work, particularly those within the Chief and Indian categories, received different pay. Thus the recruitment of an individual played a significant role in determining how much they were paid. For instance, junior assistants within the civil service received between £260 and £400 each year which was subject to tax deductions. However, army lieutenants (the most junior rank eligible to work in the Intelligence Corps) were paid £500 a year, around half of which was tax-free.[138] The same issue applied to senior assistants within the civil service, who were paid £600 a year (all of which was subject to tax) while captains in the army doing the same, or similar work, were paid £750 (nearly £300 of which was tax-free).[139]

In 1943 the problem became even more pronounced when service officers received a considerable pay rise while the civil service officers did not. As a result, 295 officers within the Services of the rank of captain or above were in receipt of a minimum of £900 per year. However, only eight out of 225 civil servants of officer rank were paid that amount or more. Despite talks with the Treasury to resolve the issue of pay by promoting some of the civil servants to a more senior rank, the problem was never fully solved and discrepancies continued throughout the war. For example, section heads if civil servants were appointed to a civil service rank equivalent to that of a major in the army, while their colleagues in similar positions within the armed services were typically of the rank of lieutenant colonel, commander or wing commander, which were both one rank senior to that of an army major.[140]

However, regardless of the discrepancies in the rates of pay for cryptographers and translators, these rates were far higher than those for GC&CS's female rank and file. A Wren, for instance, was paid only 1s 8d a day or approximately £30 a year. 1s 8d was also the base rate of pay for women in the army and in the RAF. Even the most senior non-commissioned Wrens were paid only 5s 4d a day, less than £100 a year, and Third Officers £130 a year.[141]

## Conclusion

An examination of the recruitment policies of GC&CS from its inception in 1919 through to the end of the war show remarkable achievements, in terms of both recruitment and administration, on the part of GC&CS's administrators and leaders. These individuals, during the interwar period, operated a very small agency of at most a couple of hundred individuals, yet following the outbreak of war would, in just a few years, expand that agency to several thousand employees, peaking by the latter months of the war at around 10,000 individuals at the main Bletchley war station and its surrounding outstations. Considerable foresight was also shown by GC&CS's commanding officer Alistair Denniston, when he began a pre-war recruitment campaign to sound out potential recruits from within Britain's intellectual elite as well as to build up a recruitment network within the university system to act as talent scouts. This network provided GC&CS with the opportunity to recruit academically gifted individuals with particular relevant skills to the work being conducted by the agency.

In terms of cryptanalysts, the agency began emphasising the recruitment of mathematicians as opposed to the classicists, historians and linguists it had tended to favour in its early years. This choice of candidate, who typically held a degree in mathematics, may go some way to explaining the continuing relative paucity of women employed as cryptanalysts. The primary port of call for mathematicians was Cambridge University, due to GC&CS's lengthy association with the university since the First World War, despite the fact that other universities were also producing a significant number of mathematicians.[142] As all universities in this period, Cambridge University during the interwar period produced a far smaller number of female graduates in mathematics than male graduates.[143] As a result men dominated the recruitment pool. However, considerable evidence from GC&CS's files suggests that there was also an institutional sexist attitude at play in the recruitment process. Women's colleges were excluded from recruitment drives and efforts were made to actively recruit male candidates that excluded female candidates. Unfortunately, the precise number of women employed as cryptanalysts remains unknown; however, all the evidence suggests that they were a distinct minority.

In terms of the recruitment of linguists and intelligence analysts, women saw better representation. Indeed, female translators were not uncommon in GC&CS, a policy which dated back to the agency's foundation. As in the case of mathematicians, these individuals tended to be highly educated individuals drawn from a very small pool of universities.

Female recruits overwhelmingly filled lower-grade staff positions. A sizable portion of these recruits were seconded from the female branches of the armed forces, in particular the WRNS and the WAAF. This choice of services from which to draw recruits resulted in a relatively more diverse social mixture of staff members in the lower grades than in the higher grades. That said, the nature of these two services still resulted in a preponderance of middle-class female staff members. An examination of some 15 individuals in the lower grades, while clearly an insufficient sample to make precise claims but still suggestive, implies that both grammar and boarding schools were common features in these recruits' education (Appendix 1). Many recruits also seem to have been employed by other branches of the government before finding themselves working for GC&CS. These factors suggest that lower-grade female recruits tended to be middle class, with relatively exclusive educational backgrounds.

In many respects the recruitment policies of GC&CS both before and during the war conformed to wider trends in British society during the period, particularly when it came to the employment of women.

As noted, some contemporary commentators were quick to point out that professional women with specialist qualifications were not being employed in wartime in positions relative to the skills they possessed. Penny Summerfield notes that this was common particularly in the early years of the war and that groups such as the British Federation of Business and Professional Women lobbied MPs and officials to alter the situation.[144] These efforts were met with some success: educated women did gain greater access to positions of management and promotion to officer ranks in the women's auxiliary services.[145] This success was replicated in GC&CS to a limited degree. While women never reached positions of senior management within GC&CS, there are examples of women in junior management, leading subsections or rising into the officer ranks of the women's services while working for the agency. For example, Mary Pain was an officer in the WAAF and held a junior management position in the Type-x Section.[146]

That said, with regards to GC&CS, this point does require some qualification. Whilst the agency clearly favoured educated male employees over educated women in those positions requiring key academic skills, from its foundation it did employ women in these positions. This was particularly true of those women with qualifications in foreign languages who found work in the agency as translators. In terms of cryptanalysis opportunities for women were far fewer, but were certainly not unheard of. Those women who showed particular aptitude for the work were certainly not disbarred; for instance, Mavis Lever (later Batey) was a particularly successful cryptanalyst working on the *Abwehr* Enigma under the direction of Dillwyn Knox.[147] Furthermore, when the agency was pressed hard to find recruits, it paid greater attention than it had done before to the female-only colleges of the universities. These points noted, it was still undoubtedly the case that the agency was far more disposed towards employing men in senior positions as well as those positions requiring academic skills.

To an extent, GC&CS also conformed to wider trends in terms of gendered allocation of work in its willingness to recruit women to fill lower-grade work such as machine operation and clerical work. The war had the dual effect of increasing demand on 'essential' industries as well as creating a labour shortage. The solution to these problems was to increase the recruitment of women into these industries. In 1939 women provided 14% of the labour to these industries, and by 1943 this had increased to 33%, or some 1.5 million women.[148] The primary effort among employers was to place these women into low-skilled work and to reclassify what had been considered semi-skilled labour when conducted by men as unskilled.[149] Employers maintained that women were not capable of undertaking skilled work and that women required both supervision and aid in mechanical work. This allowed them to pay women less to perform the same tasks.[150]

The Ministry of Labour and National Service, which had previously made some effort in offering relatively high-level training for women to address the increasing wartime shortage of skilled labour, found that industry was unwilling to make full use of the training it had provided women and instead opted to provide women with generalised courses in 'machine minding'.[151] As a result it is not surprising to see that GC&CS's primary solution to the growing problem of finding staff to operate the ever-growing number of machines developed to speed up the process of cryptanalysis and data storage was to employ women. Large numbers of women were drafted from the women's auxiliary services and the civil service and put to work operating machines and performing vital clerical work. Outside GC&CS women in employment in industry and factory work were typically drawn from the working classes. However, GC&CS employed typically middle-class women, from the WRNS and WAAF, to perform machine work in factory-type conditions. Thus, while GC&CS tended in many ways to conform to wider trends in Britain when it came to allocating work by gender, in terms of class the agency was different.

# 3
# On-Duty Life at the Government Code and Cypher School

## Introduction

Bletchley Park's workers are typically presented in the popular press and media as a small group of brilliant, if often somewhat eccentric, men employing the most modern machines to crack Axis codes. This picture has been developed since the 'Ultra Secret' was first revealed to the world by F. W. Winterbotham in 1974. Indeed, the preface to Winterbotham's memoir conforms to the myth by stating that the 'cipher breaking operation' was 'accomplished by a team of brilliant mathematicians and cryptographers'.[1] No individual captures this image quite like Alan Turing, who has become the archetypal Bletchley Park employee. For example, the 2014 film *The Imitation Game*, a biopic of Turing's life and wartime achievements, places Turing at the centre of a small handful of cryptanalysts.[2] The film serves as an excellent example of the popular perception of the agency and will doubtless also contribute much to maintaining an inexorable focus on Turing and cryptanalysis in popular imagination. While the work of the cryptanalysts was, of course, at the epicentre of the agency's function, it is easy to lose focus of the fact that the agency required a vast array of other forms of work in order to adequately operate. These other types of work, ranging from machine operation to cleaning, were vital support roles which facilitated the main work of the agency: cracking ciphers and reading messages.

The mechanisation and expansion of GC&CS led to the rapid development of new roles within the agency, most of a factory and clerical nature. These new forms of labour added to the work of the pre-existing cryptanalytic, translation and research roles to create a diverse array of employment types within the agency. As discussed in previous chapters, the manner in which these different sections were operated and managed varied according to the type of work performed. Machine and clerical sections tended to be operated on factory principles, while high-grade labour such as cryptanalysis was performed in a far more collegiate environment. Much of the work conducted by the agency was unique, particularly that form of work centred on cryptanalysis. However, other types of work were rather more generic. For instance, machine operation, despite the unique nature of Bletchley's machines, was hardly uncommon in wartime Britain. Meanwhile, much of the agency's work, ranging from the clerical and bureaucratic to the everyday labours of cleaners and drivers, could also be expected in any wartime facility. This chapter will explore how the agency managed its workforce and the experiences of GC&CS's wartime workers while on duty, with particular attention paid to working conditions and efforts to maintain staff morale. We will broadly follow the migration of individual messages across the major sections of the agency. As such, the chapter begins with those sections which registered messages when they first arrived, before moving onto cryptanalysis, machine operation, translation, indexing and finally security.

## Communications and traffic analysis

Intercepted messages underwent considerable processing prior to arrival at GC&CS. Axis messages were initially received by the Y Service, which operated radio interception stations across the world. Once intercepted, the messages were sent to GC&CS at Bletchley for processing. There were two means of sending the transcribed messages to Bletchley Park. First, for priority intercepts, there was the teleprinter. This method was used to quickly transmit important messages directly for processing and, in doing so, to save potentially vital time. The second method of delivering intercepts was to send them by dispatch rider. Dispatch riders not only carried all those intercepts deemed of lesser priority, but they also carried backup copies of all priority messages sent to the agency via teleprinter.[3]

The messages sent to Bletchley Park via teleprinter were received by GC&CS's Communications Section. The RAF handled the telecommunications at Bletchley Park, providing the staff to operate communications equipment.[4] These staff were members of the WAAF, and, as we have seen, over 1,000 were employed at Bletchley Park at the height of the war.[5] The Communications Section included not just teleprinter operators receiving Axis messages for decryption and analysis and forwarding deciphered and processed intelligence to relevant ministries and commands, but also the encipherment of those messages in the British cipher system, Type-x.[6]

Bletchley also liaised with, and directed, the Y Service. In Hut 6, the people who liaised with the Y Service were housed in the Control Room. By working with the Y Service British cryptanalysts could try to prioritise geographic locations and frequencies that they hoped would yield them the best results.[7] Even after the messages had been received by GC&CS, important information could still be gleaned from the radio transmission itself, which is why the Y Service was also tasked with direction finding (DF). A number of DF stations would each take a bearing on an enemy transmission which, when combined, could be used to establish the location of the transmitter. This was a useful means of tracking the location of enemy military units. In addition, research known as traffic analysis (TA) was conducted upon the signals.[8] TA was used to gather potentially valuable information from the messages independent of the actual content of those messages, for instance to expose and examine patterns in intercepted radio traffic. The individuals engaged in TA went under the title of log readers. Jimmy Thirsk, who worked as a log reader first at Beaumanor and then at Bletchley Park in Hut 6, recalled that there were around 50 log readers, mostly non-commissioned officers in the army.[9] The benefit of traffic analysis was that a considerable amount of information could be gathered from the number and point of origin of messages. For example, the lines of Axis communications could be produced, Axis military units movements could be tracked, and a build-up of forces in a specific area could be observed via radio traffic.[10]

Once the messages had been received at Bletchley they were then distributed to the various sections within GC&CS that dealt with cryptanalysis. The sections were broken down into the various agencies from which they originated. For example Hut 6, the Air Force and Army Cryptanalysis Section at Bletchley Park, analysed *Wehrmacht* and *Luftwaffe* messages, while Hut 8 did the same for German naval Enigma traffic. These sections were broken down further into various subsections, each of which was designated specific tasks necessary to analysis of the received messages. This included the aforementioned subsections that were involved in traffic analysis.

## Cryptanalysis

Once the message had been registered and prioritised, and the callsign and frequency noted, the messages went to the cryptanalysts. The cryptanalysts are the individuals who dominate the popular image of

Bletchley Park. As noted in the previous chapter on recruitment, the cryptanalysts were, with some notable exceptions such as Mavis Batey (née Lever), men educated at elite universities.[11] Initially, prior to the introduction of mechanical devices to speed up the process,[12] the entire cryptanalysis process was completed by hand. Naturally this process, even when successful, failed to achieve sufficient results quickly enough to be of much strategic use. In order to speed up the process the cryptanalysts worked on improving the methods of attacking the messages, and this led to the development of many of the mechanical systems, such as the Bombes and the Colossus machines, with which Bletchley Park has become associated.

The most common technique cryptanalysts employed to attack Axis messages was known as 'depth'. Put simply, cryptanalysts looked for examples where the teleprinter operator had made an error which could be exploited (repeated text, for example). The Enigma system also had some flaws, notably that the Enigma machines could not encipher a letter as itself. As a result the cryptanalysts had at least a foothold into the system. This could be exploited by the use of 'cribs'. A crib was a commonly used piece of text used in German transmissions. For example, a message from a German weather ship sent at the same time each day may have begun with the same line of text on each transmission. The cryptanalysts, armed with this knowledge, and the fact that the Enigma machine could not encipher the same letter as itself, could in theory extrapolate the key to the machine's settings. Careful analysis of the message in question allowed the cryptanalysts to improve the chance that they would produce a correct crib. If a crib in plain text had a single letter that corresponded with a letter in the same position in the message then that crib could be ruled out. The lengthier the crib that was not ruled out, the higher the probability that it would be correct.[13] To improve the odds further, cryptanalysts were also employed in the development of new methods of analysing messages, improving existing methods and attacking keys which had yet to be broken.[14]

The task of the majority of cryptanalysts was to attempt to work out the key being used each day. As part of this process the cryptanalysts drew upon previous messages sent. As a result, copies of messages were retained by GC&CS for future use – not least in the production of cribs. In Hut 8, which was tasked with attacking German naval messages, the individuals responsible for producing cribs were known as 'cribsters'.[15] The cribs produced would then be sent on to the Bombe room for testing; if correct, this would lead to the solution of the day's key. In Hut 6 the cryptanalysts performing this task were known as the Watch.

The Watch produced various menus which were passed on to the Bombe room for testing.

The work itself was intellectual puzzle-solving work conducted at a desk, attempting to discover patterns and apply cribs to a seemingly unintelligible string of random letters. The work was highly repetitive and required patience and meticulous attention to detail. The cryptanalysts employed and invented various extremely complex methods, with pen and paper, to apply cribs to Enigma messages.[16] The application of these methods, invented by individuals such as Dillywn Knox, became the highly repetitive daily task of the agency's cryptanalysts. One cryptanalyst described the work as being 'pretty tedious', stating that the tools and the process of the work involved working on a large piece of graph paper and adding figures together, and if, by the end of the page, they had reached a 'certain collection of numbers at the bottom [of the sheet], we'd broken it'.[17] However, the tedium of the work was broken by success. Asa Briggs recalls in his memoir the delight of having produced a successful 'crib'.[18]

Maintaining morale was an issue that many section heads, including the heads of cryptanalysis sections, took very seriously – because morale was believed to have a considerable impact on an organisation's efficiency.[19] In the cryptanalysis sections, the aim was to create a collegial managerial system in which individuals had the intellectual freedom to pursue their work, while harmoniously working together to solve problems.[20] Hugh Alexander, head of Hut 8 from 1942, noted that the idea in cryptanalysis sections like his was to achieve 'business efficiency whilst preserving the atmosphere of a cooperative voluntarily undertaken for its own sake'.[21] One of the means of achieving both high morale, and with it a harmonious and efficient working environment, was to ensure that the entire section was aware (in as much as was possible within a secret environment) of what they were doing, why they were doing it, and how their work played a vital role in the war effort. Gordon Welchman noted that he specifically kept those in his section, Hut 6, informed of various successes made by the section and the overall importance of the work being done to encourage those under his command.[22] Part of this process was to create a productive and cooperative collegiate working atmosphere within the section. Similarly, individuals within Hut 8 also reported that a collegiate atmosphere was fostered in their section. For instance, Rolf Noskwith, a veteran of Hut 8, likened his war work as 'in many ways like having an extra four years of university life'.[23]

Certainly, the sections were run with a less than military outlook. Many individuals working in the various sections were of course not technically in the military at all. Of those who were, in many cases they appear to have been under no obligation to follow conventional military etiquette such as, for example, the wearing of uniform.[24] For instance, Asa Briggs (who held the army rank of regimental sergeant major, and prior to joining Bletchley Park had been a soldier in the Royal Corps of Signals, the Intelligence Corps and the Y Service[25]) recalls that while he and his colleagues had to wear military uniform while in the military camps that housed Bletchley Park service staff members, there was no requirement that he did so in Bletchley Park itself.[26] Furthermore, military rank had little bearing on the internal hierarchy of the sections, with individuals nominally within the military working alongside individuals of lower or more senior rank as well as civilians.[27] Clearly, when it came to cryptanalysts, military status was only nominal. Fostering a collegiate working atmosphere was given priority and there was little adherence to formal military culture.

On the whole, cryptanalysts recalled the work as being fulfilling, for instance Noskwith described his work as both fascinating and satisfying.[28] However, during periods when the work yielded little in the way of results morale plummeted. In 1942, the German navy upgraded their Enigma system (codenamed 'Shark') which caused a major, if temporary, intelligence blackout until the cryptanalysts found a solution. This period of morale-crippling frustration for the cryptanalysts was further compounded by increasing pressure from the Admiralty to generate results. The Admiralty's Operational Intelligence Centre sent a memorandum to Bletchley Park stating that the Battle of the Atlantic was 'the one campaign which Bletchley Park are not influencing to any marked extent – and it is the only one in which the war can be lost unless BP *do* help'.[29] Bletchley Park's cryptanalysts were, of course, well aware of the consequences of failure. Shaun Wylie, a senior figure within Hut 8, recalled in vivid terms the loss of morale and increased pressures placed upon him and his team following the blackout: 'We were dismayed when the fourth wheel appeared. We knew it was coming. But it was a grim time. We were very much frustrated, the things we hoped to use went bad on us. We realised that our work meant lives and it ceased to be fun.'[30]

These pressures resulted in a few isolated examples of problems with the physical and mental wellbeing of staff members. For instance, Angus Wilson, a Hut 8 cryptanalyst, is reported to have attempted to commit suicide by drowning in Bletchley Park's small lake.[31] While not nearly as extreme a case, the cryptanalyst Josh Cooper confided in Gordon Welchman that he found his work an 'almost intolerable strain'.[32] However, examples of work-related stress were not uncommon throughout GC&CS as a whole, and cryptanalysts were far from unique in this respect.

## Machine operation

Once the cryptanalysts had examined a message they would draw up a menu for the Bombes, which would be sent to the Bombe room to be processed by the machine operators. Bombe operator Diana Payne described the machines as large cabinets, eight feet high and seven feet across, containing a mass of wire brushes which 'had to be meticulously adjusted with tweezers to ensure that the electrical circuits did not short', and the rear of the machine being a near-indescribable 'mass of dangling plugs on rows of letters and numbers'.[33]

The main task of the Bombe operators was to interpret complex diagrammatic instructions, called menus, received from cryptanalysts and arrange the machine accordingly.[34] Once the machine was in operation its various drums would rotate until the machine stopped. The machine would stop for two reasons, first if it had successfully found a setting that did not contain a logical contradiction, at which point the message would be run through a replica of an Enigma machine to produce plain text German, or second, if a malfunction had occurred. A Bombe machine could stop many times before the correct setting had been discovered. When a stop occurred as a result of malfunction the machine's contacts had to be meticulously cleaned, and the process restarted from the beginning.[35] The complexity of the machines ensured that the work was fiddly, and required constant and meticulous care and attention to detail.

The machines were large and physically difficult to operate. As such, the agency preferred operators to be young, physically fit and tall. Diana Payne recalled that the process of setting up the machine was 'heavy' work, and that 'All this work had to be done at top speed, and at the same time 100 per cent accuracy was essential. The Bombes made considerable noise as the drums revolved; each row at a different speed, so there was not much talking during the eight-hour spell'.[36]

Like most work beyond the opening stages of the Second World War, the demands on GC&CS dictated that Bombe operators be employed on a shift system from 8 a.m. to 4 p.m.; 4 p.m. to midnight; and midnight to 8 a.m. The WRNS would do a week of each shift and then rotate onto the next shift.[37]

Working conditions were also a difficulty. The machines became very warm and noisy in operation, which made the environment unpleasant. This stood in contrast to the work of cryptanalysts, whose work was primarily conducted with pen and paper behind a desk. These problems were compounded by the buildings which housed the Bombes. A Bombe facility at the Wavendon outstation was described by Diana Payne as being 'a building in the grounds with very little light or air from the high windows. This prevented the noise of the machines from being heard outside, but it would certainly not have passed the Factory Act'.[38] Another veteran, Alice Wolnskyj, also had similar recollections of the working conditions.

> The atmosphere was noisy and stifling, being quite airless. The windows were high and mostly blacked out. I recall a voice over the tannoy, around 9 pm, announcing, 'Wrens may remove their collars and ties and roll down their stockings!'[39]

Thus, even in the most trying of conditions, there was no relaxation of military discipline or uniform code unless specifically authorised – a reflection on the highly regimented and managed nature of the work. This was in spite of the fact that the work was also dirty. One Wren recalled that the operators were denied their request to be allocated navy blue shirt uniforms, as opposed to the standard white shirts of other Wrens, in order to mask oil stains.[40] Stringent adherence to uniform codes, in the case of Bombe operators, clearly made working conditions less tolerable. Moreover, the uniforms themselves were unfit for purpose and required additional effort to clean after a day's shift; they were more likely to hinder work and damage morale. Of course, stubborn and often unnecessary adherence to military discipline as a means for those in the officer ranks to maintain and exert control over enlisted personnel was hardly uncommon in wartime military culture.[41] This culture primarily influenced the lives of the agency's junior staff. Meanwhile, the collegiate culture imported from the universities clearly was able to insulate the cryptanalysts, even those in the military services (who were under no obligation to wear uniform at all), from the wider wartime military culture.

The 'need-to-know' system that operated within the agency in the case of those working on the Bombes meant that the actual contents of the messages remained a mystery.[42] Again this contrasts with the experiences of cryptanalysts, who were granted a greater access to information.

Of course, there was a vested interest in keeping the distribution of information to a bare minimum. However, as an explanation, fears regarding security alone are insufficient. Just as important was that in general, the senior (exclusively educated and universally male) managers of GC&CS had only limited expectations of young women. Not only were they thought to be less worthy of trust than cryptanalysts, there was also the worry that the operation of complex machinery might simply be beyond the capability of young women to master. This concern proved to have been needless. Nigel de Grey noted in 1949 that 'It was astonishing what young women could be trained to do e.g. Fish[43] and Bombe W.R.N.S.'[44] The sceptical attitude of GC&CS's male managers regarding the ability of young women to conduct technical work was hardly uncommon. Penny Summerfield notes that similarly sceptical attitudes could be observed among men in other professions in which young women were placed in a previously male-dominated workplace and asked to conduct technical work.[45]

Yet despite working on and being trained to operate the Bombe machines with considerable success, the women tasked with their operation received very little other information about their role in codebreaking. Where cryptanalysts were informed of how their successes positively influenced military operations, as a means of boosting morale, the morale of Bombe operators was afforded no such concern. The only information they were provided was the Axis service from which the message originated.[46]

Working as a Bombe operator was a monotonous, dirty and physically exacting job, in which those employed were trusted with only a comparatively small amount of information that they directly required to complete the task. The work was regimented, and the operators, all personnel from the WRNS, were subject to military discipline, including strict adherence to rank uniform code. Yet despite the limited information actually supplied to the WRNS, the agency was nevertheless still keen to emphasise the importance of secrecy despite the fact that the agency had ensured they had little access to sensitive information. Jenny Davis, a Bombe operator at the Stanmore outstation, explained how she and around 20 other women were ushered into a room and informed that they would be undertaking secret work, but could be told no more until they had decided whether they wished to work for the agency.[47]

The burden of the work, and the regularly changing shifts, in some cases had an impact upon the physical and mental health of some of the Wrens. Diana Payne reported that some of her colleagues suffered nightmares, digestive troubles and faints, and some were even invalided out of the WRNS, which she attributed to the stress of the work and shift system.[48]

Of course, the Bombe machines were not the only machines developed for use by the agency. There were in fact a large number of machines employed by GC&CS, including the 'Robinson'[49] machine but perhaps more famously the Colossus computers. The Colossus machines have been noted by historians of science and technology for the leap forward they represented in computer science; however, their impact was never really felt at the time because of the secrecy surrounding their invention and subsequent destruction after the war. The Colossus machines were developed by a team headed by the Post Office engineer Tommy Flowers. They were designed to assist GC&CS's staff break the cipher created by the Lorenz SZ-40 and SZ-42 machines which were used to protect high-grade German diplomatic communications. The purpose of these machines was to establish the wheel settings on the Lorenz machines, and in doing so massively reduce the statistical task ahead of cryptanalysts.[50] As with the Bombe machines, the primary operators of the Colossus computers were women in the WRNS.

The work of the Wrens on these machines, like that of Bombe operators, required a high degree of concentration, was highly repetitive, and demanded accuracy.[51] Also like Bombes, the Colossus machines were highly complex as was the task of preparing them. Two Wrens operated the machine under the supervision of a duty officer and a cryptanalyst. The task of the Wrens was to input information into the machine utilising a complex electrical pinboard. The messages, which were on teleprinter tape, were fed into the machine. The operators could then perform a series of different processes on the message, to quote the Colossus operator Jean Thompson:

> After you had set the thing you could do a letter count for the switches. You would make the runs for the different wheels to get the scores out which would print out on the electromatic typewriter. We were looking for a score above the random and one that was sufficiently good, you'd hope was the correct setting.[52]

Wrens and mechanics worked on these extremely complex machines under trying and occasionally dangerous conditions. On one occasion, for instance, a Wren placed a metal-framed mirror on the machine's control desk. The mirror touched two brass terminals which were live, and, following a flash the mirror melted.[53]

As noted, while Wrens operated Colossus machines they were, for the most part, not involved in cryptanalysis or maintenance jobs. That said, many Wrens appear to have become highly proficient and were able to transcend some of the boundaries placed on them by the agency. For example, Paul Gannon notes that Wrens eventually began doing some of the tasks which had previously been completed by cryptanalysts, such as choosing which tests to run on the Colossus machines.[54]

This marked an unusual extension of work beyond that machine work typically performed by women in the Second World War, described by Summerfield as 'machine minding'.[55] The extension of responsibility also extended beyond that typically assigned to female machine operators, such as Bombe operators, at Bletchley Park. Colossus Wrens also were provided with a greater degree of knowledge regarding the place of their work within the war effort and the work of their section. In the case of the Colossus Section, it was concluded that in order to operate effectively all staff members, including Wrens, should be encouraged to improve their theoretical knowledge of the principles involved in cryptanalysis and the work of the entire section. Technical documentation and lectures were offered from 1944 to ensure that section staff understood the technical and theoretical principles of the work in which they were engaged. Later, from January 1945, an education committee was formed comprising four men and 14 Wrens. The committee provided non-compulsory lectures and seminars for Colossus operators and other groups, again to ensure that the Wrens understood the principles behind the work they were doing and why they were doing it.[56]

In many ways the position of the Wrens is paradoxical. On one hand, they were employed in heavy technical work, operating and minding large, noisy, hot and dirty machines, all of which is suggestive of working-class 'blue-collar' work. On the other hand, they were largely well educated and came from respectable middle-class families. It is possible to speculate that they were selected for work at Bletchley Park precisely because of that background. Their work was conducted under a regime of military discipline, and, correspondingly, they were expected to wear their regulation military uniform while on duty – not factory overalls. In effect, the Wrens were engaged in an unusual form of 'white-collar' machine minding.

## Translation, editing and analysis

Once the encryption masking the messages had been broken, the task was to then translate and sort the messages for distribution to commands in the field and relevant ministries. To facilitate this, sections were created for each of the various Axis agencies whose messages were being scrutinised, where the messages were translated and examined for salient information.

Like cryptanalysis, the translation and analysis of messages was conducted on a production-line system of a sort. Decrypted messages would first be registered and prioritised upon their arrival before being translated. The section which conducted the translation process was known as the 'Watch'. Alec Dakin, a member of the 'Z Watch' in Hut 4, described the process in some detail.

> The sorter, often Number 2 of the group, glances at them [the incoming decrypts], quickly identifies those most important for the Admiralty, and hands them to Number 3; who rapidly writes out the German text in word-lengths, staples it to the decrypt, hands it to Number 1; who translates it into English, stamps it with a number [...], and passes it to a WAAF girl who teleprints it to the Admiralty,[57]

The work of translation, interpretation and distribution of material had only a thin line between them and often overlapped. The teams translating documents would, by necessity, also analyse their content and prioritise them for distribution.[58]

John Cairncross, the Soviet spy who operated from within Bletchley Park, described the kinds of skills that were necessary to be successful.

> I found the editing of the German decrypts much like solving a crossword puzzle, or amending a corrupt text of a classical writer such as Moliére. My work involved the correction and restoration of words blurred, distorted or omitted. This was a task which needed a generous dose of imagination, and a corkscrew mind.[59]

Cairncross also described the difficulties of the work, and how a minor error or omission could lead to considerable difficulties in producing an accurate translation of important information. The picture he painted suggests that the work could be slow and very difficult.[60] Bletchley Park's translators, both male and female, often required considerable scientific literacy in order to research the technical specifications of Axis military hardware. The growing importance of this kind of technical work and research is a particularly important point as it further highlights the shift from dilettante classics graduates to an agency widely employing scientifically literate individuals. The Bletchley Park translator, Rosemary

Morton, described working with highly technical documents, such as those for the construction of U-boats and details of German rockets, which required intensive study of English technical books to confirm the validity of the translation.[61]

Rosemary also recalled the difficulties inherent in the shift system and night work that were also common among veterans. Cairncross requested to be transferred from Bletchley Park, in spite of the considerable opportunity the agency provided him as a Soviet mole, because of the toll of the shift system on his health.[62]

Nevertheless, Cairncross certainly recalled enjoying his job before the shift system became intolerable, deriving pride, fascination and satisfaction from the work.[63] Vivienne Alford also noted the enjoyment she found in doing work that was intellectual in nature. The job stood in contrast to the gendered roles in which she had been employed prior to arriving at Bletchley Park, noting that it was the first time since leaving school that she had held a position that was intellectually stimulating.[64]

As with cryptanalysis the work of the translators was intellectual in nature and seems to have had relatively relaxed management. John Cairncross fondly recalled his own manager in his memoir. 'My team leader, a regular army officer, was one of the finest men I ever met, and, thanks to his skilful and kindly guidance, tension was conspicuously absent. Harmony was stimulated by an adolescent jocularity which recalled college days.'[65]

As with cryptanalysis, formal rank, military or civil service, had little impact on how Huts 3 and 4 were managed. Edward Thomas, a naval officer attached to Hut 3, recalled that service officers were happy to work under civilians and vice versa.[66] He also recalled that he was:

> impressed by the easy relations and lack of friction between those in, and out, of uniform. Despite the high tension of much of the work, a spirit of relaxation prevailed. Anyone of any rank or degree could approach anyone else, however venerable, with any idea or suggestion, however crazy.[67]

## Operation of the index punch card system

Over the course of the war GC&CS placed considerable resources into forming an index of captured materials. This was conducted not only by individual cryptanalysis and intelligence sections to facilitate their own work, but by the agency itself. A separate section was formed to create a punch card database of the information produced by the agency. This work grew in tandem with the increasing output of deciphered messages. The work itself was highly mechanised, with machines to produce the punch cards containing the information and further machines to sort and retrieve the information.

As in the case of the Bombe machines, women conducted the operation of the index machines while men performed the technical work and maintenance. According to Ron Gibbons, who had been at the British Tabulating Machine Company and was transferred to Bletchley Park to maintain the index machines in C Block, there were around three hundred machine operators and another hundred technicians at C Block by the end of the war.[68] The index system necessitated the delivery of truckloads of Hollerith cards to Bletchley Park each week. These fed a system which utilised hundreds of machines each capable of processing around three hundred cards per minute.[69] Like many of the other technologies utilised by the agency, the Hollerith machines were prone to occasional failure. Given the sheer number of cards they processed per minute this comes as little surprise. Mis-feeds and damaged or bent cards could jam the machine.[70] The result of the failures was that RAF mechanics were a constant presence within the section, both to repair machines but also to perform ongoing maintenance programmes in an effort to reduce failure rates. The machines also underwent an ongoing maintenance programme in an attempt to prevent machine failures.[71]

Clearly the section was highly mechanised, and both machine and labour intensive. The resulting system processed information at an extremely rapid rate. By necessity, like the agency's other sections dedicated to mechanised processes, the Hollerith Section was run on factory principles. This was reflected not only in the type of work being conducted, machine operation, but also in the manner in which it was conducted. Women operators would do the same repetitive machine work with little in the way of deviation. As Phyllis Coles, a machine operator in C Block, described her experience: 'We didn't have to do a lot ourselves; we had these pegboards, which they set up during the day to put into the machines. When the cards went through they wanted selections of them. The work was the same day or night'.[72] That noted, it is important to recognise that while this work might have been repetitive, that did not necessarily imply that it was dreary. Phyllis, for instance, went on to add that her wartime life in C Block was interesting.[73]

Unusually for women workers employed in relatively 'mundane' work, some of the veterans of the Hollerith section recalled that the work gave them a certain access to information regarding wartime developments. Margaret Martin's work primarily dealt with information regarding the capture (and escape) of prisoners of war, and she reported that her access to the information provided her with an insight into the progress of the war.[74] If women working in the Hollerith Section did gain access to the information they were organising, then they had access to an unusually high degree of information regarding the progress of the war and the products of GC&CS. As stated, that was in stark contrast to the access to information granted to many other women working at Bletchley Park, including the Bombe operators discussed above. That said, it is important not to overstate this particular facet of the work. The information they could glean from working in the section could only have been general in nature; the actual information on the cards appears to have been withheld from the Hollerith workers.[75]

Like other work at GC&CS that involved machine operation (and in contrast to the work of cryptanalysts and translators), the staff of the index punch card system was a highly regimented working environment, and workers were subject to constant supervision and a strict hierarchy. C Block was headed by a Mr Freeborn, who had been a senior figure within the British Tabulating Machine Company, the company that produced the card machines and punch cards. Freeborn had a number of deputies who maintained a constant presence to ensure that the work was being done correctly. Unsurprisingly, given both the gendered division of responsibility in both Bletchley Park and wider wartime society, the supervisors were largely male even though there were well-qualified women within the section.[76]

Nevertheless, a very few women did rise to positions of junior management within the section. For instance, Joan Allen, who, prior to being called up, had been a machine operator with Hollerith, was soon made a team leader because of her efficiency. The presence of women like Joan in positions of junior management does suggest a degree of upward mobility within the section. However, in Joan's case, that did not translate into either formal promotion or an increase in pay.[77]

Bletchley Park recruited a number of young women from the upper classes. Marion Hill notes that a significant number of debutantes were employed at Bletchley Park, many of them employed in relatively unskilled white-collar positions such as filing clerks.[78] The Hollerith Section, in post-war years, gained a reputation as having a particularly large contingent of upper-class women within its ranks. Joan Allen, when asked about that perception during an interview with a member of the Bletchley Park Trust, was quick to refute it.[79] However, she did recall a number of upper-class women at Bletchley Park, acerbically noting that 'they didn't do very much in there, these baronesses and duchesses' and 'I don't know that they did an awful lot to win the war.'[80] If the class difference was overstated, Joan was quick to suggest that nepotism was not. For example, she recalled that Mr Freeborn's two sons were section heads in C Block, which irritated her because they were of service age.[81] While titles might not have ensured a place within Bletchley Park, connections certainly did.

## Operation of the British cipher machine: Type-x

GC&CS employed a large number of women from the Women's Auxiliary Air Force. As with members of the WRNS, the WAAFs' work was primarily in machine operation. They operated communication equipment and, in some cases, in addition to women from the civil service, British cipher machines. The British Type-x cipher system was used to encipher British traffic. The traffic office enciphered the outgoing traffic from Hut 3 and deciphered the material. This process grew in scale steadily throughout the war. Frank Birch noted that at the end of 1941 a quarter of a million groups were enciphered, a tally that would rise to 3.5 million by April 1945.[82] The Type-x was also modified to decipher Axis Enigma traffic once the various daily keys had been established by the cryptanalysts.[83]

The operations of these machines could prove to be an arduous task. Mary Pain, a WAAF who had been involved in working on the machines, recalled their operation in some detail.

> The setting up, for the machine would change each night, and that, was quite hard work. It was tricky and you had to be quite strong. You had to move the machine's wheels round with your finger or thumb, and that could be extremely painful. Some girls brought in pieces of wood to help.[84]

As a result of the difficulties in using the machines, some of which were slightly easier to use than others, machine operators also had a preference for individual machines. In an effort to alleviate competition to work on specific machines a rotation system was introduced.[85]

The difficulties faced by the workers were also exacerbated by a variety of other problems. First, there was a chronic shortage of engineers to maintain the machines (unlike the Hollerith Section where engineers were a constant presence). As with other machines at Bletchley Park, the Type-x machines were operated by women but maintained by men. Mr H. L. Swatton, a Post Office engineer, maintained Type-x machines at Bletchley from 1939 with four other engineers. This figure would eventually rise to ten, but the engineers remained understaffed and in periods of crisis sometimes had to work 'virtually 24 hours at a time', in spite of their 'blinking, tired eyes'.[86]

Second, operating staff were also in relatively short supply. As with most other forms of work conducted on the site, the work was split into a three-shift system to ensure that operations continued on a 24-hour basis.[87] Yet even with a shift system, it proved impossible for any shift to be able to process every job that came in due to the scale of the workload and the shortage of staff.[88] Given the effects of the shift system, the size of the workload, and the degree of concentration required by operators, the work proved to be both physically and mentally exhausting. Mary Pain described women falling asleep at their machines, and allowing staff to take 15-minute breaks in which to sleep. Mary herself did the same, and utilised her 'gas mask as a pillow' which 'made all the difference, you could then get through the night without falling asleep again'.[89] Yet despite the bottlenecks in terms of staff numbers and the pressures of the work, the section became more efficient as time went on due to the growing proficiency of the staff.[90]

Third, the physical working environment also left much to be desired. For example, Mary Pain recalled that the building and rooms were 'not luxurious' and that they were working in a bare hut.[91] The Cypher Office, which housed many of Bletchley Park's Type-x machines, was the subject of a considerable number of complaints and internal correspondence. The Cypher Office was housed in E Block, and the building was poorly ventilated. In 1943 GC&CS investigated the complaints, and one commentator reported to Commander Bradshaw a list of problems: first, that the windows, when covered by blackout curtains, did not provide enough air, second that the slats on the windows were installed incorrectly facing the wrong direction, and third, that the fan system in one of the rooms required reversing and being provided with a channel to the open air.[92] A month later another individual sent to investigate the buildings problems commented that 'Ventilation was not good and the atmosphere was heavy'.[93]

As noted, the section operating the Type-x machines was staffed by women. Yet like all of Bletchley Park's sections, it was led by men. Initially the section had fallen under the command of the head of Hut 6 (Gordon Welchman). However, this arrangement ultimately proved to be unsatisfactory because he already had a large and increasing workload.

As such, a new section head had to be found, and the agency appointed a former bank manager to the position.[94] According to Mary Pain, the new section head had a positive effect on the running of the section, a result of both his intelligence and managerial experience.[95] That said, not all of his decisions were initially welcomed. For example, upon his appointment the new section head increased the degree of supervision within the section by appointing a number of men, also from the banking world, to supervise the women within the section. Mary Pain, who was by that point the head of a shift, was still senior to these supervisors. She, like the other women in her section, initially resented their appointment. 'We probably thought we didn't want any men there, and had all the supervision we needed.'[96] However, in Mary Pain's opinion the male supervisors ultimately proved to be successful because 'they carried a certain amount of weight with the girls'.[97] This would suggest that women also had gendered expectations about authority figures as much as men did. Conversely however, Summerfield notes that the women interviewed in her study of women during wartime tended to be placed under the authority of men and remembered them as 'old and unfit', and that men in non-combat roles in general were typically less competent and conscientious than they were.[98] It would appear, therefore, that in the case of Mary Pain's section at least, the female employees responded better to male supervisors than was often the case elsewhere in the British workplace.

Not all Type-x units within the agencies saw such impressive leadership. The Cypher Office in E Block, which housed many of Bletchley Park's Type-x machines, attracted numerous complaints, most of which revolved around poor leadership and a failure to address problematic working conditions. In 1943 the morale in the section reached rock bottom and worrying reports began to reach the desks of senior agency officials. An investigation was soon launched to probe the problems in the section. The report, while outwardly noting that there was no intention to 'cast aspersions on the current regime', was damning. It found that there was a 'tremendous lack of personal touch' among the section's managers, and that nobody in the section was 'really interested' in the welfare of its women workers. Given the type of working being conducted this was deemed problematic:

> because [the section] is so rushed and busy, there is no time to give the personal touch to the staff, which it requires, particularly as most of it is doing such concentrated and repetitive work and can see so little result for their pains.[99]

The problem lay not only in the monotony and necessarily prolonged concentration involved in operating a Type-x machine, but in the factory-style management system in place. The report recommended that in order to improve morale, a dedicated officer should be appointed to specifically address the issue of staff welfare in the section. A further investigation noted that one staff member already filled that position in an unofficial capacity – but that she failed in that capacity because the head of the section chose to deal with the problems himself, a task to which he was apparently unsuited.[100]

Unsurprisingly, the section was also beset by a high rate of both staff illness and resignations. One report suggested that this was due to the poor ventilation in the section,[101] while another flatly disagreed with that prognosis and put the problems down to poor morale. One of the solutions to the issue of morale was to introduce 'Music while you work',[102] but this soon proved problematic because a neighbouring section required a quiet working environment.[103] Captain Melrose, one of the officials investigating the problems in the section, took the unsympathetic stance that the majority of the resignations were of the 'trivial "nervous disability" type' and that the female staff members required reminding that they were 'doing war work and must be willing to put up with some discomfort'. Melrose also recommended that all certificates produced by staff members from medical professionals to excuse night work be ignored because '[I]t is no greater hardship working at night than during the day'.[104] However, as Christopher Grey notes, numerous studies have shown that shift and night work, particularly those shifts which regularly changed between night and day work, have significant impacts on both physical and mental health.[105]

Furthermore, Melrose's statement that the majority of the causes of staff resignation from within the section were due to 'nervous disability' appears to be inaccurate. First, the initial investigation in October 1943 was prompted by the fact that staff sickness rates in the section stood at between 6% and 7%, twice that of the rest of the park. GC&CS arranged for an outside doctor to examine the section's sick staff members. The doctor concluded that all the cases were genuine and furthermore noted that 'the hours are long and...there was a distinct element of strain'.[106] Second, Mr White (the head of the section in question) compiled a list of all the staff who had resigned from his section due to ill health, and of the 28 individuals only three were listed as having had either a 'nervous beak down', 'psychoneurosis' or an 'anxiety state'. The majority suffered from a variety of illnesses, not limited to debility, tuberculosis, asthma and bronchitis.[107] Of course, stress and overwork may well have been a compounding or even the causal factor in the general ill health within the section; however, no other evidence suggests that mental health problems were behind the health problems within the section. Rather, it would appear that, by the standards of Bletchley Park, Type-x work was particularly arduous and E Block, given its problematic ventilation system, was a particularly poor working environment that may have exacerbated pre-existing respiratory illnesses such as asthma.

The division of labour within the section, as noted above, was typical of the general administrative arrangement within the agency. For the most part men were tasked with the senior administrative work and positions of management, and the mechanical work that required a relatively high degree of technical proficiency. Women, for the most part, occupied positions as clerks, typists and machine operators. Mary Pain represents a relatively unusual, but by no means unique, position of lower-middle management as the head of a watch. She was in charge of the women working on her watch and their male supervisors. It is worth noting that even with this position of authority she still reported directly to her male manager. Furthermore, the men who were supervisors under her do not seem to have been actual machine operators themselves; their position would appear to have been purely to supervise female machine operators.

For the most part Mary recalled that, despite the pressure placed upon the women in her section, morale was relatively high and she rarely had to deal with any disciplinary issues. 'They were so cooperative all these girls, you hardly ever came up against anything in the way of problems of behaviour.'[108] This, it would appear, was at least in part due to the personalities within the section. Mary recalled that '[T]wo girls were Jewish, they were marvellous. Had a great sense of humour, and kept the spirits up, even when you were very depressed.'[109] Yet despite that general assertion that behavioural issues were rarely, if ever, problematic, Mary did note that in her capacity as head of watch she did have to split various staff members up, a result of differences of personality. 'You tried to make sure that you didn't put two girls who didn't like each other next to each other.'[110]

Mary also recalled an occasion when two women in her section were fired from their positions. The cause of their dismissal lay in the fact that the two women were engaged in an intimate, presumed sexual, relationship. Mary asserted that this relationship caused disruption within the section because the other women disliked them or working with them. To quote Mary's interview, 'Well, they were lesbians, and the other girls didn't like them, and they didn't like having anything to do with them, and it did disrupt the place for a while. But they weren't allowed to stay very long.'[111]

This position taken by the agency, to actively remove a homosexual couple from the working environment, is interesting for a number of reasons. The agency seemingly took little issue with the employment of homosexual men when it came to senior positions. Bletchley Park employed a number of gay men, including Angus Wilson and Alan Turing. While Turing had a fiancée, the cryptanalyst Joan Clarke, his sexuality was no secret at Bletchley Park. Bob Baker, a senior figure within Hut 6, described in an interview by the Bletchley Park Trust that he regularly dined opposite Alan Turing and Joan Clarke, at that time his girlfriend.[112] Baker then added, 'Well, I don't know where he would pick up a boy friend in Bletchley Park, it was well known that he was gay.'[113] Similarly, Margaret Chester, who worked in the Hut 6 Registration Room, suggested in an interview that homosexuality was not uncommon among the men in her section. In a story in which she was describing the attempted suicide of one individual at Bletchley Park, she noted that the victim was 'one of the boyfriends of the men many of whom had boyfriends'.[114]

It appears that the cultural and legal taboos regarding homosexuality at that time were suspended when it came to senior male figures within the agency, though not when it came to female junior staff. One likely reason was necessity. Individuals such as Alan Turing in senior positions, while known to be homosexual, had highly specialised and vital skills that were invaluable to the work of GC&CS and they were indispensable regardless of whether their sexuality made other staff members uncomfortable. Junior staff members, operating machinery, on the other hand, were easily replaced. There was undoubtedly also a cultural element at work. As Matt Cook notes, class has always played a role in governing whether homosexuality is tolerated: Oxford and Cambridge universities in particular were at that time home to 'relatively open and fashionable homosexual fraternities'.[115] The role of Oxford and Cambridge as recruitment centres for both cryptanalysts and translators was considerable, and the transfer of elements of a university common-room atmosphere to Bletchley Park has been widely noted.[116] It is unsurprising to see that the agency was willing to ignore the behaviour of its male academic recruits and the subcultures that they were recruited from and even to have allowed those subcultures to be transferred, but did not extend the same licence to junior female recruits.

## Security, secrecy and GC&CS staff

GC&CS was, of course, a highly secretive agency. This secrecy was built on the practical concern that if the Axis powers discovered that their cipher security had been compromised then they could simply alter their cipher systems and in doing so prevent GC&CS from being able to read messages. Therefore, maintaining the security of the 'Ultra Secret' was a vital consideration. This consideration dictated how Ultra intelligence was used and who, outside of GC&CS, was inducted into the secret. The question of Ultra security has been of considerable interest to historians, and a number of historians, such as R. A. Ratcliff, have examined these two issues in depth.[117] The other major security consideration was ensuring that those inducted into the Ultra Secret did not allow the secret to become public knowledge. In Britain, the largest single group of individuals inducted, at least in part, into the secret were GC&CS's own employees. As a result, the agency took particular care to ensure that employees understood the importance of security and the dangers of 'careless talk' – more on which later. The importance of security was also impressed upon staff through the signing of the Official Secrets Acts. As noted, the agency also compartmentalised work, inherently limiting the amount of information available to any one member of staff. Additionally, the sites occupied by GC&CS themselves also included a visible security presence, to prevent trespassers gaining entrance onto the grounds.

Records produced by GC&CS show that a daily password procedure was in operation on the site from October 1939 until at least 1940 for staff who wished to work late.[118] Security staff were instructed to challenge individuals at Bletchley Park in accordance with Army Council Instructions. Those individuals who could not produce a password were then escorted to other security staff for recognition. Staff were informed that if they did not cooperate, the sentry would 'endeavour to seize and detain them by hand; if that is impossible he will fire his rifle to hit low'.[119] By June 1940, a fence had been erected around the Bletchley Park site, and passes were issued to all staff members to produce for inspection by security staff every time they entered the site.[120]

The size of the security detail is difficult to determine. GC&CS's records list a category of Bletchley Park staff members employed by SIS under the title of Watchmen, Telephone and Office. In May 1942,

28 individuals were employed in this category, and by May 1943 that number had increased to 40.[121]

Interestingly, despite the documented security presence on the site, some veterans recalled that security on site was very lax. Mavis Faunch, a lettering artist employed by Hut 3, recalled that when she first arrived at Bletchley late at night on Christmas Eve she was able to enter the grounds without challenge.

> I got to Bletchley sometime round about midnight, got off the train, everything was in darkness, but there were some iron steps going over the bridge. So I went up there and that led me to a gate, which I pushed open. There wasn't a soul about, I walked through and had no idea where I was of course, but there was this big house in front of me. Nobody was about so I walked up to this big house, carrying my kit bag, up the steps into the door.[122]

However, the timing of her arrival, Christmas Eve 1942, may explain the limited security. Other veterans remember a stronger security presence. Mrs June Douglas recalled that '[T]he safety was so closely scrutinised at Bletchley, every time you came in you had to show your pass and sign in, and every time you went out you had to show your pass and then sign out'.[123]

These arrangements covered the physical security of GC&CS's war station. As noted above, efforts were made to ensure that sensitive information remained compartmentalised within the agency and that this information did not leave the agency. The primary means of achieving this was by ensuring that all members of the agency signed the Official Secrets Acts.[124] That said, there is no evidence to suggest that any individuals were prosecuted under the Official Secrets Acts for discussing their work with individuals who were not inducted into the Ultra Secret. However, there is certainly evidence that in at least two cases in 1942 prosecution was considered but decided against. Both cases involved 'careless talk': one member of staff discussed her work with family members, one of whom then repeated the information at a cocktail party, while in the other case a member of staff discussed his work with former university colleagues. The two individuals were only saved from prosecution by the personal intervention of Edward Travis who wished to prevent GC&CS from 'public discredit'.[125] Also, it was clearly within the agency's interest to remain as far below the public radar as possible, suggesting that concerns regarding the agency's reputation were slightly disingenuous.

While prosecution was to be avoided, GC&CS did have other serious disciplinary measures within its arsenal. As a result of a later incident, also in 1943, a staff member found to have breached GC&CS's security was dismissed from their position. The staff member disclosed the nature of their work to a friend, that friend then told a third person outside of GC&CS who then reported the incident to GC&CS, resulting in the staff member's dismissal.[126] Two other staff members, on separate occasions in 1942, were temporarily suspended from duty while they were investigated following an allegation of 'indiscreet talk'.[127]

Aside from disciplining offenders, the agency took a number of measures to discourage 'careless talk'. In addition to signing the Official Secrets Acts, staff were expected to watch propaganda films, including *Next of Kin*, *Chatterbox*, *Chatterbug* and *Censorship*, all of which reinforced the message of the importance of security.[128] New staff were informed upon arrival by their section heads of the importance of secrecy, and compulsory lectures were also organised for new staff members with the same purpose in mind.[129] Despite these measures, the agency repeatedly received reports of security breaches in which staff members discussed their work in public places or to non-Ultra-inducted individuals.[130] The response of the agency was to circulate memoranda repeatedly to remind staff members of the dangers of 'careless talk' and inform them of the consequences to both themselves and servicemen on the front lines should vital information reach the enemy.[131] The agency also produced secrecy guidelines, which staff were to sign, listing various forms of 'careless talk' and ending with a declaration stating, 'I hereby promise that no word of mine shall betray, however slightly, the great trust placed in me.'[132] Additionally, the guidelines on secrecy also show that even while on duty in the workplace, staff members were expected to take care that their discussions with colleagues could not be overheard by other staff members, in particular, cleaning and maintenance staff.[133]

For the most part, it would appear that Bletchley Park's staff members took the issue of security very seriously, and only on relatively rare occasions did GC&CS discover that its security regulations had been breached. Correspondingly, the security files reveal only one instance, discussed above, in which a member of staff was dismissed from the agency because of a security indiscretion, and formal prosecutions were eschewed. Of course, staff discretion is impossible to fully measure given that GC&CS disciplinary action could only be applied to those individuals who were caught. There was at least one serious security breach that GC&CS was aware of, when two staff members discussed their work in public, but the perpetrators were never discovered and therefore escaped disciplinary action.[134] The most serious known security breach, albeit of a very different calibre, by the Soviet mole John Cairncross, also went entirely undetected. Therefore, it is possible that security breaches were more common than GC&CS's security files would initially suggest. Furthermore, GC&CS was unwilling to commit to employing its most extreme sanction of prosecuting those staff who broke security regulations because of the potential discredit and unwanted publicity such revelations could bring upon the agency. One of Bletchley Park's security officers, Colonel Vivian, summed up the problem in a letter to Nigel de Grey, stating that, 'The trouble about taking any drastic action it that it is often likely to draw more attention rather than to conceal.'[135]

Given the considerable effort the agency expended drilling its importance into staff members, it is unsurprising that veterans' accounts regularly emphasise secrecy. Oliver Lawn, for instance, recalled that there was 'absolute secrecy' and that 'you didn't talk about your work to anyone outside your section'.[136] Staff were constantly reminded that they must *never* divulge what they knew.[137] The culture of secrecy was so great that the Ultra Secret itself remained largely intact until 1974. What is surprising is just how acute the psychological impact of the agency's security strategy was. Even decades after the Ultra became a matter of public record many surviving staff members remain unwilling to discuss their wartime work. For instance, in July 2001, one former WAAF refused to divulge the details of her war work, stating, 'In view of the extreme secrecy surrounding my work at Bletchley Park, I cannot give much detail other than Service life.'[138]

Considerable emphasis was also placed on workplace security. When cleaners or builders were working in buildings containing classified materials, staff members were expected to ensure that documents were not left unattended; secret documents were also not to be placed in waste paper bins where they could be retrieved. Similarly, rooms and buildings containing secret documents were supposed to be locked when not in use. Documents in transit between buildings on site were also supposed to be sealed to ensure that they had not been read by messengers.[139] Of course, these arrangements were not always adhered to, and security staff occasionally reported that unattended buildings and rooms had been left unlocked and that secret documents were readily accessible. For example, in May 1944, a security official reported that not only was he able to access Hut 4, the main door of which had been left unlocked, but he was also able to access a room which had a faulty lock and find documents classified as 'Most Secret'.[140] As it happens, GC&CS's senior staff were right to worry about document security. The failure of some sections to take the issue sufficiently seriously resulted in a breach of Ultra security of unprecedented severity. John Cairncross, the KGB mole operating from inside GC&CS, recalled in his memoir that he was able to easily smuggle thousands of Ultra classified decrypts out of Bletchley Park (hidden under his clothes), because they were simply left lying on the floor. The absence of the documents was not noticed because Hut 3 regularly destroyed documents after they had been used.[141]

On the whole, despite the occasional lapses in security, staff members were extremely conscientious when it came to security, both in terms of office security precautions or in their interactions with those outside their own section. Clearly, secrecy played a major part in the lives of GC&CS staff during the Second World War. Security concerns dictated that the work of staff members was highly compartmentalised, there was a constant security presence on site, and from the moment staff members arrived for the first time in GC&CS they were informed of the strict secrecy surrounding their work, and were repeatedly reminded throughout their time in the agency.

Of course, the security arrangements in place within GC&CS were not solely to preserve secrecy – though that was their primary function. Security staff also had the job of protecting staff members and their property. For example, the security section recorded that two female staff members were attacked by an unknown assailant a few hundred yards from Bletchley Park on their way to work for a midnight shift.[142] In 1945, security staff were asked to deal with multiple reports from female staff members that a man, Assistant Resident Engineer Bunn, had been discovered attempting to peer through the windows into their accommodation blocks in the Bletchley Park hostel, and WAAF and ATS camps, to spy on them while they were undressing. The security officials noted that the 'peeper', in an effort to facilitate his illicit behaviour, had gone to great lengths to sabotage the buildings and make it easier to catch glimpses of the young women inside. This included cutting holes in blackout curtains, disconnecting lights and vandalising window frames. Officials darkly suggested that such an individual might 'resort to more drastic measures in order to satisfy his disordered desires'.[143]

However, the most common problem not related to secrecy that security staff had to deal with was theft. GC&CS's security staff received numerous reports of minor thefts from Bletchley Park staff. In 1943 the security staff were called upon to investigate the theft of a service bicycle.[144] In 1944 GC&CS's chief administrator Commander Bradshaw circulated a memorandum requesting that any staff members who had lost property at Bletchley Park's bath house come forward to aid an ongoing investigation into thefts of a number of unspecified items which had taken place.[145] In the same year, a number of, again, unspecified items were taken from buildings at Bletchley Park that had been left unlocked and unattended overnight.[146]

## Conclusion

GC&CS was an information-processing centre that operated on a factory-style production line. Information, in the form of enciphered messages, was delivered to the agency. Individual sections were required to receive those messages, establish the means to remove the cipher masking their contents, decipher them, translate them, organise and index their contents, and then send the messages to the relevant ministries and commands. Initially, this task was conducted by small groups of people largely without any mechanical aid. However, as the war progressed and GC&CS's clients demanded greater output, and while the rate of message interception also increased, massive demands were placed on GC&CS to increase its own output accordingly. The result of these pressures was the rapid expansion of personnel and the mechanisation of every part of GC&CS. Yet, even though the agency grew in scale, added more sections, and mechanised and professionalised almost every part of its operations, the basic production-line system remained.

As discussed in earlier chapters, the division of labour at GC&CS was largely gendered and highly influenced by social status. The vast majority of staff working in cryptanalysis and research were male and held a university education. In the case of the translation and analysis of deciphered messages women did have greater representation but again men made up the bulk of the numbers. Given the language requirement these staff were also highly educated, male and female alike. The work itself could be mentally extremely difficult, as well as draining, and required considerable technical knowledge – though many staff (both male and female) clearly enjoyed the intellectual challenge presented by the work. The shift system made the work still more draining and was particularly onerous for many. This work tended to be of an intellectual, as opposed to physical, nature and many of the staff found the work, while frustrating at times, ultimately rewarding. These workers, on the whole, were granted the freedom to approach their jobs with a degree of independence, though it is also important to recognise that some regimentation did creep in. The manner in which these particular sections operated in many ways resembled a small production line within the wider production-line system operated by GC&CS; linguists and cryptanalysts provided one link in a lengthy chain. In the case of analysis, some staff would be reading the messages in order to grade their importance; others would be translating the documents; others would be checking the work; and this was overseen by a senior figure to ensure accuracy and efficiency. This ensured that, even while a considerable degree of freedom was granted to the cryptanalysts and translators to ensure an accommodating flexibility, the processes involved operated in a professional and efficient manner.

The operation of machines, such as the Bombe machines, the Colossus machines and Type-x machines, was, however, a very different story. The staff were predominantly young women. Their work was often monotonous, dirty, and physically as well as mentally exacting.[147] GC&CS's management were aware of the problem that the monotony, in particular, could have on morale. Frank Birch, in GCHQ's own official history of its wartime activities, noted that the lowest-grade labour in the Communications Section suffered (relative to other sections) low morale because they were 'unavoidably engaged in unrelieved drudgery'.[148] Women also encountered a glass ceiling that limited opportunity for promotion from beyond the Bletchley Park machine floor and into positions of management. While some women did rise to supervisory positions, it was generally over teams of other women; every major section head was male, and, for the most part, supervisors were male. That said, while it is important to recognise that there were negative impressions of wartime life among the many female workers it is easy to generalise and overlook the positive experiences and sense of satisfaction that many women workers felt. It is also easy to overlook the fact that there were discrepancies of experience between sections.

Despite the hardships the work entailed, the difficulty in gaining promotion to positions of managerial responsibility, and absence of information regarding the value of their work, memories of Bletchley Park and its outstations tend to be positive. Even when pointing out that the work was monotonous or unpleasant, many veterans still described the work in a positive manner. For example, Mary Rae, who operated a Bombe checking machine, describes the work as 'a bit monotonous, but quite interesting'.[149] Mary explains that 'Life was good thinking back on it and we were lucky.'[150] While nostalgia may play a partial role in veterans' assessments of their wartime work, the general picture painted by veterans is that they were happy regardless of the work and the conditions. Furthermore, the agency's own analysis of its own wartime performance recorded that the problems rarely impaired morale.[151]

# 4
# The Administration of Off-Duty Life and Staff Welfare

The administrative and bureaucratic challenges posed by industrialising cryptanalysis proved immense and forced a rapid *ad hoc* restructuring of the agency. The side effects of this process were not merely limited to changes to the institutional culture of the agency, the types of individual it hired, or the work they performed. The creation of a professional and industrialised intelligence agency required professional and industrialised logistics.

Increasingly large staff numbers presented numerous administrative and organisational problems for the agency. First, GC&CS had to provide adequate accommodation and billeting for staff members. Staff members were initially billeted in local hotels and pubs, before later being housed in the spare rooms of local households in Bletchley Urban District and surrounding villages. Eventually purpose-built accommodation camps were constructed near Bletchley Park. Second, the billeting issue also created another major administrative problem: transporting staff members, often from remote towns and villages, to and from Bletchley Park each day. Third, GC&CS also had to provide catering arrangements for its staff members, and, given the rapidly increasing staff numbers, that too proved to be a formidable administrative challenge over the course of the war. Fourth, GC&CS had to supply welfare provisions for its increasing pool of staff members. This included the establishment of onsite medical staff and facilities, including related amenities such as a sunray clinic. The agency also provided other amenities at Bletchley Park to aid its staff members, including bathing facilities, a laundry room and a hair salon. Tennis courts were also constructed on the site, reputedly built at the order of Winston Churchill who concluded after visiting the agency that the leisure facilities provided were inadequate.[1]

## Billeting

Providing adequate accommodation for staff members was a major and recurrent problem for the agency that became increasingly acute as the war progressed and the agency expanded. During the earlier stages of the war, when staff numbers were smaller and local billeting easier to come by, this did not present a major obstacle. The first wave of recruits was housed in local hotels and inns. It was not long until this source of accommodation was depleted and a new source of housing was required. At that stage the agency turned to the local people of Bletchley, willing or otherwise, to provide its staff with accommodation.

Within a matter of weeks, the problem of billeting had already become apparent. A potential solution to ease the strain on the billeting situation was to move the Diplomatic and Commercial Sections of GC&CS back to London. Denniston argued against that particular suggestion, pointing out that a unified cryptanalysis unit was beneficial and that splitting it into two sections would harm the agency's efficiency and ability to coordinate work. Denniston also suggested that a move back to London, while not necessarily jeopardizing the safety of his staff, would require them to spend what could otherwise have been productive hours in air raid shelters.[2]

With the option to disperse the agency jettisoned, GC&CS was forced to look beyond the immediate area of Bletchley for accommodation. This solution had its own set of problems, particularly that of transport. Some staff were billeted many miles from Bletchley and, until the institution of adequate facilities, staff members with vehicles were asked to donate their spare time to form a car pool.[3] Clearly unsatisfactory, it soon became clear that Bletchley Park required a transport service to ferry staff to and from work.

The major problem was that available housing within the town of Bletchley, and the surrounding countryside and urban areas further afield, was limited and subject to competing demands. Not only were billeting officers expected to cope with the increasingly sizable influx of GC&CS persons in need of housing, but also because Bletchley became the home to evacuees.[4] By January 1941 the population of the town had risen from a pre-war population of around 6,900 to in excess of 10,800.[5] This was at a time when the total staff contingent at Bletchley Park was less than 700.[6] In addition to the sheer number of individuals who needed to be accommodated, billeting officers were also forced to cope with the problem of uncooperative home owners and billetees. Bletchley Urban District Council repeatedly recorded throughout the war the problems inherent in billeting Bletchley Park's workers. For instance, in September 1941 the council minutes recorded that,

> Mr. G. E. Peacock, Regional Billeting Officer to the Ministry of Health attended and stated that following representations from the Government [the] Minister of Health had decided to make an Order placing restrictions on the number of persons who may come into the Bletchley Urban Area in order that accommodation may be reserved for Civil Servants and Transferred War Workers.[7]

The move to prevent further evacuees arriving in overcrowded areas, or to prioritise areas for war workers, was not uncommon. The Ministry of Aircraft Production, in particular, had pressed for measures to prioritise certain areas for war workers since 1940, and the Minister for Health was granted the power to restrict movement to certain areas by non-essential war workers in 1941.[8] This issue of billeting for Bletchley Park staff was raised in the council's minutes a few months later, but on this occasion highlighting the problem of uncooperative townspeople.

> The Clerk submitted a letter dated the 7th. January, 1942, from Mr. Jones the Council's Billeting Officer reporting that he was experiencing difficulty in obtaining voluntary billets for transferred war workers now being received into the town and had been informed by the householders that until compulsory powers were enforced they refuse to take anyone into their houses.[9]

The council then proceeded to grant billeting officers compulsory powers. However, the problem did not stop there. In May 1943 the council minutes noted,

> The Clerk reported on the present position of billeting in the urban area to the fact that in the near future large numbers of transferred war workers would be sent into the urban district for building work at Bletchley Park, followed by additional civil servants. The Clerk stated that the Council's and the Bletchley Park's Billeting Officers were now meeting difficulties in obtaining billets in the town owing to the attitude of certain householders who had consistently refused to take any one into their homes.[10]

By June 1943 the situation had escalated and the council recorded that it had taken the decision to prosecute households that refused to take in billetees, and on 6 July a minute noted that a legal case against a household was being prepared.[11]

Some of the billets also lacked basic amenities or were in relatively remote locations, making it difficult for staff to find the time to visit laundry facilities, among other services. As a result, facilities were built on site to provide staff with a number of amenities that were otherwise unavailable or in short supply. One of the major additions in this respect was the construction of bathing facilities. The bath house was opened in December 1943 and contained eight bathrooms for the use of female staff members and a further four bathrooms for male members. The bath house also contained facilities for laundry, ironing and hairdressing.[12] However, these facilities were provided only for civilian staff who were in billets. It was not extended to staff members housed within military camps or those within civilian hostels.

During the opening years of the war military personnel, particularly those in the Royal Air Force and the army, were billeted in the nearby towns and villages. Members of the WRNS, on the other hand, were often billeted together on large sites, such as the Woburn Abbey estate. The WRNS provided the largest share of the women employed by GC&CS in uniform (by September 1942 there were in excess of 400 Wrens, nearly 50% of the total number of female staff members in uniform). By placing large numbers of Wrens together on single sites the agency relieved pressure on billeting officers. This initiative was initially unique to the Navy until 1943, when the construction of camps for army and RAF personnel began. Members of the WRNS were in some ways a little different from other employees, in that not only did many of them work at Bletchley Park but many more worked at the various outstations. As such, Wrens employed at the outstations in North London, Eastcote and Stanmore were accommodated together nearby. The bulk of Wrens employed at Bletchley, or the very close outstations, were housed in nine different nearby locations. From 1943 onwards this included Woburn Abbey, the stately home of the Duke of Bedford. Wren officers were billeted together at Walton Hall, and the rest of the Wrens were billeted in seven other locations as far away as the village of Steeple Claydon, a village 12 miles southwest of Bletchley.[13]

By May 1943 approximately 50% of GC&CSs personnel, which by that stage exceeded 4,000 individuals, were attached to the agency from the armed forces. It was only then that plans were drawn up to start housing as many of these individuals as possible in communal accommodation.[14] In this instance the agency did not turn to various nearby halls or stately homes, as it did for the Wrens, but instead built its own accommodation blocks.[15] Accommodation in Bletchley was rapidly becoming sparse, and many of the nearby halls and stately homes had been commandeered for other government purposes.

On May 11 1943 the minutes of Bletchley Urban District Council recorded that Bletchley Park wished to requisition a further 15 acres of land 'from Rickley Lane to Shenley Road for extensions to Bletchley Park'.[16] The Shenley Road Military Camp was opened in January 1944 and came to house the majority of Bletchley Park's army personnel.[17] The decision to construct a camp to house staff members was not restricted to army personnel. On June 8 1943 the decision was taken to reroute a local footpath to make way for an RAF accommodation camp.[18] RAF Church Green started admitting its first residents on June 6 1943.[19] Between them the Shenley camp and the Church Green camp would by 1944 house around 2,000 individuals.[20]

The communal housing of employees was not restricted only to the military. While the bulk of the civilian employees of GC&CS were housed with the civilian population of the town of Bletchley and its surrounding towns and villages, a number of people were housed at the nearby Elmer's School and in a wartime block on Wilton Avenue. These two locations between them housed several hundred people from 1943 onwards until the end of the war, peaking in September 1944 with a total of 392 individuals.[21] The majority, however, were forced upon the civilian population and remained so until the end of the war.

The range and numbers of individuals who required billets was a considerable task for billeting officers. By 1945, GC&CS had placed workers in at least 31 nearby villages and towns.[22] These included villages in the immediate proximity of Bletchley, but other workers were located a little further away. To the northeast billets were located in Bedford, some 14 miles from Bletchley. Similarly, the village of Steeple Claydon, 12 miles to the southwest of Bletchley, also housed agency staff.

Ultimately, while the problem of accommodating staff members was a major concern for GC&CS, it was certainly not unique. The war required that millions of people be transplanted from their homes and transferred across the country and beyond. Between June and September 1939, some 3.5 to 3.75 million people were evacuated from their city homes and sent to live in smaller towns and villages where the threat of aerial bombardment was considered remote.[23] Others, both in the armed services and part of the civilian workforce, found themselves employed far away from their homes.

During the opening months of the war the accommodation of transferred war workers proved to be a major problem. The Ministry of

Labour offered mobile workers a little help by providing lists of potential lodgings, but otherwise typically left workers to fend for themselves. The lack of practical arrangements proved to be a major factor in discouraging workers to migrate to where their labour was most useful. According to H. M. D. Parker, the historian commissioned by the British government to write the official history of manpower issues during the Second World War, between a quarter and a third of all migrants to the Midlands[24] returned to their homes because of a lack of reception arrangements and because lodging was either unavailable, too expensive or too uncomfortable.[25] Steps were made to combat these problems by sending hopeful migrants relevant accommodation information prior to their departure. Their details, including travel times, were also supplied to local offices in the reception area in order for them to be met and assisted in the transition.[26] By contrast, GC&CS does not appear to have made similar efforts on behalf of its workers. For instance, James Thirsk recalled he was ordered to report to Bletchley Park and once there was simply assigned a billet in the local community.[27]

Despite these measures, finding migrant workers suitable lodgings remained a difficult task. The challenge was exacerbated by the wider national policy to evacuate the major cities. Evacuees transplanted to Bletchley took lodgings which could otherwise have been taken by workers employed in essential war work. As noted earlier, in January 1941 the Minister for Health acquired powers to regulate the letting of lodgings in particular areas where accommodation was most urgently required by war workers, to prevent vital spaces being taken by evacuees. It became clear to the government that the only method of providing suitable accommodation was to construct residential hostels, particularly in those instances where factories providing essential war materials were built in isolated locations.[28]

In a number of key respects GC&CS faced administrative challenges typical of those of many wartime organisations evacuated to the countryside. Growing staff numbers, combined with an influx of civilian evacuees into the same region, placed considerable pressure on billeting officers within the region who had to look further and further afield to accommodate war workers. This in turn created considerable logistical problems in order to transport those workers to and from their billets. The initial solution by the state was to restrict the influx of non-war workers into these regions, a solution that was also applied to the Bletchley area. The state also turned towards communal accommodation to relieve the pressure on local communities, a solution also eventually adopted by GC&CS. However, the change in the agency's response was gradual. The problem of finding accommodation for staff had been noted as early as 1939, yet because there was no plan in place to govern the agency's expansion (which grew in a haphazard fashion to address specific problems) there was no initiative in place to house new workers once they arrived. It was not until 1943 that serious building work took place to resolve the issue permanently.

## Transport

The by-product of accommodating employees in ever-increasing distances from Bletchley Park was significant transport problems. The initial solution by GC&CS was to ask individuals within the organisation in possession of cars to volunteer their time and vehicle to transport their colleagues. It was not long before Alistair Denniston began to consider the acquisition of official vehicles, drawn from SIS, for transporting staff billeted outside of Bletchley.[29]

Soon, the agency had acquired a fleet of vehicles and drivers to transport staff members and cater for any other transportation needs as they arose. By March 1942 the agency already had 50 drivers on its books who covered between them 19,362 miles each week.[30] The duties of the drivers included providing transport for senior staff and visiting officialdom, conveying workers, and carrying dispatches. The issue of providing timely and efficient transport was also integral to the work of the Y Service, and the process of delivering intercepted wireless messages to the agency required a small army of motorcycle dispatch riders. Despite typically being overlooked or taken for granted in histories of the agency, an efficient transport system was an integral component of the entire Ultra infrastructure. Without it the entire system would have collapsed; if raw enciphered messages were not swiftly delivered to Bletchley Park, much of GC&CS's work would have been of little value as the intelligence derived would have soon been out of date. Similarly, without transport for workers, the Bletchley Park factory would have ground to an immediate halt.

The drivers were recruited from a wide variety of different backgrounds. Ann Witherbird (née Graham) was recruited as a teenager into the ATS, trained as a driver and eventually posted to Bletchley Park. Her recollections provide interesting insights into the type of individual employed as a driver and the different driver pools utilised by the agency. '[T]here was another Graham, a Lady Jean Graham and I've seen a picture of her in one of the rooms. There was Lady Rowsbotham, Dianne Sou, all volunteer drivers, they weren't in uniform, and we were the only two ATS.'[31] The implication of Mrs Witherbird's statement suggests that those individuals who drove staff cars were predominantly female civilians, including several debutantes. This stands in contrast to those drivers in the main Services Transport Section (bus drivers who ferried staff members to and from their billets), in which by the midpoint of the war, the numbers of men and women employed as drivers were near equal. Over the following war years the proportion of men steadily increased until they outnumbered their female colleagues by nearly two to one.[32]

As noted above, the distances between the various towns and villages which accommodated GC&CS staff members could be considerable. The distance between Steeple Claydon and Bedford, the two furthest settlements from Bletchley Park utilised for accommodation, is twenty-five miles. To cater for transport across such distances, at all times both day and night, required a large number of drivers and vehicles which regularly covered significant distances. In January 1945 the drivers collectively covered 34,567 miles in a single week. That week the agency recorded a total of 128 drivers in the Transport Service, who on average each travelled 272 miles, and between them drove in total 29,915 passenger journeys.[33]

As in the case of billeting, transport was a national problem and the challenges faced by GC&CS were by no means unique. In fact failure to provide adequate transport arrangements for war workers was a source of considerable nationwide anger on the part of the workers.[34] For example, in December 1943 a Mass Observation poll placed the blackout and transport as being the two wartime problems that were most inconvenient.[35] Workers, in addition to spending extended hours in the workplace, were forced in many cases to endure long waits for transport which would then prove to be both slow and uncomfortable.[36] The problem of transport was exacerbated by a lack of drivers, conductors and vehicles, as many of the former two were recruited into the armed services and the latter were requisitioned by those same services. Much essential war work was also conducted in isolated areas which demanded that many workers be transported long distances each day.

Among the national solutions to these problems was an initiative to supply new buses, expand the capacity of existing buses and stagger working hours to reduce traffic congestion. Additionally, as occurred in the case of GC&CS, drivers were assigned, typically from the armed forces, to operate the vehicles. Furthermore, women were encouraged to participate in solving the problems by becoming conductresses.[37] In this respect GC&CS had arrived at the same solution to a very similar transport problem. By 1944 GC&CS's transport service, at least a third of which was made up of female staff members, had acquired around 40 buses to transport its thousands of staff to and from billets.[38]

## Catering

If the logistical issues of finding accommodation and transport for workers were major administrative obstacles for the agency, then perhaps even more challenging was the question of feeding them. Catering was not only a practical necessity, but, as we shall see in the next chapter, it was also a key component in maintaining morale. The efforts made to ensure a smooth catering service also provide a fascinating story in their own right. The task of GC&CS's caterers was one which not only expanded as staff numbers swelled, but also required significant adaptation and compromise over the course of the war. The caterers were faced with the problem of how to feed many hundreds, if not thousands, of individuals, in some cases several times a day, over the period of a full 24-hour day, every single day.

### Meal numbers and meal subscriptions

At the beginning of the war, when GC&CS first evacuated to Bletchley, the caterers had only to provide meals for some two hundred or so individuals. As we have seen, in the early days of the war many of the new recruits were drafted from the common rooms of Britain's elite universities. With the limited numbers of staff members the decision was taken to recruit caterers befitting the social rank and lifestyle of the individuals being fed. For Admiral Hugh Sinclair, the head of MI6 and Director General of GC&CS, this meant hiring one of his favourite London chefs to provide lavish meals for the staff.[39] When GC&CS first arrived at Bletchley Park, the staff sat at long tables to enjoy the food provided by the chef together.[40] However, this arrangement could not last. The agency was gaining new recruits by the day, and the demands on the chef proved too demanding.[41]

So instead, GC&CS provided a self-service cafeteria on the ground floor of the mansion, replacing the previously lavish catering system in place.[42] However, the pressures of growth were already taking their toll on the catering system in the opening weeks of the war. In October 1939 the agency took to internal memoranda to point out to staff that there was no obligation for employees to take lunch at the site and those who did were expected to pay a full month's rate. Individuals who failed to attend could not expect reimbursement and the agency further reminded staff that the rates charged were less than the cost.[43] Staff were also regularly prompted to pay for their lunches.[44] The demands on the caterers were not restricted to normal working hours either. Even within the first few months of the war a shift system had been introduced. This meant that the caterers were required to provide not only lunches and dinners, but also breakfasts and other meals for those individuals employed on shifts during unconventional hours. Until at least 1940, for those on night shifts, meals were free of charge; however, staff on the day shift had to pay for their lunches.[45] Staff were invited, provided they paid and took the offer in limited numbers only, to also dine at Bletchley Park while off duty. For example, one memo circulated across the agency asked, 'Will all those not on duty please pay for their dinner as soon as possible.'[46] The same message also informed staff that meals for those not on duty were a concession that could be maintained only if numbers remained small, and that it could be withdrawn at any time. Clearly, the catering arrangements were barely coping and additional strains were not to be encouraged.

It is also clear that, during the opening months of the war, the agency paid for the catering it provided on behalf of its staff working unconventional hours, and subsidised the meals of its day staff. Those charges were determined by the amount a staff member was paid. Staff who earned more were expected to contribute accordingly (see Table 4.1).

With staff paying for monthly meal subscriptions, the issue of non-payment generated an even larger number of internal memos asking defaulting staff members to pay their dues. Despite the agency's efforts

Table 4.1  Monthly lunch charges according to seniority

| Staff description where applicable | Rate of pay | Monthly lunch charge |
| --- | --- | --- |
| Serving officers and other personnel | £300 or greater per annum | £1.10.0 |
| Personnel | £3 per week or greater | £1.0.0 |
| Personnel (WRNS, WAAF, ATS) | Below £3 per week | £0.15.0 |
| Persons aged 17 (military other ranks) | Not stated | £0.10.0 |
| Personnel aged 15 or 16. All personnel on provincial rates (other than locally recruited personnel living at their homes who pay for lunch) according to their grade) | Not stated | Free |

Note: Alistair Denniston, 'Meals at Warstation' [Day obscured] August 1940, HW 64/56, TNA.

to encourage timely payment, in November 1941 there were still 100 individuals who had failed to pay their October meal subscription.[47] This was clearly problematic, however, given the size of Bletchley Park's staff contingent, which by that stage numbered more than 1,600 individuals, 100 defaulters represented only 6% of staff numbers. Most staff members were compliant, paying in full and on time.[48]

Excluding lunch, three other main types of meals were provided for those individuals on site at different times: dinner, midnight supper and breakfast. The cost to an individual not on duty, but eating on site for convenience, was 1s for both lunch and dinner and 9d for breakfast.[49] Tea was also served in the mess, and from January 1941 a charge of 1$^{1/2}$d was placed on tea to subsidise meal subscriptions.[50] These rates were to rise by May 1941 for the majority of personnel, with the exception of the top category which saw a reduction when the top two categories were melded together. As a result those earning in excess of £300 p.a. saw a reduction in monthly meal rates of 7s 6d, while all the other categories saw their charges increase by 2s 6d, with the exception of those who received free meals, which remained free of charge. Another exception to this were those Wrens who ceased being charged a monthly rate and instead were charged 9d per meal. This meant that any member of the WRNS who worked in excess of five days a week would be charged more per meal than their counterparts in the ATS or WAAF. These charges were to remain the same for the rest of the war.[51]

As a rule, the charges for the catering were higher for those individuals in senior positions. This was in spite of the fact that the catering provided was the same regardless of rank or income. Not only was the food provided the same, there was no distinction in the physical geography of the cafeteria. Senior officers and staff were not provided alternative facilities or food to those of their-lower ranking colleagues: everybody ate in the same hall.[52] Therefore, meal prices were determined by the ability to pay, which in turn was determined by rank.

With the growth of the agency in every respect, particularly in terms of geography and staff numbers, the task of providing catering naturally became a major challenge for the agency. In March 1942 when the agency began making regular weekly records which detailed staff numbers, they also began noting the number of meals provided each week both at Bletchley Park and its outstations. By that point in the war GC&CS already employed around 1,500 at Bletchley Park (still considerably less than the 9,000 or so individuals employed there by January 1945), and the agency in turn provided nearly 1,500 meals each day (10,187 meals during the week ending 22 March 1942 alone). These meals were split into six different categories: lunches, snacks, dinners, suppers, breakfasts and high teas. Of these the most numerous were lunches which accounted for 4,524 of the 10,187 meals provided.[53]

The number of meals provided does not neatly fit the rise in staff numbers. The highest recorded number of staff at Bletchley Park was in the week ending 14 January 1945 with a total of 8,995 staff members recorded.[54] The number of meals provided that week numbered 24,742, or a little over 3,500 meals a day for nearly 9,000 staff members. Additionally, at some stages when staff numbers were lower the number of meals provided were actually greater. For instance, on 30 April 1944 GC&CS recorded that it had provided 30,126 meals that week for a staff of 7,586, or just under four meals per week per staff member. However, by 5 November 1944 staff numbers had increased by 1,022, yet the number of meals provided that week had only risen by 1,007 to 31,133. That meant that GC&CS was now only providing 3.6 meals per week per staff member.[55] This was because staff in the armed forces housed in the purpose-built accommodation camps (which opened in January 1944), with the exception of officers, were not permitted to eat at the cafeteria without gaining prior permission.[56] As it was, the camps already had their own mess facilities.[57]

These figures show that the catering for an agency the size of GC&CS was a vast operation, at its peak providing 32,140 meals in a single week. The figures also make it plain that demands on the caterers could have been considerably higher from 1944 onwards, as the pressure upon them was relieved as many military personnel received catering elsewhere. Even at their peak in the week ending 25 June 1944, the average number of meals served per day came to only a little less than 4,600. Excluding SIS members, some 8,054 staff members are recorded as having been employed on the Bletchley Park site that week, nearly double the number of meals provided.[58]

Nevertheless, the popularity of these meals resulted in the establishment of multiple sittings despite a large number of employees using alternative catering arrangements. For example, in October 1940 staff were informed that both dinner and supper had been expanded into two separate sittings held at regular times each day, dinners at 7 p.m. and 7.30 p.m. and supper 2 a.m. and 2.30 a.m.[59] As the demands upon the catering system increased the number of times slots increased accordingly; by May 1941 the number of slots was increased again to three.[60] Lunches, the most popular meal, were provided over four individual sittings each day, and the agency operated seven days a week.[61]

## The administration of catering

In the summer of 1940 GC&CS's Joint Management Committee (JMC), Bletchley Park's main organisational body consisting of representatives from both GC&CS and SIS, made the decision to formalise and professionalise the ever-expanding catering operation at Bletchley Park. Stewart Menzies ordered the formation of a mess committee – an arrangement common in the armed forces.[62] The committee consisted of Commander Denniston as its president, Captain Ridley of the SIS as its secretary, and Commander Bradshaw as its paymaster. In addition to these three, a further three individuals, voted for by staff members, were added to the committee. Their role was to deal with issues arising regarding the catering at Bletchley Park and respond to any suggestions or queries made by staff members regarding the station's catering.[63] The elected staff representatives were to hold their positions for a year, at which point new elections would take place.[64]

In October 1940, soon after the establishment of the mess committee, the JMC announced that given the rapid increase in the demands on the catering system at Bletchley Park, a full-time catering manager was to be appointed. The catering manager, Mr Crawley, was mandated to oversee catering at the agency and reported directly to the JMC.[65] This move was designed to improve the catering system and ensure the efficient use of catering supplies.[66] The development was indicative of the general reorganisation, and professionalisation, of the catering systems in place and indicative of the *ad hoc* growth of GC&CS. Rapid growth of various sections, particularly in terms of personnel, evidently was permitted with little consideration of the demands on the auxiliary sections such as catering, which had only limited staff and facilities. For example, the construction of a new cafeteria (scheduled to begin operation in April 1942) and the reorganisation of the catering services were the result of GC&CS's recognition that its growth in staff numbers had placed considerable strain on the catering service.[67] Belatedly, GC&CS's senior staff informed Bletchley Park's workers, who were beginning to complain about the catering situation, that they too had recognised the problems and that steps were being taken to solve them before they became still more acute.[68] In short, by the summer of 1941 the caterers simply could not meet the demands of the agency without swift reform and expansion. The system was at breaking point. For example, in September 1941 soup was temporarily made unavailable because there were not enough staff to physically serve it or fulfil washing-up duties.[69] Growth-related issues had not been anticipated and, therefore, no consideration had been given to building a catering system that could cope with sustained growth. Until the proposed measures were put into place, including the construction of the new cafeteria, the situation continued to decline. For three weeks in March 1942 there were not enough hot meals to fulfil requirements. This was because the agency lacked the facilities to provide those meals. As a result, the catering services provided an extra 180 sandwiches daily to fill the gap and once a week staff members were asked to forgo a hot meal and have a sandwich instead until the completion of the cafeteria in April 1942.[70]

The ongoing problems, particularly prior to the expansion of the catering facilities in April 1942, were outlined by Alistair Denniston in September 1941.[71] Chief among them were the kitchen facilities, which, Denniston lamented, were wholly inadequate for an agency the size of GC&CS whose staff at that time daily consumed in excess of a thousand meals. The cost and availability of catering supplies also severely limited the range and quality of the food available. Finally, there were only a limited number of staff available to the catering department. This shortage was attributed to competition arising from the railway and factories which were able to offer would-be caterers abnormally high wages beyond the means of GC&CS. The solution to these latter problems was an increase in the supply of un-rationed foodstuffs, and new dining facilities, run on cafeteria principles, to alleviate the problems regarding staffing.[72] These problems, and the subsequent professionalising solutions proposed to combat them, were symptomatic of GC&CS's retroactive approach to growth. Moreover, the incremental steps made were also symptomatic of its wider gradual metamorphosis into a professional information factory.

Of course, the issue of providing supplies for catering extended beyond acquiring food and cooking materials. Also necessary was the provision of cutlery, crockery and hot drinks, which again show, in microcosm, the wider *ad hoc* processes of the agency's professionalization and indeed mechanisation. Memos were regularly circulated around the agency regarding the loss and breakages of cups and mugs in particular. Staff were provided with hot beverages during breaks and, at least those within cryptanalysis and translation sections, in their huts. The provision of these drinks was clearly designed to maintain morale. However, by 1941 staff were encouraged to consume their drinks in their huts in order to reduce the number of working hours lost to breaks.[73] But the provision of these drinks came with its own problems; for instance, the agency circulated a memorandum in February 1940 stating:

It is regretted that, owing to losses, it is no longer possible to provide service crockery etc. for morning and afternoon teas. From Wednesday next, 14th February, those wanting tea must provide their own gear. All those cups, saucers and spoons are to be returned to the Kitchen by 5 p.m., on Tuesday 13th February.[74]

Nevertheless, the issue of lost or damaged crockery continued to pose a problem. In August 1940 Captain Ridley, one of the agency's site managers, reminded staff members that the tea room was run by volunteers. Part of the problem was that the loss of the various items of crockery, which were government property, was the personal responsibility of those volunteers running the tea room. Ridley complained that crockery had been 'found pushed into the shrubberies and left about in offices, many of them broken'.[75] Ridley further estimated that the loss of crockery was five times that expected on a man-of-war, and that it had become necessary to prohibit taking government property from the mess.[76]

Despite the implementation of these measures to prevent staff members from removing crockery from the mess, the problem did not end there. In January 1942 Alistair Denniston requested that all section heads perform a search of the various cupboards in their huts and return any borrowed service cutlery and crockery.[77] Again, in April 1944, senior figures within the agency were requesting that, due again to the short supply of crockery, staff members provide their own cups for taking tea because the provision of crockery could not be guaranteed.[78] This same message was repeated to staff in December that year.[79]

In addition to facing periodic shortages of resources, including foods, staff and space, limiting the extent of meals available, the same was true of hot beverages. For example, following a message from the Ministry of Food, a memo was circulated around the agency which requested (rather than ordered) staff forwent their morning cup of tea in the light of national shortages.[80] The problem of providing enough tea, and the time tea breaks wasted when tea was provided at central locations such as the cafeteria, led to the entire system for distributing tea being rearranged.

In May 1942 the agency circulated a memorandum outlining the new arrangements. The memo outlined a number of important issues: first, it made note of the rationing of tea within the agency; second, it also clearly highlighted the *ad hoc* nature of the catering system. As the demand grew over time the agency was forced to develop new schemes to provide tea to staff more quickly, ration the resources available and ensure that the tea was paid for. As such, the memo is worth quoting at length:

> Owing to the amount of time now being taken in collecting afternoon teas, arrangements are being made to obtain a limited number of tea urns which will be supplied to Heads of the larger Sections so that they can make their own arrangements, if and as desired, for the serving of tea in their huts.
> These urns have a capacity of about 70 cups.
> 1. tea (in kind) would be available for collection in bulk over a week at 10 a.m. on Mondays from the Cafeteria and milk daily at 2 p.m. from the cafeteria in exchange for tea tickets at 0 1d. per head. The present allowance of tea is 1 lb. for 200 persons and ½ pint of milk for 10.[81]

Introducing urns into the huts was not the only method the agency devised to ensure that tea was available, while reducing the loss of both time and funds. In the same month as the urns were incorporated the agency began the process of automating the distribution of tea and coffee tickets, with machines placed in the cafeteria.[82] A series of crises in the catering system led the agency to turn to (partial) mechanisation, both literally and metaphorically – just as it had with its primary cryptanalytic sections.

In summary, the catering arrangements very much followed along the same lines as the billeting and transport situation. The catering system began on small and, very soon, obsolete principles, as it attempted to provide high-quality, even luxurious standards of food to a limited number of individuals. Given the class and backgrounds of many of the individuals employed in the opening days of the war, the attempt to provide catering to the standard to which many were accustomed is not surprising. However, given the rate of staff growth that GC&CS experienced it soon became apparent that this approach was impractical. The result was the institution of a new self-service catering system in the mansion, which in time also eventually proved inadequate as staff numbers continued to rise. It too was eventually replaced and a new purpose-built cafeteria was constructed. Over the course of the war the catering system radically altered. These changes were made on an *ad hoc* basis as the existing systems became increasingly strained. This process of gradual evolution led to what was, by 1942, a formalised professional catering system that operated in a manner designed to maximise efficiency with the limited resources available to the agency. This involved the construction of new facilities as well as new management, including the introduction of a mess committee to liaise with staff members, the appointment of a catering manager, and even the automation of the distribution of tea and coffee tickets. In many ways the catering system was symptomatic of the wider trends within GC&CS, which saw gradual periodic *ad hoc* changes which in time transformed GC&CS from an organisation with an amateur ethos into a professional bureaucratised information-processing agency.

## Illness and medical facilities

As in any workplace, illness was commonplace at Bletchley Park, and, as noted in previous chapters, was the source of a number of resignations. Over the course of the war the number of staff taking time off due to illness fluctuated between 1% and 6%, the winter months understandably seeing the highest levels.[83] While a relatively low percentage, this still represented a significant loss of working hours. For an agency of 9,000 people by 1944, the wastage of 5% of the workforce to illness for a day represented a loss of 3,600 hours.

The occasional accident also led to staff members requiring medical attention, seemingly the most common being minor traffic accidents involving GC&CS transport vehicles bringing staff members to and from work.[84] This, like illness, was also not uncommon. The introduction of the blackout led to a rise in traffic accidents. As Angus Calder notes, this was most acute in the first month of the war when the number of fatal incidents nearly doubled.[85]

The inevitable occurrence of both accidents and illness among Bletchley Park's staff members led to the provision of onsite medical services. A sickbay and first aid post were located in Hut 1 at least as early as March 1940.[86] However, in a now familiar fashion, the growth of the agency soon rendered these facilities insufficient. This led to the agency adopting a series of *ad hoc* alterations to the medical system in place in order to match the increasing number of staff members. In June 1942 the agency considered arranging for a medical officer from RAF Chicksands to periodically visit the station. That solution was ultimately rejected because the projected growth of the agency was such that a visiting medical officer would make little practical difference to the level of care provided.[87] Instead, the agency acquired its own medical officer in August 1942. A new sickbay was constructed in 1942; it was headed by a nurse, Mrs Meade, who acted as matron and who presided over what was at that time an unspecified number of trained and auxiliary nurses. A doctor was also invited to inspect the sickbay each week.[88] In March 1943 the agency hired a fully trained nurse, a Miss A. M. C. Jones, to act as the superintendent matron for the agency. Her role was to organise all the civilian nursing and first aid services at Bletchley Park. In addition to Miss Jones, a number of other nurses and first aiders were also added to the books.[89] By May 1943 GC&CS had acquired a medical staff of ten and had gained an additional five by October 1944.[90] The introduction of Miss Jones to head the medical facilities at Bletchley Park soon led to unexpected problems. Her predecessor, Mrs Meade, took umbrage at the loss of authority over what had, until then, been her sickbay and promptly complained to the Acting Director of Administration (AD(A)), Paymaster Commander Bradshaw. Bradshaw's response was less than cordial; he wrote to the Deputy Director of Services, the then head of Bletchley Park, Edward Travis, suggesting that he talk to Mrs Meade and inform her that unless she learned to cooperate with Miss Jones she would soon be out of a job.[91]

The sickbay itself consisted of two small wards, four single rooms, facilities for dining, and living quarters for the matron. The aim was to cater for those illnesses which were not serious enough to warrant hospital treatment, but could not conveniently be treated at the patient's billet.[92] By 1943, Bletchley Park also had a sunray clinic that was provided to offer staff members, many of whom regularly worked on night shifts, free courses of treatment under ultra-violet lamps. This was prompted by the loss of working hours to illness, which was partly put down to the taxing three-shift system. Workers in industry, many of whom were also engaged in night work, were offered treatment under ultra-violet light and provided with cod liver oil capsules in order to combat sickness rates. Initially, Bletchley Park offered sunray courses to those on the three-shift system,[93] and in 1944 the facilities were offered to all staff members upon request, and provided patients with 15-minute courses of treatment under an ultra-violet lamp. Bletchley Park's chief medical officer advised staff members that such a course of treatment was a 'valuable tonic' and ultra-violet light aided recipients in resisting disease.[94]

## Conclusion

The administration of GC&CS was a major undertaking, and the organisation of the agency constantly had to adapt itself in order to accommodate a large, and growing, staff contingent. The problems of finding accommodation for staff members, transporting them to and from that accommodation, providing them with meals and facilities for their health and general welfare, proved a significant and evolving logistical headache.

Each of these case studies reveals a similar pattern. The pressures of staff growth placed considerable stress on GC&CS's auxiliary, logistical and welfare sections. Increasingly professional solutions were imposed to relieve that pressure and remove bottlenecks. However, these solutions tended to be *ad hoc* in nature, and put in place with only limited planning and consideration of GC&CS's potential future requirements. The agency's response to administrative and logistical problems was remarkably similar to its response to the major problems in its central functions of cryptanalysis and data storage: to address them as they emerged, and to provide short-term salves that partly resolved immediate irritations but rarely, if ever, invested in long-term planning to facilitate growth.

# 5
# Off-Duty Life: Staff Experience

The administration of GC&CS's support services, ranging from the catering facilities and welfare to the provision of accommodation and transport, were essential to maintaining a successful intelligence agency. The primary challenge faced by GC&CS in this arena was the rapid expansion of the agency over the course of the war. The efforts to implement these support services were hampered by a shortage of resources, but also by a lack of long-term planning or a coherent vision for the agency's future.

The central purpose of the support services was to ensure the smooth operation of the agency's major functions: cryptanalysis; translation and analysis; and communicating intelligence to the agency's clients. The failure of the support services would spell failure in the agency's central mandate. Also of importance was that the smooth operation of the support services would also directly influence morale within the agency.

Of course, there was not, and indeed could not be, a uniform experience of wartime life at Bletchley Park – though different accounts by veterans of the agency often contain familiar echoes. Ultimately, however, the agency's *ad hoc* solutions to the provision of support services meant that employees experienced the war in a variety of different ways dependent on a wide variety of factors. For instance, because the billeting situation was often chaotic, those who arrived at the agency early, or simply happened to be blessed with good fortune, could very well receive a far higher quality billet than later arrivals. Rank, social class, and status within the agency also played their parts. A senior cryptanalyst recruited from a university's senior common room early in the war, comfortably billeted in one of Bletchley's hotels or inns, would have had a remarkably different experience to an individual placed into one of the large military camps constructed outside the gates of Bletchley Park. Taste and expectations also governed an individual's experience. For instance, the catering, which was uniform after the construction of the cafeteria system, elicited a variety of responses from staff.

Also important was how staff chose to utilise their time when off duty. Aware of the importance of morale, the agency encouraged and facilitated a wide variety of leisure activities. This included, for instance, the formation of a recreational club that organised and arranged numerous social groups engaging in a wide variety of activities, ranging from music groups and amateur dramatics to niche interests such as Scottish dancing. Staff members also looked beyond the agency to stave off the boredom and discomforts of wartime life. Many staff regularly attended locally held dances, frequented local pubs and explored the surrounding countryside. While on leave they also travelled further afield, visiting their hometowns and villages, or travelled to large towns and cities, London in particular, to take advantage of their leisure amenities.

## Reactions to GC&CS's catering

Unsurprisingly, the initially lavish catering arrangements adopted by the agency upon its arrival at Bletchley Park were well appreciated. Phoebe Senyard, a GC&CS veteran, recalled the 'wonderful' food provided: '[B]owls of fruit, sherry trifles, jellies and cream were on the tables and we had chicken, ham and wonderful beefsteak puddings, etc. We certainly could not grumble about food.'[1]

However, as noted in the previous chapter, the banquet-style catering system was not to survive long and was soon replaced by a cafeteria system. The agency also had to deal with the problem of rationing, which naturally reduced the menu that the Bletchley caterers were able to offer.[2] The new standards of catering were not appreciated by all members of staff. For example, one Wren recalled how at 'Three o'clock in the morning they used to feed us, on the night watch they used to feed us corned beef and prunes, I've never touched either since.'[3] Another individual asserted that Bletchley Park food 'wasn't very good' and 'institutional type food', then added that a colleague would describe anything placed on his plate with the mysterious (though doubtless unflattering) descriptions of 'harse' and 'wadge'.[4] Similarly, Irene Young, a veteran, wrote in her memoirs that she vividly remembered, due to their unpleasantness, having pastry fruit tarts.[5] The standard of catering also led to a number of formal complaints being made by staff members. One complainant stated, 'The two main dishes in the canteen consist of mince, which is chopped gristle and slime, and fishcakes, which are made of mashed bones and breadcrumbs.'[6] Some veterans also recalled that the food rarely varied. For example, one recalled that the meals she had on the site were usually sausages, dried eggs, carrots and cabbage.[7]

Some veterans even asserted that the poor quality and limited variety of food had an adverse effect on health. For instance, a volunteer in the sickbay recalled treating 'an awful lot of boils and I had to bathe these wretched things. Looking back I think they were caused by malnutrition.'[8] However, these negative views on the quality of the catering at Bletchley Park were far from universal. For instance, Jimmy Thirsk recalled that the meals he was offered included foods, such as salads, that had been unavailable to him in the army before he was posted to Bletchley Park, and described the catering as being 'fantastic' in comparison to that he had experienced while in the army.[9]

Jimmy was not alone in his positive assessment of the food provided by GC&CS. Jean Valentine, a Wren posted to the agency, recalled that the food at Bletchley Park was 'great'.[10] Similarly, in her memoir *Cracking the Luftwaffe Codes*, Gwen Watkins wrote a seven-page appendix on the food at Bletchley Park's cafeteria, as a rebuttal of the unflattering depiction of the agency's food in Robert Harris's novel *Enigma*.[11] The food was, she asserts, sufficiently wide in variety to be deemed 'exotic' to 'the young British person who had never been abroad'.[12] Clearly then, staff had very different impressions of the food that was provided by GC&CS.

In addition to feeding staff members, the cafeteria system also provided another invaluable social function at Bletchley Park. The cafeteria was a social mixing pot, which allowed staff members to congregate beyond the confines of their work. For example, John Croft, who worked as a cryptanalyst at Bletchley in 1939 and 1940, noted that he got to meet and know a number of the mathematicians, including Alan Turing, via the canteen.[13] He also noted that the canteen served as a hub for social life and interaction.[14] Moreover, unlike in the armed services, the mess at Bletchley Park catered for all staff regardless of rank. As a result, low-grade junior staff members could find themselves eating alongside their senior colleagues.

Of course, for those who found the catering provided by the agency unsatisfactory, there were always local options. One Wren noted that when money was available she would take trips to the train station where the Women's Voluntary Service 'supplied sausage meat and chips, or lucky us, perhaps a corned beef sandwich – such bliss'.[15] Similarly, Gordon Welchman recalled being a frequent patron of the local fish and chip shops, largely because fish and chips were not rationed.[16] Not, of course, that the local cuisine was necessarily superior to that provided by the agency. One veteran, Irene Young, wrote in her memoir that she and others would occasionally have their supper at the local station café.

> It was a gloomy place, almost a replica of the film set for *Brief Encounter*. But nothing so romantic ever transpired there, and the coffee was as bad as railway coffee has ever been, and much worse than it is now. I cannot image why we chose this post-prandial pleasure, except that it was the only place available as a change from the B.P. cafeteria.[17]

## Billets

As discussed in the previous chapter, the billeting arrangements for GC&CS staff altered over the course of the war. Initially, staff members were accommodated in local hotels and inns. Once these places were filled, the agency then began placing staff members in the town of Bletchley and expanded outwards towards the nearby villages. Ultimately even this measure proved insufficient to house all of GC&CS's staff members, and the agency built a number of camps and blocks to accommodate its personnel.

Unsurprisingly some billets were better than others, making the billeting system something of a lottery, in terms not only in quality of housing, but in how home owners treated their billetees. One veteran described his landlady as 'a horror', who wanted 'an assurance from the Park that I wasn't a conscientious objector'.[18] Other landlords also denied their billitees access to either sufficient food and amenities: 'We were billeted in Aspley Guise [a nearby village]. The family treated us like dirt – they wouldn't give us baths and wouldn't feed us properly.'[19] Another veteran noted that she had trouble sleeping because she was billeted with a family including noisy young children.[20]

Others also noted that they were placed with unreasonable or otherwise objectionable landlords and ladies. For example, one staff member recalled that the billet was 'beautifully furnished' and in an 'idyllic' location, but was however owned by an 'obnoxious landlady [who] inspected our every move'.[21] Similarly, Jimmy Thirsk had problems with his landlady:

> Trouble came when she complained that I was consuming too much electricity when reading in bed. I pointed out to her that the 40-watt bulb in the bedside lamp consumed very little electricity, but she

continued to grumble and I continued reading after midnight. One night, plunged into darkness in mid-sentence, I realised Mrs. B. had turned off the main switch in the meter cupboard.[22]

One of the primary concerns of the agency was the physical standard of the billets. Billets were often cold, lacking adequate heating. One veteran recalled that their billet had access to neither gas nor electricity; instead they had to make do with oil lamps, oil and paraffin heaters, and if they could acquire it, coal.[23] Another veteran described their billet as 'a cold, cheerless house'.[24]

Billets were also often lacking in terms of both physical space and basic furniture. One member of staff recalled that the billet provided lacked any furniture, and that the agency had to provide a bed, wardrobe and other items to the billet.[25] Yet another veteran, Ann Harding, also recalled a basic billet with an outdoor toilet: 'My room was very small with an iron bedstead, feather mattress and two very thin blankets. There was no bathroom, just a washbowl and cold water on a washstand.'[26] In one, perhaps extreme, example, a member of Bletchley Park staff was forced for a time to share a bed with a colleague, because while the billeting officers had ascertained that the billet contained enough space for multiple billetees, they had not checked to ensure that it had enough beds. The result was that she shared 'a bed with a 6-foot lesbian ballet-photographer, who, since her measurements were larger than anything the manufacturers of WAAF uniforms had allowed for, continued for some time to wear her long black cloak and black sombrero'.[27]

A number of the billets lacked ablution facilities, and in 1943 the agency addressed the issue and constructed its own bath and shower blocks. The move to construct these facilities was preceded by complaints from staff members that the conditions of billets were inadequate and too far from Bletchley Park. For instance, one complaint from 1942 noted that 'You are considered extremely lucky if you are within 10 miles of Bletchley and have indoor sanitation and a bathroom, the general rule being an E. C. [sic] in the backyard and a cold tap.' Furthermore, the billet was described as extremely cramped, to the extent that it was impossible to even fit both a chair and a bed into the room.[28]

One of Bletchley Park's own officers, M. P. Vivian, responding to the complaint, conceded that, 'There are several drawbacks [to billets], not necessarily common to all, and the lack of baths is the chief and most common.' However, she contested the claim that the sanitation facilities were typically poor: 'There are a very few billets in some of the villages where sanitation is primitive, but in the rest the arrangements are modern.'[29] Certainly, it is clear that some the homes of working-class people living in and around Bletchley came as a surprise to the predominantly middle-class workforce employed at Bletchley Park, and who arrived at Bletchley with accommodation expectations commensurate to their backgrounds.

Similarly, not all staff recalled that their billets were disagreeable. June Douglas, a WAAF working at Bletchley Park, was billeted in the nearby village of Great Brickhill in a 'lovely house and garden' with four other members of her section. She also recalled that the location was very safe, and that despite never locking the house nothing was ever taken and that 'there was no hassle of any sort. It was the most peaceful time in the middle of the war.'[30]

Just as the condition of billets varied, so too did the landlords and landladies. While Jimmy Thirsk had initially been housed with an unpleasant proprietor, soon afterwards he moved to a rather more agreeable billet with a far more amicable family.

> For meals and accommodation she [Mrs Jones, Mr Thirsk's landlady] was paid just over £1 (twenty-one shilling a week). What meals they were! With a husband and four children Mrs Jones had six ration books. She also had mine. For nearly fifteen months I lived on the fat of the land. Sometimes, when Mr Jones had gone to work and the children to school, I enjoyed a large breakfast of egg, bacon and mushrooms (which one of the boys had collected in the fields not far from the house), followed by bread, butter and marmalade. If I arrived home at 0045 after an evening shift, a light snack would be waiting for me, which I ate quietly, with all the family asleep upstairs.[31]

Beryl Lawry described being billeted in a small terrace house with a 'very kind landlady' and a taciturn husband who was nevertheless 'very good to me'.[32] Similarly, Irene McPearson, who initially was billeted in an unpleasant house, moved to a new, far better, billet in a nearby village with a landlady who was 'a dear old soul' and 'very kind' to her.[33] Likewise, Mrs L. P. Holliday recalled being billeted in Bletchley 'with a pleasant homely family consisting of husband and wife and married daughter with a husband in the forces [sic]. They were very good to me and I was very happy there.'[34] Even those billets which were basic and lacked amenities could also be pleasant places to live. For example, Elizabeth Laura Persival described being billeted in a 'primitive' country billet, that was nevertheless a pleasant experience because her landlady provided excellent food, she was billeted in the company of her sister who also worked at Bletchley Park, and the billet itself was 'a lovely place'.[35]

Overall however, if there is a general impression of the billets in and around Bletchley, it is that more often than not they were unsatisfactory in some way or other. Many lacked suitable facilities, were too small, too distant from the workplace or had unwilling and uncooperative landlords. In confirmation of the general memories of veterans, M. P. Vivian, one of Bletchley Park's officials, noted in 1942 that her job had taken him to 'more of the inferior type of billets than to the good ones'.[36] Vivian was hopeful that the new accommodation blocks, which were under construction in 1942, would solve many of the problems. By 1943 individuals were beginning to be accommodated in these large military housing facilities constructed near Bletchley Park. However, contrary to Vivian's hopes that the new camps would solve the issue of accommodation quality, the conditions of these billets appears to have been relatively poor. For instance, Jimmy Thirsk described the accommodation in the Shenley Road Military Camp, where he was accommodated from 1944, in bleak terms. The accommodation huts were overcrowded, built to house 16 to 18 individuals, yet in some cases quartered 32. The staff also found themselves at the mercy of the weather, because the huts were poorly insulated: freezing in winters and uncomfortably hot during summer months.[37]

Yet despite the conditions he claimed to have enjoyed his time in the camp, a result of the varied and interesting people he lived with.[38] Individuals, both men and women, within the army were not alone in being housed *en masse* in purpose-built military facilities. The Navy and Royal Air Force provided similar accommodation for their service personnel, male and female. Members of the RAF at Bletchley Park were stationed just outside the park grounds in the purpose-built RAF Church Green, while many of the Wrens were housed at the stately home of Woburn Abbey. Further afield, at the various outstations, service personnel were again housed *en masse* either in pre-existing facilities large enough to accommodate them, or in newly constructed facilities. The shared accommodation provided was reminiscent of that experienced by Jimmy Thirsk. For instance, Anne Lewis-Smith, a Wren posted to Bletchley Park's satellite station at Gayhurst Manor, lived in a small cabin, which she shared with 15 other Wrens.[39] In her memoir she depicts the problems associated with shared accommodation with individuals all on varying shifts. Individuals clambered over one another into their bunks to get to bed, while the person beneath them, on a different shift, attempted to sleep.[40]

## Time off

### Escaping Bletchley

Perhaps unsurprisingly, given the sometimes unpopular standard of catering and often dismal accommodation provided by GC&CS, staff would often attempt to escape the confines of Bletchley Park and its satellite stations, in order to return home or elsewhere. Such breaks were facilitated by the shift system in place. Staff would typically have a week on watch, and then receive a day and a half off work. For those individuals who lived relatively nearby these brief breaks from work were used for short breaks but also to visit nearby towns or travel south to London. Jimmy Thirsk summed up the pull of London:

> Those of us in the army camp found it too depressing to stay there and although there was nothing to stop you leaving the camp and sitting by the lake at BP on a summer's day with a good book, the lure of London enticed many of us to spend our days off there. With its concerts, theatres, cinemas, restaurants, even in wartime its glamour remained. To those like me, who had lived only in country towns, London was the romantic 'Baghdad of the west' that Robert Louis Stevenson knew.[41]

Likewise, a veteran of the WAAF wrote, 'By train we would usually travel to Luton or Dunstable. [It] all helped to give us relaxation in our off duty periods and to keep the anxieties of war at bay.'[42] In addition to London, and local towns such as Dunstable, staff would also travel to other relatively nearby attractions such as the theatres of Stratford-upon-Avon.[43] Similarly, Asa Briggs recalled that staff members would travel to Bedford to attend concerts held at the Bedford Corn Exchange.[44]

Often such trips were made on a limited budget and staff would hitchhike some of the way.[45] The recorded memories of GC&CS veterans are littered with references to hitchhiking. For instance, Beryl Robertson recalled, 'We did a lot of hitchhiking in those days, which was very safe. The drivers used to feed us on the way up to London on the old A1. We always tried to flag down a staff-car with a flag on the front of it.'[46] Similarly, Mavis Faunch recalled hitchhiking from the nearby village of Fenny Stratford to London.[47]

Hitchhiking was not uncommon during the war. The practice had its origins during the interwar period and was popularised during the Depression of the 1930s. This was a result of the mobile workforce, travelling around the country in the search of work, in combination with the growing number of commercial travellers and hauliers using the nation's roads in that time.[48] During the war the government actively encouraged hitchhikers because it saved petrol and provided a means for service personnel, such as those employed by GC&CS, to return to their stations.[49]

## Onsite entertainment: the Bletchley Park Recreational Club

The agency itself also tried to facilitate off-duty leisure activities for staff in addition to amenities to provide for their general welfare. As such, the agency made its buildings available for various leisure and educational activities. Hut 2 initially served as a tea room, providing hot beverages, sandwiches and lunch vouchers. The hut also contained a lending library and was the home of the Bletchley Park Recreational Club from its formation in October 1940. The aim of the club was 'to provide, for all members of B.P., facilities for recreation and amusement which otherwise do not exist in Bletchley, and in particular, to cater for junior members of the joint organisation whose billets are often poor and whose resources are limited'.[50] Both the library and recreational club remained in Hut 2 until May 1942 and the departure of SIS from the mansion, at which point both the recreation club and library occupied rooms in the mansion.[51]

By November 1940 the recreational club had 150 subscribing members, a figure which was to rise to 340 by January 1941.[52] This was no small number, at that time representing approximately 50% of the agency's staff members.[53] Despite the initial success of the recreational club it did suffer a number of serious problems, including attendance and retaining members. The most pressing of these problems was created by the workload of staff members; regular attendance was limited by the unorthodox hours placed on staff by the shift system, and the transfer of members to other sections. Not only did these factors limit attendance but they also had an impact on the organisers of the club, which included:

> (a) [...] the resignations of both the Hon. Secretary and the Hon. Treasurer, who have found it impossible to devote the requisite amount of time to their voluntary work connected with the Club; and (b) to the collectors being unable to collect fully and regularly without loss of working time.[54]

Those problems saw a decline of membership to 130 by April 1941.[55] The proposed solution was the recruitment of a full-time club official to actively manage the operation of the club. However, the funds available from subscription were limited and instead the wife of a staff member was recruited on a voluntary basis.[56] Despite the problems faced by the recreational club in the first months of its existence, it continued to operate until April 1946.[57]

The club offered its members a number of different recreational activities. From December 1942, the club had sections offering dance, badminton, drama, music, squash, art, golf and fencing. From early 1943, the club also used facilities at Bletchley Senior School to provide its members with the opportunity to play table tennis.[58] In February 1943 the club was permitted to serve beer.[59] It also apparently served other, stronger, alcoholic beverages. For instance, one veteran recalled that her first introduction to alcoholic spirits was gin acquired from the recreational club.[60]

The off-duty cultural activities of staff members posted to Bletchley Park, facilitated by the recreational club, has been widely commented on in the literature on Bletchley Park. For example, Sinclair McKay includes a chapter dedicated specifically to this facet of Bletchley Park.[61] McKay notes that these activities were typically highbrow, a result of GC&CS's recruitment policy which drew staff members from educational establishments that placed an emphasis on the arts.[62]

Staff members have recalled many of these cultural activities. For instance, Scottish dancing was popular and regularly appears in the recollections of former staff. Similarly, Beryl Lawry recalled being introduced to that form of dancing while at Bletchley Park, as did Muriel Gallilee.[63] Others, including Oliver and Sheila Lawn, recalled the amateur dramatics and music performed by other staff members.[64] Similarly, fellow veteran Wendy Munro recalled attending several of the revues performed by members of the staff.[65] Performances of this nature commonly appear in veterans' recollections, often as being of a high quality. For instance, one veteran recalled that the 'Social life at BP was very full – an excellent dramatic society with many professional actors and actresses employed at the Park.' Furthermore, 'There were many concerts and recitals, poetry readings, country dances and language courses.'[66]

Due to the wartime restriction of materials such as textiles, performers produced innovative solutions to produce props and costumes. One solution was to buy blackout curtains with which to make dresses. Similarly,

> Bunting as used for carnivals and draping stages etc, and butter muslin, also unbleached calico were all 'not on' coupons. We would dye these materials in every colour we could lay our hands on. One

act we used to do which was always a winner wherever we went, was a chorus line doing the Can Can. We made the dresses from blackout material and dyed bandages different colours for each dress.[67]

Doreen Luke's recollections suggest that Bletchley Park staff placed considerable effort and indeed expense into the production of their shows. Doreen also suggests, by stating that an act was highly successful whereever it was presented, that these performances were not restricted to those at Bletchley Park, but were held around the community.

Bletchley Park also had its own chess club. Given the number of highly skilled chess players, including a number of individuals from the British chess team such as Harry Golombek, C. H. O'D. Alexander, P. Stuart Milner-Barry, as well as the Scottish chess champion, James Macrae Aitken and N. Anthony Perkins, who would go on to represent Scotland in the 1958 Munich Chess Olympiad, the establishment of a chess club was natural. Given GC&CS's policy of recruiting a number of chess players to work as cryptanalysts, the formation of a chess club is among the least surprising cultural developments at Bletchley Park. Perhaps more odd, given the stringent secrecy surrounding GC&CS, was the appearance of the Bletchley Park chess team in a victorious match against the Oxford University chess team in December 1944, subsequently reported in February 1945 by the magazine *CHESS*. As Alan McGowan highlighted, writing in *Scottish Chess* in 2005, an observant reader may well have found it odd that a small and obscure town in central England had a chess team that contained so many distinguished players and that was able to defeat the Oxford team 8–4.[68]

### The assembly hall

The agency actively encouraged staff to create opportunities for recreation. When the decision was made to build an assembly hall in 1942, just outside the gates of the park, one of the key points made to justify its construction was the facilitation of social activity. It was understood by the agency that recreation was necessary to maintain morale and with it a high level of productivity within the workplace. This reasoning was made clear in a letter by an unnamed official (though probably Stuart Menzies, the head of SIS and GC&CS) to the treasury official Herbert Brittain, asking for funds for just such a facility.

> We have over 3,000 people working in a small township without recreational facilities. They are mostly billeted in neighbouring villages.

There is no getting around the fact that all work and no play makes Jack a very dull boy, and while no one wishes for extravagance in war time, unless some recreation is available, work suffers. By recreational facilities, I mean the occasional showing of films. Actually, I arranged for 'Next of Kin'[69] to be put on the screen for B.P., for security reasons, but owing to the lack of accommodation, it took an incredible amount of extra work to ensure that the staff all saw it.

I hope, therefore, you will see your way to acquiescing in this expenditure, which I can only endorse in the genuine belief that it will assist in the work of this all important establishment.[70]

The assembly hall was subsequently constructed, seating up to 400 people, and was used from August 1943.[71] One of the recreational functions the author suggested that the assembly hall facilitate was the showing of films.[72] However, projecting films proved to be only a small part of the recreational activity for which the hall was utilised. From its opening month the Bletchley Park recreation club's dance group held weekly sessions for three hours each Monday evening. Additionally, every Friday between 1 p.m. and 1.30 p.m. the hall would host 'lunch time music'. The music group and dance group both had nights reserved, once a month, for formal concerts and performances.[73] The hall was also open for reservation by individual GC&CS sections for their own social events.[74] Furthermore, outside 'star performers' were also approached to appear, though restrictions on bookings greater than two months in advance made that difficult (though in the case of the recreational club it was extended to three months). That restriction was put in place because the hall proved so popular and was regularly fully booked.[75]

### Sport at Bletchley Park

While off duty, some staff members also enjoyed playing sport with colleagues. The journalist Malcolm Muggeridge, who served as an intelligence officer in the SIS, occasionally visited Bletchley Park. In his memoir, he recalled that staff members regularly played rounders on Bletchley Park's lawns, and that the Oxbridge dons:

> would dispute some point about the game with the same fervour as they might the question of free-will or determinism, or whether the world began with a big bang or a process of continuing creation. Shaking their heads ponderously, sucking air noisily into their noses between words – 'I thought mine was the surer stroke'.[76]

Sinclair McKay notes that the use of the lawns at Bletchley Park for sporting purposes was popular in 1939.[77] However, it seems unlikely that this practice continued much beyond that point given the considerable workload the agency placed on its staff members once expansion began in earnest. But there is evidence that Bletchley Park's staff members did enjoy a number of different sports with their colleagues while on the Bletchley Park grounds. The social club also included sections dedicated to badminton, fencing, table tennis, squash and golf.[78] The social club, on the behalf of its members, also arranged facilities off site for use by its sports sections. For example, its members used a local school hall for table tennis from 1943 onwards.[79]

Given the social background of many of GC&CS's employees, the sports veterans recall playing at Bletchley Park were those typically played by the middle classes. Ross McKibbin notes that golf, in particular, was popular among the upper elements of the British middle class, in no small part due to the relative cost of acquiring equipment, as for the same reason were racquet sports.[80] As noted in Chapter 4, the agency, purportedly on the instructions of Winston Churchill, also built tennis courts at Bletchley Park for staff use.[81] McKay notes that the tennis club was particularly popular and that there is archival evidence to suggest that the agency permitted the tennis club access to site buildings, specifically a summer house, to use as changing rooms.[82]

## Bletchley town

For those who did not have either the opportunity or perhaps the inclination to employ the station's organised recreational facilities, clubs and societies, there were only limited other recreational activities available. Wendy Munro, despite attending the occasional revue, recalled that she 'didn't really have a tremendous social life'.[83] Instead she, like others, took weekend trips to London or spent time exploring the countryside.[84] Similarly, veteran John Croft's recollections suggest that there was very little to do in wartime, and that he spent his time largely reading, spending time with friends and taking country walks.[85]

Moreover, the efforts of the agency and its staff members to provide a social life in Bletchley did not suit all tastes. For example, the common pastime of dancing did not appeal to Marjory Campbell. However, she did take advantage of the occasional shows put on by staff members.[86] Distaste for events was not the only problem; some impediments were logistical. Wendy Munro stated that she was billeted too far away to really take part in social events.[87] Instead she invented her own entertainment, as did John Croft. Elizabeth Laura Persival and her friends similarly created their own social life. Persival recalled that she and her friends hosted a party one evening at which they, despite the limitations created by rationing, all contributed a number of different dishes.[88]

As in the rest of Britain, cinema was an important pastime.[89] Bletchley had two cinemas, both of which were regularly frequented by agency staff.[90] Asa Briggs recalls that there were other cinemas in settlements surrounding Bletchley, in villages such as the nearby Wolverton and Fenny Stratford, and also made reference to a film society within Bletchley Park that showed foreign films and documentaries.[91]

The local pubs were also frequented by some staff members. For instance, Sheila Lancaster, who worked for MI6 at Bletchley Park during the war, recalled frequenting the local pub.[92] Pub attendance did, however, entail a certain 'town–gown' divide. As Asa Briggs recalls, 'There was little mixing between railwaymen, who played games like darts, shuffleboard, shove ha'penny and dominoes, and BPites. Some "hostelries" were very much railwaymen's pubs, and I do not remember seeing anyone playing chess in any pub.' Moreover, there were three pubs with highly educated clientele '[where it] was reputed that a few of their customers spoke classical Greek to each other over their beers.'[93]

Of course, pubs were not necessarily available to all members of GC&CS's staff. Drinking and pub culture were identified as being distinctly male,[94] and Britain's military services took a paternalistic attitude towards its female recruits and actively sought to prevent them from engaging in activities deemed socially inappropriate for women. Female members of the armed forces posted to GC&CS were no exception. Alice Wolynskyj, a veteran of the WRNS, recalled that all the pubs within a 12-mile radius of her accommodation were banned.[95] Therefore, while female civilians working for GC&CS were able to visit local pubs, the majority of women at Bletchley Park were actively discouraged from doing so. However, obviously, the policy was only preventative and designed to make visiting pubs difficult though not impossible; there was nothing stopping Wrens like Alice travelling beyond the restricted 12-mile area.

### Dances

A popular pastime for many GC&CS staff members was attending social functions, such as dances. As noted, GC&CS's assembly hall was used once a month to hold evening dances for its staff members. Furthermore, staff members also attended dances in the local community as well as neighbouring military facilities. Attending dances was an extremely popular pastime among GC&CS's staff members. Shelia Lancaster told her interviewer that, 'We all got together for dances at the school and for drinks at the pub because we were not allowed to drink in the school.'[96] Similarly, Joan Marr (formerly Tollet), a Wren at Bletchley Park, attended dances while billeted at Woburn Abbey.[97] Staff members would travel considerable distances to attend dances. June Douglas, a WAAF posted to Bletchley Park, recalled that she and her colleagues would travel by train to London to enjoy the entertainment available, which included dances.[98]

While the demographic makeup of Bletchley Park meant that the female contingent far outnumbered the men, Bletchley Park and its outstations brought many people into regular contact with those of the opposite gender. Young women were able to gain contact with men outside of the work setting by travelling to the dances regularly held on other nearby military establishments. Many women have noted that the American servicemen, on relatively nearby bases, invited them to their dances. To add to the attraction the American troops were able to offer the British women items they had not been able to easily acquire once rationing was introduced. Joan Collins, a Wren posted to Bletchley Park, recalled that, 'We always used to go [to dances hosted by American troops] because they had beautiful food and ice-cream.'[99]

## Romance

An unintended consequence of bringing a large number of young men and women together was that GC&CS facilitated a number of romantic relationships. Joan Watkins met, and subsequently married, Jimmy Thirsk during their time at Bletchley Park.[100] In 1943 two Bletchley Park employees, Ann Graham and Arthur Witherbird, met at a local dance and by the March of 1944 they had married.[101] Sinclair McKay's history of Bletchley Park lists numerous other romantic attachments among staff members, many of which led to marriage. In addition to the Thirsks and the Witherbirds, Harry Hinsley and his wife met at Bletchley Park, as did Sheila and Oliver Lawn, and Mavis Lever and Keith Batey. These relationships were often aided by the numerous recreational events and social activities facilitated by the agency.

The Bletchley Park veteran Gorley Putt described the formation of romantic relationships as being the inevitable product of the intensive working environment at Bletchley Park; indeed it is Putt's implicit assumption that the agency's conditions rendered staff unusually susceptible to romance as well as conflict. 'Nerve tautened to breaking point by round-the-clock speedy exactitude would fumble, in off-hours, for emotional nourishment.' The 'emotional nourishment', he suggests, manifested itself in various ways ranging from sexual attraction to fallings out, both taken to the extreme; 'In the hothouse secret confinement of Bletchley Park, personal relations were as grotesquely falsified as in an Iris Murdoch novel. Sexual infatuations and personality clashes alike became obsessional.'[102]

Oliver Lawn described the relationships at Bletchley Park in more sober terms, stating that there was 'quite a bit of romance' at Bletchley Park, and then noted that he was aware of several marriages formed within Hut 6, including his own.[103] However, relationships were not, despite the strict compartmentalisation of work, confined only to romance within individual sections. For instance, Harry Hinsley worked in Hut 4 while Hilary Brett-Smith, whom he went on to marry, worked in Hut 8. This is of course unsurprising given the ample opportunity for individuals within different sections to meet and socialise outside of the working environment, be it the canteen, social clubs or other leisure facilities. There was also no bar to prevent these relationships being formalised by marriage, the only caveat being that civil service regulations demanded that married couples within individual sections work in separate rooms.[104]

Interestingly, despite the potential security risk, no effort was made by the agency to prevent romantic attachments among its staff members. For instance, Mavis Lever and Keith Batey's relationship, which they initially had attempted to keep private, did not go unnoticed by her colleagues or her section head, Dillywn Knox. In fact, when they announced their engagement, despite having tried to keep the relationship a secret, Mavis discovered that her colleagues had already placed bets on when the announcement would be made.[105] Indeed, anecdotal evidence suggests that section heads were willing to reorganise individuals' shifts, if they were in a relationship, in order to maximise a couple's off-duty time together. Conversely, if a relationship was breaking down, the individuals would be placed on separate shifts to make the situation less difficult.[106]

On the other hand, some veterans report finding that the ratio of male to female staff was a prohibiting factor in being able to enjoy a relatively full social life. Mavis Cannon, a former WAAF teleprinter operator employed at Bletchley Park between 1943 and 1944, rarely attended any of the dances at the assembly hall. The reason given was that there were few men at the events.[107]

Nevertheless, despite the gender imbalance, it appears that romance was relatively common among GC&CS staff members. The blossoming romances within the agency, despite a widespread anxiety that the war would contribute towards growing moral vice (particularly sexual promiscuity), most relationships were purely romantic in nature. McKay argues that this was because the largely middle-class makeup of GC&CS's staff meant that the majority of the young men and women at Bletchley Park arrived at the agency with certain preconceptions regarding romantic relationships prior to marriage. Certainly, premarital sex carried with it a social stigma that, for many young middle-class GC&CS recruits, made sexual relationships untenable. The potential results of such sexual relationships could have profound negative consequences, including family disgrace, for young middle-class women in particular. McKay quotes an unnamed Wren who describes how the news of an illegitimate pregnancy would be received by a young woman's parents. 'If, heaven forfend, you were to come home pregnant, your mother would have banished you from the house. It would have been unthinkable.'[108] Nevertheless, there is some anecdotal evidence that such relationships were at least possible. For instance, Marion Hill quotes, though does not name, a veteran who stated,

> Of course you couldn't actually share a room with a man in a hotel. They asked to see your marriage certificate first. But where you will, you find a way. There was plenty of opportunity for walks in the countryside, bike rides. I can remember drinking champagne on hilltops with young men.[109]

Of course, this veteran does not obviously refer to a relationship between staff members, and could equally have been referring to a relationship forged outside of the agency. However, it does certainly suggest that despite the prevailing moral attitudes towards sexual relationships between unmarried couples of the time such relationships, including those of members of GC&CS's staff, could and on occasion did occur.

Similarly, there were rumours of pregnancies among unmarried staff members and illegitimate births that circulated Bletchley Park.[110] These rumours were not entirely without foundation. B. Brister, the superintendent of Bletchley Park's hostel (which housed some of the agencies' female Foreign Office staff), wrote to Commander Bradshaw in March 1943 regarding arrangements for an unmarried woman, Miss M. Dalley, who had become pregnant.[111] The agency attempted to deal with such pregnancies with some delicacy. For instance, arrangements were made for pregnant unmarried staff members to take unpaid maternity leave for up to six months, and in exceptional circumstances up to 12 months. Therefore, illegitimate pregnancy did not disbar continued employment at GC&CS, and arrangements for extended (unpaid) maternity leave could be made as the circumstances dictated.[112] Given the prevailing social stigma towards premarital sexual relationships GC&CS's sympathetic attitude towards its unmarried pregnant staff members may seem surprising, but it is necessary to note that GC&CS's policy was, in fact, dictated by the guidelines provided by the Treasury.[113] Overall, evidence of illegitimate pregnancies is scant. Barring the very real possibility that such references were largely omitted from agency records, or masked in euphemism, illegitimate pregnancy was a rare phenomenon among GC&CS's staff.

Ultimately, as McKay suggests, the entire issue of sex was, for many of Bletchley Park's staff members, a subject that was not openly discussed and 'the whole business remained shrouded in mystery'. Certainly, the Bombe veteran, Anne Lewis-Smith, in her memoir, recalled an event suggestive of a certain naivety surrounding sex.

> I was surprised to see a girl called Vera kneeling on the floor. Her overnight bag was open beside her.
>
> 'Look' she exclaimed, 'an American friend must have put all these balloons in my bag as a present.' Already she had blown some up, the ends knotted, and bouncing around the floor...odd sausage things. Alas, all one colour, beige, which I thought, as a present, inconsiderate.
>
> We were laughing with delight, and I was about to help blow up some more, when an older Wren came down the steps.
>
> 'What are you doing?' she said severely. Vera told her about a kind airman she met who must have put them in her bag when she was in Bedford on an overnight pass.
>
> She explained they were French Letters. We looked totally blankly at her.
>
> Then she told us clearly and plainly what they were and why they were used. Both of us were horrified and gladly helped her stamp on them – not at all easy! Eventually the jolly bouncing balloons became sordid bits of rubber.[114]

The general emphasis among GC&CS staff members to engage in romantic as opposed to sexual relationships largely conforms to the general trends within Britain during the Second World War. For instance, Gerard DeGroot has argued that women within the Services were far more likely to seek romantic as opposed to sexual encounters, and that the women interviewed in his study of sexual and romantic relationships among British servicewomen during the Second World War claimed not to have indulged in such behaviour and nor did they believe it was prevalent among their colleagues.[115]

There was, however, a moral panic during the 1930s and the Second World War regarding increasing moral laxity among young women in regard to sexual activity.[116] One of the fears was that young men and women, in a wartime setting, with pay and without proper supervision would engage in 'immoral' activity. DeGroot notes that the typical stereotype was that 'young women, removed from parental control, and aroused by a range of erotic stimuli (danger, uniforms, guns, alcohol), offer themselves willingly to randy warriors'.[117] The war, which took a large number of young men and women outside of the sphere of parental influence, many for the first time in their lives, fuelled fears of a rise in moral laxity. Neither the government nor the press were immune to such fear. In 1943, *The Spectator* published an article on the threat of venereal disease, by Colonel L. W. Harrison, an advisor to the Ministry of Health. Harrison suggested that the main catalyst in the spread of venereal disease lay in the moral failings of young women. Promiscuity, he argued, was the result of the attitude of 'girls' whose wartime work took them away from parental influence and provided them with an income allowing them to indulge in excessive consumption of alcohol. This, he argued, led to 'multitudes of reckless, unstable girls who drink far too much and are determined to have a good time come what may'.[118]

However, as noted, DeGroot has found that young women engaged in war work in the women's services did not in fact behave in the manner Harrison suggests – rather, they sought purely romantic relationships. Similarly, there is little evidence that among the thousands of young women working at Bletchley Park and its outstations sexual promiscuity was common or that that sex was a component common in the premarital romantic relationships formed. By extension illegitimate pregnancies were uncommon and there is no evidence that venereal disease was a problem.

## Conclusion

In February 1943 Commander Edward Travis, by then the head of Bletchley Park, concluded that, 'The workers' lives at BP consist almost entirely of work, meals, transport and billets, in invariable succession.'[119] In Travis' view, the primary means of improving the lives of staff members living under these monotonous circumstances was to improve the administration of the agency, making the situation as easy and painless as possible.

With the aid of the agency, as well as their own initiative, staff members broke the monotony of their work by engaging in a numerous recreational pursuits. They formed clubs and societies that catered for a wide variety of hobbies and interests. Many of these groups, in particular those dedicated to performance, be it musical or theatrical, also regularly conducted well-attended revues and recitals – often of high quality – that were open to Bletchley Park's staff members. Given the typically educated middle-class backgrounds of GC&CS staff members, many of these clubs and groups engaged in relatively 'high brow' recreational pursuits. These groups were not only sanctioned by the agency, but actively facilitated by it. The agency constructed buildings and facilities specifically with staff welfare in mind.

The activities hosted by the recreation club feature widely in the memories of the agency veterans, both in memoirs and oral history interviews, which is suggestive of the popularity of these events and groups. This stands in contrast to similar recreation groups within other wartime institutions staffed by transplanted war workers. For instance, *War Factory* by the social research organisation Mass Observation records that the social centre for workers formed by the authorities of the factory under observation was a largely unsuccessful enterprise. Like the Bletchley Park recreation club, the social centre was formed to provide numerous recreational activities for off-duty factory staff – it included a bar, dances, lectures, reading rooms and so on, and also encouraged clubs dedicated to recreational activities, including dramatic groups, walking and cycling. However, there was little demand outside the white-collar office staff and the factory's management staff.[120] Therefore, it appears that these facilities were popular with the middle-class contingent of the factory's workforce, but not the working-class, lower-grade staff members for whom the facilities were built. Bletchley Park's workforce was primarily middle class, and the social and recreational facilities proved to be popular among all groups of staff members, both high and low grade.

However, understandably, many staff members looked beyond Bletchley Park to enjoy their leisure time. Cinema was a popular pastime in wartime Britain, and Bletchley was no exception. The town of Bletchley and its surrounding villages had a number of cinemas, supplemented by the on-site cinema, that were widely attended.[121] Wartime cinema attendance was high with 70% of civilian adults occasionally attending the cinema.[122] Similarly, GC&CS's staff also regularly attended dances, which also were regular recreational pastimes for other transplanted workforces in Britain during the Second World War.[123] However, while it seems that many GC&CS staff found recreational pursuits to fill their off-duty time that was not spent in billets, other transplanted workforces often found very little available recreational activity.[124]

In regard to the broader issue of social change, the GC&CS case study provides a number of revelations. The war brought a new independence to a whole generation of young people, uprooting them from their homes, schools and families, and placing them in a new environment of places and people they would not have met before. People of various backgrounds and educations were forced to interact. So at the least, from a social perspective, GC&CS expanded the horizons of its employees.

This gain in terms of independence was also enjoyed in other ways. For example, at least as far as GC&CS was concerned, though the Ministry of Health official Colonel L. W. Harrison was largely mistaken in his prediction that the war would result in the spread in venereal disease, he was, however, correct that many young people had access to both greater personal income and more opportunity to spend it. As Harrison also predicted, the newly found independence also resulted in indulgence, in some cases, of alcohol.[125] In the light of the fears surrounding the impact of war on morality, the armed forces took a rather paternalistic approach to the moral welfare of their female employees, and thus limited the leisure activities of the servicewomen seconded to GC&CS.

Ina Zweiniger-Bargielowska notes that, certainly in terms of food consumption, the Second World War had a levelling effect on social class. The standard of food consumed by the middle classes 'deteriorated' while the working classes benefited from a larger nutrient, calorie and vitamin intake.[126] Given that GC&CS primarily drew on the middle classes to source its recruits, this thesis is difficult to test via analysis of Bletchley Park. However, if applied to agency hierarchy an interesting observation can be made: staff, regardless of their background and position within GC&CS's hierarchy, ate precisely the same food in the canteen, and the fees charged to staff clearly favoured those on wages and lower salaries.

Similarly, the problem of accommodation invites interesting observation. With the exception of those individuals who arrived at Bletchley very early on, the accommodation crisis saw individuals being placed in whatever accommodation was available regardless of the standards they had previously enjoyed. That factor was magnified still further when the military personnel were transplanted from their civilian billets in town and placed into large purpose-built military accommodation. As the Y Service veteran Geoffrey Pidgeon noted, 'you have the situation of "girls of quality" going into a room with a twenty-five watt bulb, and the instruction that they are to only have one bath a week. And there is lino everywhere.'[127]

# 6
# Bletchley Park and Its Impact on the Local Community

Prior to the outbreak of war Bletchley was a small railway town. The town marked the junction between the major rail link between London and Birmingham and the 'Varsity Line' running from Oxford to Cambridge. More importantly, the town was also situated near to a major trunk of the nation's communications cable network, and the Fenny Stratford repeater station provided GC&CS with easy access to the heart of the British communications network.[1] The small neighbouring town of Fenny Stratford was the larger of the two urban areas and would provide much of GC&CS's billeting during the Second World War. Like Bletchley, Fenny Stratford had grown because of the national transport infrastructure. While Bletchley was centred around the rail infrastructure, Fenny Stratford had benefited from stage coaches travelling on the Roman road of Watling Street and the barges employing the Grand Junction Canal. While the dominance of rail travel would eventually lead Bletchley to grow into, and ultimately dominate, Fenny Stratford, at the outbreak of the war Fenny Stratford was still the larger of the two small towns.

Despite Fenny Stratford being the larger of the two towns, by the opening years of the twentieth century Bletchley had already begun to dominate its neighbour. On 16 May 1911 the Bletchley Urban District Council formally took responsibility for Fenny Stratford. This move signified a shift in administrative dominance between the two towns that had become increasingly inevitable since Robert Stephenson directed his London–Birmingham line through Bletchley in 1846. Further importance was granted to Bletchley when Thomas Brassey's Oxford branch reached the town in 1855. Bletchley became an important junction connecting the London and Birmingham Railway to the Varsity Line between Oxford and Cambridge.[2]

The 1931 census recorded that there were 6,170 individuals within the Bletchley Urban District; an area which included both Bletchley and Fenny Stratford.[3] Such was the importance of the railway network to the town it had become the single largest employer of the local male workforce, employing 416 men. By contrast, agricultural occupations, including farming, gardening and agricultural labour, employed only 247 men, and the production of bricks, pottery and glass only occupied 38 individuals. Nevertheless, Ron Hellier, a local resident who grew up in Bletchley during the war, vividly recalls the importance of the sizable agricultural sector that also heavily contributed to local employment in the years leading up to the Second World War.[4] In the case of female members of the workforce, the largest single occupation was domestic service which occupied 201 individuals.[5]

Bletchley was, in many ways, typical of a great many small towns in the region during the period. It was built on a small number of common local industries which provided goods and services to larger towns and cities. Bletchley was also typical in that it contained the minor estate of Bletchley Park. There were a number of large houses, with sizable grounds, in the local area. The most notable of these is Woburn Abbey, the stately home and extensive estates of the Duke of Bedford, situated close to the nearby village of Woburn. However, there was a considerable number of other large residences nearby, including Chicheley Hall, a large baroque-style home built in the early eighteenth century; the country mansion of Whaddon Hall; Hanslope Park, another local manorial estate; and, of course, Bletchley Park.

In many ways Bletchley Park was an obvious choice to house GC&CS. The estate included the relatively spacious country house in which to work, and the picturesque grounds offered relief from work, and, fortuitously once the war had begun in earnest, were large enough to accommodate considerable expansion. The rail and road networks, which had facilitated the growth of both Bletchley and Fenny Stratford, made for easy transportation. The local towns and villages also provided a welcome supply of hotels and inns in which to house GC&CS's initially small workforce. Significantly, as noted in earlier chapters, the town was also situated on a major trunk of Britain's communications network.

## The impact on the local area

Given the limited size of Bletchley and its surrounding towns and villages, it seems a logical assumption that an agency eventually numbering nearly 9,000 individuals being housed nearby would have a drastic effect on the area. Local historian Robert Cook drew just that conclusion when he noted that the evacuation of GC&CS forever altered the town, stating 'a hive of activity, focusing on Bletchley Park and Rickley Lane RAF camp, meant there was no going back'.[6]

Certainly, the arrival of GC&CS at Bletchley Park did have an influence on the town and surrounding area. This was not just in terms of physical change, but also in a variety of other subtle ways. Bletchley Park's employees lived locally, they ate locally, they patronised local services and amenities, and the arrival of a government facility in the community did not go unnoticed by locals. From the outset the question of what the government wanted with Bletchley Park aroused local interest. One of the weekly local newspapers, the *North Bucks Times and Country Observer*, ran a story in June 1938 with the headline, '"Bletchley Park Puzzle", "Air Ministry or War Office Purchase?"'[7] The article detailed the paper's fruitless attempts to discover not merely what purpose the estate was to be put to but which ministry had acquired it. The paper had 'learned' that the estate had been acquired for the purpose of air defence. Yet when, the paper informed readers, the Buckingham Member of Parliament Major J. P. Whiteley had contacted Sir Edward Campbell, the Parliamentary Private Secretary to the Secretary of State for Air, he was informed that the Air Ministry had no plans for Bletchley Park. Instead he was advised to contact with War Office. Some days later, the paper was telephoned by the Air Ministry to confirm that, after all, purchase of the estate was indeed connected to air defence.[8]

The article was followed, three weeks later, by a second piece which reported that the mystery had still to be resolved. The Air Ministry, though initially stating that the estate was to be utilised in air defence, denied that they were behind the purchase of the estate; enquiries to the War Office were equally unsuccessful.[9] Rival local newspaper *The Bucks Standard* was also interested in the mysterious fate of Bletchley Park. The paper also reported in June 1938 that the Air Ministry was rumoured to be behind the government's purchase of the property, though like the *North Bucks Times and Country Observer*, it had uncovered no specific information. The paper reported the various rumours afoot regarding the purchase, one contender being that the estate was to be the location of searchlight defences. The only solid information the paper could give readers was that work was afoot on the local communications network, and that new telephone cables were being laid. Though it could not confirm the rumour, the paper suggested that the cable was a direct line to Whitehall.[10]

Ultimately, however, the local papers ceased reporting the question; we can speculate that this was either because they lost interest or because they were warned off by the agency. The belief that a government department had acquired the estate for various military purposes was maintained until long after the war. A 1965 book on Bletchley, published by a local historian, D. C. Low, declared that the estate had been acquired by the Foreign Office and was employed by all of the services for military training.[11] Even after the publication of Frederick Winterbotham's *Ultra Secret* in 1974, which brought the true purpose of Bletchley Park to national attention, there remained confusion as to just which government department had purchased the estate. For instance, in a 1979 history of Bletchley, Ivy Fisher, another local historian, stated that the War Office had acquired the house and grounds.[12]

As the *The Bucks Standard* made clear, the relocation of GC&CS was followed by a flurry of activity which was not limited to the digging up of the local roads to connect the estate to necessary physical lines of communication. The arrival of the agency was hardly inconspicuous, and considerable building work was done on the Bletchley Park site and surrounding area. Work on the utilities did not cease after the outbreak of war either. For example, Bletchley Urban District Council noted in June 1940 that a new water main for the estate had also been laid.[13] The site itself underwent considerable physical change over the course of the war. From the outset construction work began to increase the amount of workspace available. Initially, prefabricated huts were built, and later on large concrete blocks. By the end of the war dozens of new buildings adorned the site.[14]

Throughout the war, GC&CS continued to make major physical alternations not only on the grounds of the estate, but beyond. For example, the nearby Elmer's Grammar School had been requisitioned by GC&CS in 1939.[15] Over the course of the war the agency continued to requisition nearby land. In May 1943 the Bletchley Urban District Council recorded that requisition proceedings had begun to further extend the site by 15 acres.[16] On 8 June 1943 the council's minutes noted that the construction of an RAF camp had been proposed.[17] Such expansion and building work had further consequences, not only on the local scenery, but for the people as well. The requisition of the land, and the construction of RAF Church Green to house the agency's RAF personnel, meant that a local right of way that shared the same area had to be moved.[18] In addition to the RAF camp, the agency also built a military camp, on the nearby Shenley Road, to house army personnel.

The hive of activity at Bletchley Park was also visible in other ways. As noted in earlier chapters, the site received a great deal of vehicle traffic on a day-to-day basis. GC&CS's Transport Section ferried employees to and from billets several times a day, and by 1944 the Transport Section accumulated weekly mileage totals which typically exceeded 30,000.[19]

Traffic to and from the site also included dispatch riders bringing encrypted messages for cryptanalysis from the various Y intercept and direction finding stations. From September 1943 onwards the agency had a contingent of over 110 drivers until the end of the war, between them carrying no less than 20,000 passengers each week to and from the park.[20] These individuals were transported in buses with a capacity of 40 individuals per bus and by 1944 each individual shift required 40 buses.[21] Of course, these figures exclude other unrecorded and unquantifiable miscellaneous traffic arriving on site each day as well as dispatch riders. Thus, the estimates of daily traffic recorded by the Transport Section represent only a portion of the vehicles that arrived at, and departed from, Bletchley Park each day. The three-shift system must also be taken into account – the bulk of the passenger traffic would have been centred around the those hours which staff started and ended their shifts, concentrating traffic at 9 a.m. each morning, 4 p.m. each evening and midnight each night.[22] The roads to and from Bletchley Park were small residential streets and were in plain view of the local people. Ron Hellier, for instance, specifically recalled 'big blue RAF buses' taking some of the many RAF personnel on the site to and from their billets.[23]

While in light of the physical alterations that occurred, not only to the site but also to the land surrounding Bletchley Park, the arrival of GC&CS was clearly highly visible. GC&CS also became a significant local employer. Most notably, local builders and tradesmen were employed to construct and maintain the physical structures erected by the agency. There were 25 building tradesmen working on site, including local carpenter Bob Watson who published an account of his experiences in 1993. Watson had already been employed on the site by the previous owners and continued to offer his services to GC&CS, both at Bletchley Park and its outstations, throughout the war.[24] The agency also made use of other local services. For example, when the Naval Section organised a dance at the station's assembly hall, the catering and provision of alcoholic beverages was arranged through a nearby local pub.[25]

Interaction between staff members and the outside world were not always as pleasant. The security files compiled by GC&CS report one incident when an unknown assailant, presumably a local resident though potentially a staff member of GC&CS, attacked two female members of staff while they were returning to their billets after a late-night shift.[26] As we have seen, local landlords and landladies often showed evident displeasure at the additional cost and inconvenience that they were forced to endure by taking on agency billitees.[27]

Meanwhile, GC&CS personnel interacted in turn with local people in various local organisations and functions. This included enrolling in organisations such as the Home Guard. The Home Guard had premises, including a rifle range, on the Bletchley Park site.[28] In addition to involvement in the Home Guard, Bletchley Park employees and social groups participated in various local functions and similarly local groups also used the park's facilities. For example, in 1943 the National Savings Committee organised an event in which the Bletchley Park Drama Group agreed to perform.[29] Furthermore, after some negotiation, the institution also made its own assembly hall available to host the event.[30] That event was by no means unique; evidence exists of other local events held within the grounds of the site. For example, Ron Hellier recalled, as a child during the war, attending local band practice on site most weekends and playing in concerts for the staff members.[31] Further emphasising the contact between locals and staff members, the pianist in the band was actually an employee of the agency. In the light of the sensitivity of the work being conducted at Bletchley Park, the fact that local individuals otherwise unconnected with the site or its work is highly surprising. However, one potential explanation is that by entirely cutting off the local community GC&CS would in fact attract greater attention and interest. In other words, GC&CS hid its activities in plain sight.

Certainly, Ron Hellier confirmed that while at Bletchley Park for band practice he saw nothing sensitive and stated that, 'we didn't know [about site activities]', and that site activities were 'so understated that nobody knew what was going on'.[32] Ron also recalled that he and his colleagues in the band never knew what their pianist did professionally, and that the most he ever told them was that he worked for the Diplomatic Wireless Service.[33] It also seems that, for the most part, local people did not ask. Jimmy Thirsk's memoir fails to mention any example of the local people he was staying with ever showing an interest in his work. In fact, one of the families he stayed with were openly hostile to 'careless talk', reporting to him that people were discussing Bletchley Park's business openly in a public train carriage.[34]

That said, while most residents appear to have been incurious, there were some locals, intrigued by the arrival of a military installation in their town, who attempted to discover what was going on. One such example was reported to GC&CS's security staff, who recorded the incident in some detail:

> There is a parson in this neighbourhood whose name is the Rev. Harry L. Clothier, The Rectory, Aspley Guise. We have had a number of people billeted there from time to time and as a host he is very kind. He has, however, apparently acquired a good deal of information about Bletchley Park, some of which gets rather close to the knuckle. The four girls who are billeted there now are getting a good deal disturbed about him because he not only seems to try and catch them out with the idea of obtaining a little more information, but he repeats what he knows to everyone that comes into the house and seems to take a quite unchristian delight in getting the girls into an awkward position when introducing strangers.[35]

The result of Reverend Clothier's interest in the activities of his tenants was an issue which the agency's security took seriously. However, there was some concern regarding how to deal with the problem of outsiders learning too much about GC&CS. Just as the agency was keen to avoid the unwanted attention that might be generated if it prosecuted those staff members who breached security regulations, it also took a measured stance against local gossip: if the agency was too heavy handed with offenders then that, in and of itself, would be revealing.[36] As a result, GC&CS appears to have taken a policy of trying to frighten offenders into silence as opposed to resorting to legal action. In the case of the Reverend Clothier, it was decided that the best course of action was that he be 'officially warned to keep his mouth shut'. Rather ominously, the security official suggested that what the Reverend required was 'a thorough frightening'.[37]

The problem of overly interested individuals from outside the agency was not restricted only to local residents. Individuals in other governmental or military organisations were also intrigued by the secret activities of GC&CS, and the same policy to ensure that they lost interest was followed. For example, Wrens working at the Stanmore outstation attended a number of dances at which a US Air Force pilot showed an unhealthy interest in and knowledge of their work. The pilot, Lieutenant Skalak, not only seemed to have gathered a vague idea of the activities being conducted by the agency but was asking questions and making comments with the clear intention of learning more.[38] As in the case of Reverend Clothier, GC&CS was keen to dissuade Lieutenant Skalak from probing the issue further by subjecting Skalak to as 'big a fright as possible'.[39]

For the most part, however, the majority of recorded issues typically related to members of staff breaching security through minor acts of 'careless talk'. There is evidence that these acts of careless talk did make an impact on some local residents and others outside the agency. The case of Lieutenant Skalak led Nigel de Grey to conclude that, 'The U.S.A. case revealed that the officers of Thurleigh were aware of the W.R.N.S. activity and I wonder if they provide the local parties with something to gossip about.'[40]

Similarly, veteran intelligence officer Ewen Montagu's memoir account of his first visit to Bletchley Park is revealing:

> I was to go down to the deciphering headquarters at Bletchley Park in Buckinghamshire. On no account was I to go in Uniform, it was far too secret. Having arrived at Bletchley Junction I asked the taxi-driver to take me to Bletchley Park. 'Oh, the cloak and dagger centre,' he replied – so much for secrecy![41]

Of course, Montagu's example suggests only that local individuals were aware that something secret was occurring, but little beyond that – certainly not the specifics of the work. That said, the use of the term 'cloak and dagger' suggests that the taxi driver suspected that the activities at Bletchley Park were related to intelligence work. The agency was worried about the extent of 'careless talk' among staff and within the local community. Nigel de Grey, in a letter largely regarding security breaches at the Stanmore outstation, made a passing, but telling, comment regarding the security situation at Bletchley Park. 'It is all much on a par with local gossip here. Odd bits of "talk" are constantly reported to me – which is good in one way as showing some people as being on the alert and as showing how much does in fact get about.'[42]

Local people were well aware that the agency existed and were even aware that it was conducting war work that was secret in nature. Patchy and fragmented information regarding the general activities of the agency disseminated among the local population. That said, there is no evidence that this illicit information was anything other than vague in nature. As de Grey's letter suggests, local knowledge was restricted to rumour based on 'Odd bits of "talk"'.[43] First, this limited degree of local knowledge can be attributed to the apparently high degree of security discipline maintained by GC&CS staff members. Second, with a few exceptions, most locals took very little interest in the agency.

## Contextualising local attitudes

So why were the local inhabitants of Bletchley largely unconcerned with the activities going on in Bletchley Park? Not even the local press took much interest, and they invested comparatively few column inches to considering the busy government agency housed in the heart of the town. Understandably the agency actively discouraged journalistic efforts concerning its affairs. The agency's attitude towards journalistic interest was highlighted when two bombs landed on Bletchley Park in November 1940. Unsurprisingly, this immediately attracted the attentions of the local press, keen to report that the *Luftwaffe*'s strategic bombing campaign had reached sleepy suburban Bletchley. However, when a local journalist, Ron Staniford, arrived at Bletchley Park to investigate he was promptly evicted by agency officials.[44]

However, this instance was relatively isolated and little other evidence survives in GC&CS's security files to suggest that the agency leaned heavily upon the local press. Rather, with the exception of some early interest when the agency first arrived at the estate in 1938, the local press and the local population remained indifferent to Bletchley Park and GC&CS's workforce.

To elaborate on the issue of local indifference, Ron Hellier, when asked about the impact of wartime government facilities such as Bletchley Park and war workers on local life, did not recall much impact at all. Instead, Ron recalled the arrival of German prisoners of war, displaced foreign immigrants from Eastern Europe and immigrants from the West Indies in the immediate post-war era as having had a far greater impact on the local community. He suggested that this was due, in particular, to the impact they were perceived to have had on the local job market.[45] For many local people like him, the activities at Bletchley Park were only of passing interest. When asked whether he knew anything about the activities on the site, Ron responded, 'Nothing, we weren't allowed to know.'[46] However, he did recall various side effects of the agency on the town, such as the example of war workers being delivered to and from their billets. He also specifically recalled there being 'quite a few RAF personnel in and around Bletchley Park'.[47] To take another example, the war diary of local resident Herbert Bennett included 43 entries, selected by local historian John A. Taylor, documenting his observations of the town during war. Of those 43, only a single entry passed comment on

Bletchley Park. Of the changes the war had brought to the town was 'the great number of strangers there are in Bletchley now. We have here a branch of the War Office. I don't know how many thousands are employed there, but it's still growing and they keep building.'[48]

More noticeable in Herbert's diary was, with the exception of occasional shortages as a result of rationing, the limited impact of the war on Bletchley. However, these examples collectively emphasise that while local residents were aware of the presence of the agency and that it did have a noticeable impact on the town, they were largely unaware of what was being done on the site. In fact, they even began constructing imaginative explanations for the park activity that was visible. For example, Ron recalled believing that the RAF personnel and buses he saw in and around Bletchley were there to distract locals from knowing what was going on at the site.

> A lot of us thought that it was just a cover for what was going on in Bletchley Park. It didn't occur to us until quite a few years later that these people, RAF personnel, weren't doing anything other than riding around in buses, and a lot of us got the idea that it was just a cover for what was going on at Bletchley Park.[49]

Where local residents did recall (in oral history interviews) Bletchley Park's wartime role, this often centres around the billeting situation or the occasionally striking difference between themselves and many of the newcomers. For example, one local man, Baden Powell,[50] recalled that his mother-in-law's billetee was Angus Wilson (later the famous novelist), and that Wilson was 'educated but hadn't a clue about everyday, ordinary, common things'.[51] Baden's next-door neighbours were also Bletchley Park employees, whom he recollected were well-educated individuals. Baden noted that they were pleasant, but that they never spoke about their jobs.[52] In some cases the alien quality and the difference in social class of the new arrivals could be intimidating. Local historian Marion Hill quotes an anonymous local individual who recalled, 'A Wren was billeted with my boyfriend's mother. We all went for a drink one evening, although as a factory worker I felt a little inadequate, more so after our shandy – she said she liked "cherry brandy". I did not even know of it.'[53] Some locals were also rather suspicious of Bletchley Park's staff members. Gwen Blane, a local resident who worked at Bletchley Park, recalled, '[T]he locals never knew who these strange people were and were rather suspicious. All their boys had gone off to war and were fighting. What were this queer lot at Bletchley Park? Skiving?'[54]

Another Bletchley resident, Martin Blane, summed up the situation: 'We locals used to think Bletchley Park was like a holiday camp. We didn't realize what was going on there. We used to see people, they were billeted out.'[55] Some accounts of Bletchley wartime life do not make even passing comment on the park. For example, a history of wartime Bletchley by John Taylor includes four firsthand accounts of wartime life by children. There is no mention of Bletchley Park in any of these accounts.[56]

Given the size of the agency relative to Bletchley's population, it may seem counter-intuitive that local people entertained only a vague or passing interest in the activities on the site. Part of GC&CS's success in keeping locals from knowing about onsite activities was down to their own policy of actively warning staff against discussing their work in public. Ron Hellier stated that nobody asked questions about Bletchley Park 'because there were no questions to ask. Nobody prompted the questions. Nothing that was going on around prompted any questions, we all thought that was part of the game; don't let anybody know and they just won't ask questions.'[57] However, there are a number of other factors on both a regional and national level that help to explain not only how the secret was kept, but also the general absence of overt interest.

## GC&CS, Bletchley and evacuation

The outbreak of war resulted in massive upheaval in rural regions across the country. The small towns and villages of East Anglia, the Midlands and the Home Counties north of London, such as Buckinghamshire, were no exception. The limited industry, relatively small population centres and extensive transport links made Buckinghamshire an ideal candidate for placing evacuees. Buckinghamshire alone became the home of 31,000 children, mothers and teachers in September 1939,[58] as part of the evacuation programme, which saw the transplantation of some 3.5 to 3.75 million people from areas deemed at risk within the first week of September 1939.[59]

Bletchley, being directly on the major train line between London and Birmingham, was a prime location to receive evacuees. The town's population increased by 3,900 between the outbreak of war and January 1941.[60] GC&CS had recorded its employee totals the month before, in December 1940, and the staff numbers were lower than 700 individuals.[61] As such the major impact to Bletchley, particularly in the opening years of the war, came not from the imposition of an incoming government workforce but from the arrival of thousands of evacuees departing the cities.

Certainly, evacuation of children and mothers to Bletchley received considerable coverage in *The North Bucks Times*. The arrangements for the evacuation programme filled numerous columns both before and after the outbreak of war, and at least five articles were dedicated to the preparations for the arrival of evacuees to Bletchley in 1939 prior to the outbreak of war itself.[62] The paper also continued this interest in the impact of evacuation throughout the war, including a lengthy story on the arrival of the evacuees. By the end of 1939 a further ten articles had been published detailing the various arrangements that had been made for the evacuees, and the impact their arrival had on the town.[63] A further 11 articles would appear in 1940.[64] However, the arrival of GC&CS, as noted, received only muted interest from the local press.

If GC&CS seemingly had relatively little impact on the memories of local people, this was not true of evacuation. For example, Monica Austin recalled the considerable activity that greeted the arrival of the evacuees, describing a 'swarm' of adults with clipboards and children carrying their gas masks. Monica recalled that her mother 'without saying a word, went out into the street and a few minutes later came back with two girls in tow'.[65] Similarly, local historian John Taylor included an extract concerned with evacuation from Herbert Bennett's wartime diary.[66] Ron Hellier, when asked about civilian evacuees from London, stated,

> I can well recall the, [pause] 'social workers' we'll call them, trundling around the roads, street and houses with crowds of kiddies with little suitcases on them, and knocking on doors and just asking can [pause], you know, [pause] not can you take, but what room have you got? How many live here? What room have you got? And if there was room, obviously, room for an evacuee, then you had one or two, as the case maybe. Not a nice time. We didn't. We had a house full anyway where I lived, but the people next door had a couple and several down the street had kids thrust on them and didn't get the option. But they were paid. And that's the beginning of another horror story because I'm quite sure a lot did it for the money and no other reason.[67]

The arrival of several thousand evacuees into a relatively small community and hundreds more at a time, periodically over the first year and a half of the war, must have had a diminishing effect on the impact of the arrival of incoming war workers. By mid-1941 when the staff numbers of Bletchley Park began to exceed 1,000 individuals, the local inhabitants of Bletchley had already been living with, and adjusting to, the presence of a considerable external population for around two years. New faces in the town had, by that juncture, ceased to be remarkable. Furthermore, the trickle of recruitment to Bletchley Park further reduced the impact of the agency's staff on the town. If GC&CS arrived at Bletchley with 8,000 staff members in 1939, then the effect on the town would have been, like the arrival of hundreds of evacuees at a time, considerable. As it was, GC&CS grew in numbers relatively gradually and its initial arrival was overshadowed by the influx of civilian evacuees.

## Bletchley and other secret institutions

The presence of uniformed personnel was also not uncommon in and around Bletchley. There were numerous nearby military bases,[68] and the town, being a railway junction, saw considerable traffic. One local resident, Dennis Comerford, described not only the increase in the number of people passing through Bletchley, but also his mistrust of these strangers:

> Winslow was about nine miles up the Oxford branch from Bletchley. They were busy days during the war. Troops were passing through and trainloads of tanks were a common sight. I kept a sharp eye out for suspicious characters. One memory is of a pair of Canadians chasing a couple of girls who were not keen on their acquaintance.[69]

Clearly, GC&CS was by no means the only new arrival on the doorstep of Bletchley residents. Not only did they have to contend with a considerable influx of new neighbours as a result of the nationwide evacuation programme at the beginning of the war, but the location of their town brought them into close proximity to military personnel.

The war did not just provoke the mass movement of people; it also saw the uprooting of numerous institutions, both governmental and private. One notable feature of the countryside surrounding London was its sudden acquisition of a whole range of facilities, including various other shadowy government agencies engaged in clandestine and semi-clandestine activities. GC&CS's move to Bletchley may have been among the most obvious examples of this trend of institutional migration, but it certainly was not unique. Indeed, GC&CS was not the only agency to occupy Bletchley Park. At the outbreak of the war both SIS and SOE had a presence on the estate. SOE established an experimental section, to develop sabotage weapons, at Bletchley Park in 1939. However, the expansion of GC&CS and the shortage of accommodation soon forced SOE to relocate its section elsewhere.[70]

Meanwhile, the Political Intelligence Department (PID) of the Foreign Office, an institution tasked with acquiring information on the conditions of various European nations, was located at the nearby building Marylands, just a few miles from Bletchley. However, this move only came about after the PID had temporarily inhabited several other large homes in the nearby countryside. Initially, the PID selected Froxfield Lodge, the former home of Lady Ampthill, as its home. However, the location soon proved insufficient in size and the organisation required a new home. Marylands, originally founded as a cottage hospital by the Duchess of Bedford in 1903, was selected and the institution remained there briefly until 1940 before eventually returning to London.[71]

The region also housed a number of agencies which produced black propaganda as opposed to the information-gathering function of PID and GC&CS. Department Electra House, also under the Foreign Office aegis, was an offensive propaganda organisation that produced wireless propaganda and written propaganda, both of which were destined for Germany. In 1940 the organisation eventually became the Special Operations Executive's propaganda wing – the Political Warfare Executive (PWE).[72] 'Electra House' was evacuated to the Woburn Abbey riding school less than five miles from Bletchley, and following the death of the Duke of Bedford in August 1940, occupied the stately home itself. Part of the organisation's role was to produce leaflets in German which were dropped over Germany. The institution's print unit, which had initially also been housed on the estate, soon relocated to Marylands following the departure of PID back to London.[73]

Other elements of the Special Operations Executive, which occupied a large number of different stately homes across the British countryside, were also housed in the region. Chicheley Hall, located a few miles north of Newport Pagnell, now a suburb of Milton Keynes, was used as an SOE training site. The airfields employed to deliver SOE agents to their mission sites were also relatively closely located, a little north of Bedford. Radio sets for use by these agents were also produced at the nearby Whaddon Hall, which was the headquarters of the Secret Intelligence Service radio communications. The primary purpose of Whaddon Hall was to broadcast black propaganda programmes to Germany. These programmes were transmitted by small shortwave broadcast transmitters located in a field nearby to the village of Gawcott near to the town of Buckingham.

These programmes were recorded at Wavendon Towers, a relatively large property located a few miles northwest of the Woburn estate.[74]

The fact was that Bletchley Park was not unique in being home to a covert government institution. In that respect, it was not unique nationally or even regionally. Numerous large homes in and around the region had been occupied by institutions, many within a few miles of Bletchley Park. As a result, from the local perspective, Bletchley Park can only have been one of many small secret wartime institutions that suddenly appeared in the large country homes in and around the town. It is possible to speculate that this, in itself, decreased the extent to which local people would have paid interest in GC&CS. After all, it was just one of several anonymous government organisations occupying familiar local sites.

## Bletchley and 'careless talk'

The British government had been concerned, particularly following the fall of France, that rumour could be damaging to public morale and, worse still, could arm hostile elements within Britain with potentially damaging strategic and logistical information.[75] These concerns were tied into a paranoid fear of 'Fifth Columnists'. The Fifth Column was a largely imaginary covert group of pro-Nazi agitators within Britain that conspired to bring about British defeat. The belief in a Fifth Column held considerable currency, especially after the defeat of the British Expeditionary Force following the German invasion of France.[76] However, the reality was that there were very few actual examples of British citizens attempting to undermine the war effort or provide the German state with sensitive information regarding Britain – as Angus Calder notes, German intelligence regarding Britain was, in fact, poor.[77]

Interestingly, the efforts to undermine British security, particularly by the *Abwehr*, were largely unsuccessful, in no small part due to the efforts of GC&CS. *Abwehr* agents working within Britain communicated with Germany via wireless. The cipher system used by *Abwehr* agents was broken by March 1940. These efforts allowed British security forces to swiftly arrest agents and offer them the choice of either execution or employment with the British security services feeding the *Abwehr* information vetted and, in some cases, invented by those security forces.[78] The system was so successful that by 1943 MI5 controlled every *Abwehr* agent in Britain.[79]

However, despite this the government was not immune to unwarranted paranoia regarding a Fifth Column. Of particular relevance were the propaganda campaigns mounted by the government to suppress morale-damaging rumour and discussion of sensitive information related to the war effort, including the ill-advised 'Silent Column' campaign mounted by the Ministry of Information beginning in July 1940 at the behest of the Prime Minister. The campaign encouraged citizens to invite stereotypical rumour spreaders to 'join Britain's Silent Column'.[80] In the last resort, people were encouraged to inform the police of any individual who caused 'worry and anxiety by passing on rumour and who says things persistently that might help the enemy'.[81]

As the war progressed the government continued to campaign against rumour, specifically those rumours thought of value to the enemy.[82] The most memorable campaign was 'Careless Talk Costs Lives' which featured, among others, the popular posters of the *Punch* artist Fougasse.[83] As McLaine explains, Fougasse's posters employed a 'light touch' and 'avoided browbeating the public', while the Silent Column 'created the impression that the authorities regarded almost any exchange of information or opinion on the war as unpatriotic and dangerous'.[84] The 'Be Like Dad, Keep Mum' campaign also saw its origins in 1940, and like the Silent Column and Careless Talk Costs Lives (a phrase which Keep Mum also incorporated) warned citizens of the dangers of discussing information potentially valuable to the enemy. These campaigns continued throughout the war; for example, the most famous of the Keep Mum posters, 'Keep Mum, She's Not So Dumb' by the artist Gerald Lacoste, was issued in 1942.[85]

Of course, the underlying message of all these campaigns, successful or otherwise, was that German agents were ubiquitous and any inadvertent slip by a member of the public could have catastrophic results for combat troops on the front lines.[86] The posters, slogans and statements were also accompanied by wartime films including the Ealing production *Next of Kin* (1942).[87] *Next of Kin* depicted the defeat of a commando raid because of careless talk. The use of cinema as a tool for spreading propaganda was highly important. In 1939 there were over 4,000 cinemas operating in Britain, which were attended by 19 million individuals each week, a figure that would rise to 30 million by 1945. To take advantage of this popular medium the Ministry of Information produced 3,000 newsreels and nearly 2,000 official films.[88] Radio, as a medium for transmitting important news and propaganda, was of even greater importance. While over 70% of civilian adults occasionally attended the cinema, 90% of households possessed a radio; this brought the BBC directly into the homes of the vast majority of the British population.[89] This placed the

BBC at the front line in the war against the imaginary, yet powerful, Fifth Column.

Thus, every medium for the dissemination of propaganda extolling the dangers of discussing war work and spreading rumour was utilised. Of course, this propaganda was also employed by GC&CS to discourage its own staff from discussing their work. The message, being a national one, also reached Bletchley and the agency was quick to forcefully remind members of the public suspected of knowing too much to mind their own business.

The full effect of these anti-rumour campaigns on the Bletchley community is hard to fully gauge because, as Siân Nicholas notes, it is difficult to quantify the success of the British government's propaganda campaigns.[90] However, in the case of Bletchley, as noted, only limited evidence has come to light indicating that local people attempted to spread rumour about Bletchley Park or attempted to discover what was going on inside. Indeed, there is some anecdotal evidence that the anti-rumour campaigns actively discouraged rumour spreading. As noted in an earlier discussion of Bletchley Park's security arrangements, James Thirsk recalled that his landlady informed him that she had overheard an instance of 'careless talk' while on a train returning to Bletchley, which he in turn duly reported to GC&CS's security staff. He specifically attributed his landlady's decision to report the conversation she overheard to the anti-gossip poster campaigns, and he discussed them in some detail.[91] In many ways this is unsurprising: the poster campaigns to discourage discussion of potentially sensitive subjects was targeted particularly at individuals within Britain's transport network, such as lorry drivers and railway workers, and Bletchley was a town built around a railway junction.[92] The apparent deference of Bletchley's largely working-class local population to the government's instructions, which attempted to induce a wartime etiquette of silence regarding military matters, seems to have aided GC&CS in maintaining its wall of secrecy.

## Conclusion

The failure of the people living nearby to Bletchley Park, and the various GC&CS outstations, to take a great deal of interest in the activities of GC&CS is relatively unsurprising. On a national level, discussion of wartime work was severely discouraged. On the regional level, the arrival of semi-clandestine organisations engaging in war work was common. Numerous organisations occupied large stately homes in the counties immediately north of London, making the new arrivals at Bletchley Park hardly unorthodox. Nor was the wartime migration of large parts of the British workforce. On a local level, the arrival of new individuals into the town of Bletchley as a direct result of the war was also common. In the opening months, and indeed years, of the war the evacuation of school children, mothers and teachers was far more pronounced than the new arrivals at Bletchley Park, who only appeared in the town gradually. Finally, the agency itself was quick to track down and rebuke those members of staff who broke their silence. Those few members of the local community who did try to discover the true nature of the agency were paid frightening visits by menacing security officers.

The war brought many changes to life in Bletchley, and ironically enough given the legacy of the agency, the arrival of GC&CS was not among the most conspicuous. It was only in the later years of the war that GC&CS began to number in the many thousands, and by that time it had already occupied Bletchley Park for several years. Had the organisation numbered in excess of 8,000 individuals at the outbreak of war and had this mass of people suddenly arrived in this town that normally was home to only 6,000 to 7,000 people then it would have been far more likely that the town's inhabitants would have paid it considerably more attention.

# Conclusion

Over the course of the war GC&CS grew from a small organisation with an amateur ethos into a large, bureaucratic and highly mechanised information factory. The height of Bletchley Park's expansion between 1 January and 6 May 1945 saw staff numbers hover between 8,800 and 9,000 employees.[1] This required a massive support structure, which grew, like the number of the agency's employees, throughout the war. At that time, driver numbers fluctuated between 127 and 132 with a combined weekly mileage of no less than 32,000 miles.[2] The number of meals provided each week, though down from the peak of over 32,000 meals in July 1944, still hovered at 22,000–24,000 until April 1945.[3] Following the unconditional surrender of the German armed forces on 7 May 1945, the scale of GC&CS's operations went into immediate decline. By the capitulation of Japan on 15 August 1945 the number of staff at Bletchley Park had already decreased by approximately 2,000,[4] the number of meals provided each week by 10,000, and miles covered by 6,500.[5]

Staff were transferred out of GC&CS into other military and civil positions, others into urgent civilian work and many more were made redundant and provided with 'a week's pay and out'.[6] The Government Communications Headquarters (GCHQ), the cover name that replaced GC&CS in the post-war period, projected total staff numbers for 1946 at 1,010, and relocated to Bletchley Park's old outstation of Eastcote in North London in early 1946.[7] The files stored at Bletchley Park soon followed, and the empty huts and blocks were the only reminders of Bletchley Park's wartime activities; relics of a hidden war.

After the departure of GC&CS, Bletchley Park faded into obscurity. The important wartime activities that had occurred there remained a closely guarded secret until 1974. Even after the revelation of the Ultra secret,

Conclusion 159

the estate retained a relatively anonymous profile. During the intervening years the estate was inhabited by a variety of different groups, including British Telecom, a teacher training college and the Civil Aviation Authority. However, by the late 1980s most of these tenants had left the estate, and the wartime huts and blocks entered a state of disrepair and, soon after, decay. By the early 1990s plans were afoot to demolish the site to make way for a housing development. It was not until efforts in the 1990s and 2000s to rescue the site from demolition that the historical legacy of the physical estate began to become widely appreciated.[8]

## The development of GC&CS

Upon the outbreak of the Second World War Bletchley Park became the new home of GC&CS. At that time GC&CS was a small organisation still recovering from the retrenchment of Britain's cryptanalytic efforts following the conclusion of the First World War. In addition to its modest resources in 1939, GC&CS also faced several other major problems that limited its growth. First, the solution to the huge technical problem of regularly, and quickly, breaking military Enigma traffic initially proved elusive. Second, GC&CS's clients, Britain's various ministries and military commands, initially failed to appreciate the potential benefits of Ultra intelligence and even ignored it when it did have important information to contribute.[9] Third, GC&CS remained partially entrenched in a mentality that had emerged during the First World War. Cryptanalysts from the days of Room 40 had long established methods and ethos derived from the Oxbridge environment from which many staff members had been recruited, and this was reflected in the GC&CS that arrived at Bletchley Park in 1939.

Yet by the end of the war GC&CS, and Bletchley Park for that matter, had changed remarkably. The organisation had become hugely successful and had expanded its staff numbers to nearly 9,000 at Bletchley Park with over 2,000 more working at outstations.[10] This growth went hand in hand with a radical shift in how GC&CS operated, as it switched from a relatively collegiate ethos dominated by academics who pursued GC&CS's work as a scholarly exercise, into a mechanised and professionalised bureaucracy. However, these changes did not occur swiftly and nor were they incorporated across the agency – various sections, most notably those engaged in cryptanalysis, kept much of their original collegiate ethos. Instead GC&CS only gradually transformed and grew over the course of the Second

World War. There was little in the way of major foresight and planning in its development, and the existing administrative and logistical apparatus were beset by constant bottlenecks that GC&CS was invariably reluctant to alter until the situation became untenable. At that point, GC&CS would implement *ad hoc* measures to release pressure. Yet these measures were typically developed to address existing problems. Once in place, as the organisation grew, the pressure would mount once more and the cycle continued. This method of addressing growth permeated every aspect of GC&CS's operations examined, be it staff recruitment, the provision of billeting or the construction of buildings at Bletchley Park.

The manner in which GC&CS operated also underwent a remarkable transformation. While initially the work of cryptanalysts was done by hand, the birth of the machine cipher called for machine-based solutions to quicken the process of code breaking. This process of mechanisation was extremely pervasive and came to feature in nearly every aspect of GC&CS's primary functions. Teleprinters were used to communicate priority messages to GC&CS and then distribute intelligence derived from those messages to the outside world. Complex electromechanical devices such as the Bombe and Colossus machines were designed and built to aid the cryptanalytic process, while Type-x machines were modified and other new machines built to mechanise the processing of messages once the various day's keys had been established. Finally, a vast punch-card tabulating machine system was built to collate, store and retrieve information derived from deciphered signals.

GC&CS's staff had also changed. While the academics drawn from Britain's intellectual elite, who dominated initial wartime waves of recruitment, remained in their roles as cryptanalysts and translators, thousands of machine operators, technicians and clerical workers joined them. Of course, GC&CS had always held a sizable administrative overhead representing around half the staff members in 1919. However, wartime mechanisation and growth led to the recruitment of over 4,100 women from Britain's armed forces (two thirds of whom were members of the WRNS) the vast majority of women from the armed forces would have been engaged in machine operation at Bletchley Park and its nearby outstations. There were also approximately 250 male mechanics employed at the outstations to maintain these machines, and another 250 working in the Tabulating Section. Therefore, machine work, which was primarily a wartime development, came to dominate how GC&CS operated and that is reflected in the huge demand for staff that mechanisation required.

The work of the senior tiers of Bletchley Park's staff members, who fell into the 'Chiefs and Indians' categories identified by Peter Calvocoressi, also underwent a process of professionalisation. In his study of government, Jon Agar identifies the attribution of machine-like qualities as being an important phase in any later process of mechanisation.[11] Agar actually employed Bletchley Park as a case study, identifying its internal organisational solidification and then the actual mechanisation of many of its processes with particular regard to the processes involved in breaking codes and then storing information. Over the course of the war the agency was, Agar argues,

> transformed from a collegiate to an industrialised bureaucracy: an organisation marked by an intricate division of labour, very high staff numbers, an emphasis on through-put, and innovative mechanisation at bottlenecks, all directed to speeding up and making more efficient processes of manipulating symbols.[12]

Certainly, there is much to be said for Agar's analysis. During wartime, GC&CS did restructure itself into a more rigidly structured production line with clearly defined components at each stage of that line. It was also the case that GC&CS's structural and organisational reforms were also complemented by the mechanisation of many of its processes.

The methods and working culture of the 'Old Guard' staff, who had been attached to British cryptanalysis bureaus from as early as the First World War, were gradually replaced over the course of the Second World War. The scholarly approach of individuals such as Dillwyn Knox, which approached the task of cryptanalysis and translation as a single exercise, in which Knox researched the cipher system, broke messages and translated them, was replaced by a production-line system. Various staff members, with particular cryptanalytic skills, were tasked with the process of researching ciphers and formulating new methods to crack them, others would apply those methods to break Axis ciphers, and the messages were then passed on to other sections with the specific task of translating them and prioritising them for wider distribution to Britain's various commands and ministries. Individual cryptanalytic sections, such as Hut 8 and Hut 4, also formed their own internal production lines. Individual subsections were tasked with cataloguing enciphered messages, directing the efforts of the Y Service and ensuring that key messages had been correctly transcribed, formulating cribs and breaking ciphers, and fusing the information gathered from decryption with data obtained from Traffic Analysis. Similar production lines were also established in those sections dedicated to the translation of intercepted messages. This process of compartmentalising work into production lines within a larger production line allowed individuals to become highly proficient in their small role while vastly reducing those individuals' knowledge of the overall scope of GC&CS's work, and in doing so added a layer of security to the operation.

While Agar's analysis examines the formalisation of GC&CS's internal organisation and its adoption of machines in the context of cryptanalysis and data storage, this book has also examined other aspects of GC&CS's evolving wartime character. In particular the patterns identified by Agar in GC&CS's primary work actually permeated to virtually every other aspect of its operations. The catering system, for instance, initially provided luxury banquet food for GC&CS's staff members, to complement the 'university common room' approach adopted by the agency in terms of both staffing and approach. However, the gradual process of professionalisation, which saw the introduction of a wider variety of staff and, more pertinently, vast numbers of them, led to the formation of a cafeteria system to provide mass catering. These measures were necessary not only to feed considerable and growing staff numbers but also to maximise GC&CS's limited catering facilities and resources during a period of rationing. The results of these efforts met with mixed reaction from staff members, some of whom detested the quality of the food or complained of a lack of variety, while others remembered it favourably and contended that it was largely of higher quality than might be expected in other wartime institutions – particularly the armed services. Even something as apparently minor as the provision of hot beverages created significant administrative problems which required repeated restructuring of GC&CS's facilities. The bureaucratisation and partial mechanisation of tea provision is testament to Agar's point regarding government bureaucracies.

However, in other respects Agar's argument is less convincing when GC&CS is inspected in detail. First, it is certainly the case that wartime GC&CS saw a considerable increase in staff numbers. Yet it is important to also note that even before its expansion as the war progressed, in September 1939 the agency was still larger than either of its constituent elements. GC&CS had more staff members at the outbreak of the Second World War than Room 40 and MI1b had accumulated by the close of the First World War combined. With 200 staff members it was still, by the standard set by the previous war, a considerable cryptanalysis operation – suggesting that the organisation was already, before the first British troops had fired a rifle in anger, characterised by high staff numbers. The same point can be made regarding the agency's emphasis on through-put, and its division of labour.

During the interwar period, GC&CS had already split its operational organisation into different categories. Staff were employed to work on specific intercepted messages dependant on the origin of the message. Thus there were distinct sections which dealt with naval traffic, military traffic, commercial traffic, diplomatic traffic, and so on. Furthermore, staff were also subdivided in other key areas, often according to gender and social background. Well-educated men tended to handle cryptanalysis, while similarly well-educated women were employed as linguists to translate messages, but not as cryptanalysts. Meanwhile women, typically without the same exclusive educations, were employed in clerical and administrative roles. This shows that there was already a significant division of labour, but moreover, also shows the extent to which GC&CS placed an emphasis on through-put. The aim of the agency was, and always had been since its inception, engaged in the process of collecting one type of information (the enciphered messages of foreign powers) and performing a number of different discrete processes on that information, to produce a useful product which could be gainfully employed by other branches of the British state. Even before the outbreak of the Second World War, a production-line process was in operation. However, Agar is certainly correct to note that the various processes along the production line became vastly more complex, more discrete, and more numerous as the agency developed in wartime.

A considerable element of this development in GC&CS's production-line system was the process of mechanisation. It is in this respect that Agar's description of GC&CS's transformation is most compelling. GC&CS certainly began, as war became an increasingly likely prospect in the late 1930s, to start recruiting scientifically minded specialists to augment its cryptanalytic staff. That group, in particular key figures such as Turing and Welchman, developed new methods of analysing messages, and developed complex mechanical solutions to the problems posed by the advent of mechanical cipher systems, with the aid of fruitful collaboration with outside institutions such as the British Tabulating Machine Company and the General Post Office. The agency also mechanised many other elements of its work, including the indexing system where it again turned to the British Tabulating Machine Company, and even to its auxiliary and logistical services – such as the implementation of ticket machines to better facilitate the smooth operation of the catering service.

It is necessary to depart from Agar on this issue, and also from the wider conclusions of David Edgerton regarding the centrality of technology within the British state, in respect to how and why processes of mechanisation occurred. Edgerton argues that the British state was dominated from its highest levels by individuals with a technocratic attitude – powerful figures such as Winston Churchill, who surrounded himself with scientists and favoured 'machines over manpower'.[13] Meanwhile, Agar points to a powerful middle-ranking group of technocratic specialists within the civil service. In the case of GC&CS the evidence suggests that it was, in fact, neither the most senior officials nor their middle-ranking subordinates who made the agency receptive to technology and mechanisation. The evidence suggests, perhaps counter-intuitively, that GC&CS was, in fact, not receptive to new technology or mechanisation at all and that analyses of the agency which place emphasis on such facets over-simplify the complexities of GC&CS's evolution.

The recurring theme highlighted in detailed analysis of GC&CS on a forensic level – whether it is in examination of broad administrative change, the growth and development of new and existing sections, geographical expansion, development of the catering and billeting systems, recruitment policy, the mechanisation and professionalization of key processes – suggests that development was carried out in an extremely *ad hoc* fashion, without evidence of prior planning or consideration of future needs. In every instance, GC&CS adopted change because the existing structures in place had collapsed or were on the verge of collapse. For instance, mathematicians and other scientists were recruited in increasingly large numbers because the existing staff, primarily made up of linguists, classicists and historians, had proved unable to solve the problem of the Enigma system; and a war with Germany, which chiefly employed the Enigma system, was on the horizon. The arrival of these new, typically young scientists also caused considerable hostility within GC&CS, as the veterans of the First World War and interwar period were gradually side-lined, and GC&CS's organisational infrastructure and processes altered – again, in an *ad hoc* fashion.

These developments were slow to take place, and the growing tensions and pressures on GC&CS ultimately led to the major reorganisation of GC&CS, and the purge of a number of its key personnel, in 1942. Again, this reorganisation occurred because the agency had proven incapable of adequately meeting the expectations placed upon it from its client ministries and services, and nor, for that matter, could it solve its internal disputes. Crises had grown to such proportions that major change became necessary. With that change came the appointment of staff with key administrative experience and aptitude (drawn from both within and outside the agency) to ensure smooth operation. To take a final example, before the war had even begun there were those at GC&CS who had correctly concluded that a mechanical solution to the Enigma problem would have to be developed,[14] yet it was not until March 1940 that the first British Bombe machine began operating. The German military had been employing the system since 1926, yet it was a full 14 years before a mechanical solution (to a machine-based problem) was developed. The Polish cryptanalysts, who were scientists, on the other hand, had developed a mechanical solution, the *Bomba*, the first of which entered service in 1938.

Of course, GC&CS's resistance to altering its existing systems was, in part, because of the considerable pressures placed upon it which stretched already limited resources. However, it is also partly explained by its unwillingness to alter its existing methods and internal structures unless it was absolutely necessitated by unfolding events. This explains the course of the agency's development, which was characterised by a series of impending crises which forced the agency to adopt incremental changes to its operation once the existing structures in place had been irrevocably compromised. The result was that the growth of staff numbers and the introduction of mechanisation was gradual and that administrative restructuring was haphazard. As the organisation theorist Christopher Grey has noted, the organisation became 'chaotic' in structure, as the meritocratic and collegiate sections were partnered with newly formed and tightly structured and managed sections which operated on factory principles.[15]

In short, GC&CS mechanised and professionalised, not because a growing contingent of technocrats drove its wartime development in that direction, but because wartime developments left the otherwise resistant agency with no other option. The technocrats were then, and only then, mandated to place their skills into action. Indeed, the technocrats were only recruited in large numbers because the agency had been left with no option but to increasingly turn to science for a solution to its problems. Agar dismisses the notion that 'bureaucratic inertia' and a cultural 'resistance to mechanisation' were in evidence in the civil service.[16] However, in a forensic examination of GC&CS, one of Agar's case studies, they most certainly were.

Similar processes of professionalisation and bureaucratisation of other essential services can be observed across GC&CS's administrative and logistical apparatus. The intertwined problems of billeting and transportation are worthy of particular note. Initially, workers were housed in the town of Bletchley, in local hotels and inns. However, the rapid growth of GC&CS's staff members soon rendered this solution impractical as places filled. The initial solution to the problem was to begin billeting staff members in spare rooms of the town's population. In turn these rooms were soon filled and billeting officers began placing workers in nearby villages and towns at ever-increasing distances from the Bletchley Park estate. The administrative difficulties faced by the agency in the provision of distant billets resulted in the housing of staff members in accommodation of varying quality and in some cases many miles from Bletchley Park. The many staff unfortunate enough to be placed in a low-quality billet, with limited facilities and unpleasant landlords, had very little recourse because of the limited availability of accommodation. Efforts were made by the agency to improve the situation of staff members by constructing welfare facilities onsite, such as laundry and bathing facilities to cater for the needs of staff members placed in homes which lacked these basic amenities. The distances between billets and Bletchley Park required workers to be transported to and from those billets at the beginning and end of their shifts, and those shifts operated over the entire 24-hour period of each day. Again, while initially transport was provided by members of the workforce who owned their own cars, by 1944 GC&CS had acquired its own Transport Section, which collectively covered in excess of 30,000 miles each week.[17]

The management of individual sections adds to the picture of GC&CS as an agency that, over time, professionalised and mechanised its processes into a machine-like form – particularly in regard to machine sections. The majority of staff were highly regimented, subject to military regulations (such as uniform attire) and discipline, and regulated with clearly delineated lines of authority. In particular, this applied to those sections tasked with Bombe, Type-x and communications machine operation. Staff had highly particular and repetitive work with little, if any, scope to approach it in a personalised fashion or on their own initiative. They were also heavily supervised, and provided with little, if any, knowledge of where their role fit into the wider picture of GC&CS's work. For many thousands of workers at Bletchley Park and its outstations, their wartime role was to perform a precise and undeviating process in a large bureaucratic information-processing machine.

However, in the case of the 'Chiefs and Indians' the situation was a little different. While the gradual professionalisation of the agency also reduced their roles into performing a specific process, the method in which they were managed was very different. It was understood that in order to gain the best results from cryptanalysts and translators, who were often engaged in highly complex intellectually challenging work, it was still necessary to grant them a considerable degree of freedom to approach the work in the manner which best suited that individual. Similarly, the collegiate atmosphere which had developed during the First World War was retained to a considerable degree. Formal military or civil service rank had little bearing on these individuals' status within GC&CS, and neither did pay, which varied considerably even between individuals performing the same tasks. For the most part seniority was determined by ability, and highly skilled workers quickly rose through the ranks of GC&CS's sections, leading to individuals such as Gordon Welchman and Alan Turing heading their own sections.

However, the process of professionalisation did eventually curtail this meritocratic practice to an extent. It was discovered that while individuals such as Turing might be excellent cryptanalysts, their ability to liaise with outside agencies and manage their sections was questionable. The failure of GC&CS to adequately address the administrative problems arising from increasing demand from client ministries, limited resources and significant organisational growth resulted in several internal disputes within GC&CS and mounting dissatisfaction with GC&CS's management from external agencies. These pressures led to the removal of several of GC&CS's senior figures from positions of management and their replacement by highly competent administrators. Malcolm Saunders, the head of Hut 3, was replaced by the professional businessman Eric Jones. Similarly, Turing was replaced by Hugh Alexander, who as Turing's former second-in-command had a proven track record as a skilled manager. However, perhaps the most notable individual to be replaced was GC&CS's head, Commander Alistair Denniston, by his deputy Edward Travis. While practical ability had, in the initial stages of the Second World War, seen the displacement of GC&CS's 'Old Guard', by 1942 the ability to effectively manage a workforce had become paramount and ineffectual leaders were replaced regardless of their skill in cryptanalysis. However, even with this important caveat, it is important to note that while the incremental and invariably *ad hoc* process of bureaucratisation and professionalisation was clearly in evidence within these key sections of GC&CS, these sections still retained a very different, far more collegiate, working atmosphere to those highly regimented machine sections run on factory principles.

The overriding theme is that, despite the differences in management style between various sections, GC&CS underwent significant professionalisation, mechanisation and bureaucratisation throughout the

Second World War, typically through the implementation of *ad hoc* solutions to resolve various individual administrative and logistical problems. Yet despite this emerging professionalisation, GC&CS became increasingly complex, as various methods of organisation and management were, to utilise Christopher Grey's term 'twisted together', which led the agency to gain what he describes as a 'chaotic and anarchic character'.[18] The agency repeatedly altered how it operated its existing sections, created new sections, reorganised its internal structure, and expanded. All the while, the vast majority of staff members had no idea of the scale of the operation or the extent of GC&CS's successes. Perhaps the most illustrative example of GC&CS's chaotic and *ad hoc* evolution, apparent in every aspect of its development from catering arrangements to the administration of cryptanalysis sections, is in the actual physical geography of Bletchley Park and its relationship to GC&CS's internal organisational structure. The relative rapidity in which individual sections and subsections migrated around Bletchley Park was testament to the general lack of long-term planning and *ad hoc* response to the logistical problems generated by rapid institutional expansion.

## Social class and gender

Attitudes towards gender and social class also had a major influence on the development of GC&CS during the Second World War. Both factors helped to determine how staff were recruited and how work was allocated within the agency. Higher-grade staff were predominantly very well educated upper and middle-class men. The trend of employing this type of individual was forged long before the Second World War because well-placed individuals within Britain's ancient universities acted as recruiters for the agency. Many of these recruiters were former cryptanalysts from the First World War, and the agency exploited its connection to these universities extensively. The result was that the vast majority of 'Chiefs and Indians', senior figures within the agency, and those individuals working in cryptanalysis and translation, were drawn from the same recruitment pools. As a result, the social makeup of the ancient universities was reflected in GC&CS's high-grade staff, which typically (though certainly not exclusively) comprised young, highly intelligent, upper and middle-class men. This was particularly true of GC&CS's cryptanalysis sections; however, sections working on the translation and distribution of messages conformed to this trend to a lesser extent, having recruiting women in larger numbers than their sibling cryptanalysis sections. The work conducted in these sections was often of an intellectual nature, and required that the staff member have (or acquire) considerable technical proficiency in cryptanalytic techniques or languages. Many veterans have described the work as requiring considerable patience and a lateral approach to problem solving, and they were given considerable freedom to approach their work with a degree of flexibility.

Those sections comprised primarily of lower-grade staff, particularly those engaged in machine operation, were very different in some respects, yet surprisingly similar in others. Primarily, it was young women drawn from Britain's military services who staffed these sections. They were recruited to conduct relatively low-skilled labour – in many cases, particularly in Bombe and Colossus operation, a form of 'machine minding'.[19] They had limited scope, in comparison to their colleagues working in cryptanalysis and translation, to approach the work in a flexible manner and instead followed highly specific procedures 'programming' the machines. The work, a form of manual labour, though not classed as such, was both physically exacting and, in the case of Bombe operation in particular, dirty. Machines were also often very noisy and radiated considerable heat, making working conditions difficult. The lower-grade staff were also generally paid far less than their colleagues engaged in cryptanalysis or translation. However, despite the obvious differences listed above, work conditions were often similar to that of cryptanalysis and translation. For instance, staff members worked in the same types of buildings, namely prefabricated wooden huts and concrete blocks which were often extremely cold during winter months. In both instances work was also often extremely high pressured, was conducted on 24-hour shift systems, and was monotonous, even though the work itself was of an entirely different type.

Certainly in terms of gendered division of labour, clear parallels can be drawn between GC&CS's practices and wider wartime attitudes towards employment. Men filled positions of seniority and management in all GC&CS's sections, and women could rarely expect to rise beyond positions of junior management and never to senior management. Men dominated high-skilled work, be it cryptanalysis, translation or technical maintenance of machinery, and comparatively few women were employed in these roles. Machine labour and low-grade clerical work, on the other hand, were dominated by female labour. A similar pattern had emerged in the wider British workplace as increasing amounts of female labour entered the male-dominated industrial workplace, but restricted to work typically classified as both low skilled and low status.[20]

Furthermore, that work which had primarily been considered 'men's work' was reclassified as 'women's work', suggesting that gendered divisions in the workplace did not break down but instead shifted position.[21] This allocation of low-status work to women was certainly replicated by GC&CS.

However, at that point the similarities begin to break down. The increasing numbers of female workers in Britain's industrial workforce were typically working-class women who had previously held employment and returned to the workplace during wartime.[22] GC&CS, on the other hand, overwhelmingly employed young middle-class women to perform its machine work. This was because the female workforce was primarily drawn from the WAAF, the WRNS and the civil service, which predominantly recruited young well-educated middle-class women. As a result the young women operating Bombes and communications equipment came from middle-class homes and often had attained an education to Higher School Certificate standard as a minimum, and many also had college or university experience. The fact that the young women who were recruited from these pools were typically middle class and from 'good families' (as opposed to the more working-class ATS) suggests that GC&CS selected these recruiting grounds precisely because it could be assured of receiving predominantly middle-class recruits.

GC&CS's emphasis on recruiting educated middle-class individuals was partially reflected by the belief among senior staff that less-educated individuals, even in the most junior roles, would be incapable of mastering work. However, it also lay in the intelligence community's assumptions regarding middle-class characteristics. The patriotism and discretion of gentlemen who had been educated at Britain's public schools and prestigious universities could be relied upon. As a result individuals such as John Cairncross were recruited without question, while an individual with a less prestigious education and different social background would have received considerably closer inspection – Cairncross's patriotism and trustworthiness were simply (and in his case mistakenly) taken for granted. It was no coincidence that the typically less well educated young women, most of whom had not travelled in the same social circles as Bletchley Park's senior officials despite their middle-class backgrounds, were not afforded the same trust and were afforded diminished knowledge of GC&CS's operation. However, they were still primarily middle as opposed to working-class and presumably therefore could be trusted in the less, though still somewhat, sensitive roles to which they had been assigned. Speculation aside, GC&CS was certainly dominated by recruits from the middle classes.

The predominantly middle-class background of GC&CS's recruits also had a considerable impact on staff members' after-work activities and how the agency approached the issue of leisure and welfare. Mindful of the negative consequences of low morale, GC&CS attempted to provide sport and other leisure facilities. This included the construction of tennis courts, the provision of a bar, and the facilitation of various clubs and societies dedicated to a range of sporting and leisure activities. Unsurprisingly, given the social class of the majority of its recruits, these tended to be relatively high-brow activities, ranging from typically middle-class sports, such as golf and racquet sports, to music recitals and amateur dramatics, all of which were highly popular. The location of Bletchley Park also offered recruits a variety of after-work activities. Staff members were able to easily travel, via the train or often by hitchhiking, to towns and cities which offered extensive leisure amenities – London in particular. Staff members were also able to use Bletchley's own limited leisure facilities and attended local dances and community events, as well as local pubs and cinemas, and, failing that, to enjoy the Buckinghamshire countryside. In many respects it appears that Bletchley Park's staff had a relatively rich variety of social activities in which to engage while off duty compared to other wartime facilities, in particular factories, many of which were located in remote areas.

## Bletchley Park and Bletchley town

One of the most striking features of the agency was its relationship with the wider community in which it was housed. GC&CS had a massive impact on the local community in and around Bletchley. The local community shared their local facilities, roads, food and homes with Bletchley Park's staff, yet there is only limited evidence that they took any interest in the work being conducted at Bletchley Park. While Bletchley Park's security files describe instances in which local individuals attempted to extract illicit information from staff members, these were relatively rare. What very little information did emerge from Bletchley Park regarding its work was typically the result of 'careless talk' by staff members themselves.

Perhaps most surprising in this respect was the policy of GC&CS itself, which, rather than completely close off Bletchley Park, instead actually allowed locals occasional access to the site and facilitated a number of community functions. In effect, GC&CS hid in plain sight, and did not attempt to hide its existence, but rather its purpose. On the whole, locals accepted the vague cover stories provided by GC&CS, or if they did not, still did not press the issue. GC&CS was just one of many wartime facilities that had arrived in the region. The state also attempted to popularise a wartime etiquette which demanded that people patriotically refrain from discussion and rumour regarding war work and activities in case they revealed potentially damaging information. In the case of Bletchley, people appear to have accepted this etiquette and dutifully refrained from investigating and discussing Bletchley Park; in fact some locals actually went a step further and informed on some of those few individuals who did discuss the agency. Of course, the people of Bletchley also had plenty of wartime concerns, including caring for a considerable number of evacuees who had arrived in the town at the outbreak of the war. Evacuees in particular appear to have had a far greater impact on the wartime lives and consciousness of Bletchley's citizens than the gradually growing wartime agency housed at Bletchley Park ever did.

## Conclusion

In many respects Bletchley Park was simultaneously both unique and commonplace. It conducted highly important work, saw the development of innovative new technologies, and its very wartime purpose was a heavily guarded state secret that remained largely intact for nearly 30 years. Yet the prevailing attitudes and trends of the day ensured that many of the key decisions in its development were remarkably similar to those seen in other wartime institutions. Those similarities ranged from the decision to transplant GC&CS from London to the north Buckinghamshire countryside, to recruitment and working arrangements which were coloured by prevailing attitudes towards social class and gender. The development of Bletchley Park was also driven by the extreme circumstances and demands placed upon it during wartime. Change, growth and demand exceeded any ability for long-term plans to be made and the result was a series of *ad hoc* solutions to complex administrative and logistical problems, which created an equally complex machine-like institution, which grew over time and comprised multiple cogs, each with their own specific function.

The result of the incremental changes to the agency was the development of a very different culture within the agency. Where it had once been amateurish it had become professional. This did not go without notice by those within the agency. Though commenting specifically on cipher machine research and development, Gordon Welchman's candid reflections, written in July 1944, could apply across the board. 'We can claim to have made a pretty good show, but we must admit that in the early stages our handling of the production was rather amateur and we did not realise the problem of the maintenance problem.'[23]

# Appendices

# Appendix 1 Table of Individuals

*Table 1* Senior/managerial staff (arranged by age)

| Name | Year of Birth/ Age at 1 Jan 1940 | Education | Academic subject/occupation prior to GC&CS | Wartime role(s) at GC&S |
|---|---|---|---|---|
| Alastair Denniston | 1881 (58) | Bowden College Cheshire<br>Bonn University<br>Paris University | Foreign languages<br>Teacher at RN College, Osborne | Head of GC&CS 1919–Feb1942<br>Head of Diplomatic & Commercial Section in London, Feb 1942–May 1945 |
| A. Dillwyn Knox | 1884 (55) | Eton<br>King's College, Cambridge | Classics<br>Fellow of King's College, Cambridge, researching Greek Papyri | Chief cryptographer<br>Cryptographer of unsteckered Enigma.<br>Broke Italian naval and German *Abwehr* Enigma |
| (Sir) Edward Travis | 1888 (51) | School in Blackheath | Enlisted in Royal Navy 1906<br>Commissioned 1909<br>Naval staff officer<br>Admiralty cryptographer 1916–1918 | Responsibility for construction team & Enigma teams<br>Deputy head of GC&CS<br>Head of Bletchley Park from Feb 1942<br>Director of GC&CS from March 1944 |
| Francis Birch | 1889 (50) | Eton<br>King's College, Cambridge | Modern languages<br>Historian | Head of German Naval Section Sept 1939–June 1941.<br>Head of Naval Section June 1941–Nov 1945<br>Organiser of end-of-war Bletchley Park Reports 1945/1946 |

*Continued*

Table 1 Continued

| Name | Year of Birth/Age at 1 Jan 1940 | Education | Academic subject/occupation prior to GC&CS | Wartime role(s) at GC&S |
|---|---|---|---|---|
| John Tiltman | 1894 (45) | Charterhouse (offered place at Oxford aged 13 but had to refuse due to lack of funds) | Schoolteacher 1912–1914 Soldier WW1 Russian translator GC&CS 1920 GC&CS cryptographer | Head of Military Section 1929–1944 Chief cryptographer 1942–1945 |
| Max Newman | 1897 (42) | City of London School St John's College, Cambridge | Mathematics Served in army WW1 Mathematician, Fellow at Cambridge and Princeton universities | Testery Section Aug 1942–Feb 1943 Head of Newmanry Section Feb 1943–June 1945 |
| Hugh Foss | 1902 (37) | Marlborough Christ's College, Cambridge | Japanese language, Mathematics Joined GC&CS direct from Cambridge 1924 | Head of Japanese Naval Section |
| Gordon Welchman | 1906 (33) | Marlborough Trinity College, Cambridge | Mathematics Fellow of Sidney Sussex College, Cambridge | Enigma research Head of Hut 6 Feb 1940–1943 Assistant director (mechanisation) 1943–1954 |
| (Sir) Stuart Milner-Barry | 1906 (33) | Cheltenham College Trinity College, Cambridge | Classics/moral sciences Stockbroker; also international chess player | Hut 6 head cribster Head of Hut 6 Sep 1943–June 1945 |
| (Sir) Eric Jones | 1907 (32) | King's School, Macclesfield | Joined family textile firm aged 15; built own textile agency 1925 Enlisted RAF Volunteer Reserve 1940 Air Ministry Intelligence | Temporary head of Hut 3 Air Section Triumvirate head of Hut 3 March–July 1942 Head of Hut 3 July 1942–Nov 1945 |

| Name | Year (Age) | Education | Subject | Role at Bletchley Park |
|---|---|---|---|---|
| Hugh O'Donel Alexander | 1909 (30) | King Edward's, Birmingham; King's College, Cambridge | Mathematics; Maths teacher, Winchester College, 1932–1939 | Hut 6 Feb 1940–March 1941; Hut 8 March 1941–Sep 1944; Head of Hut 8 from Nov 1942; Head of Japanese Naval Section Aug 1944–1945 |
| Alan Turing | 1912 (27) | Sherborne; King's College, Cambridge | Mathematics; Research Fellow, King's College, Cambridge, & Princeton 1936–1938 | Research team Dec 1939; Head of Hut 8 Dec 1940–1942; Research 1942–1945 |
| Peter Twinn | 1916 (23) | Manchester Grammar School; Dulwich College; Brasenose College, Oxford | Mathematics and physics; Began PhD in physics | Worked on Enigma research in Cottage 3; Co-founder of Hut 8; Head of ISK Section – *Abwehr* Enigma |
| William 'Bill' Tutte | 1917 (22) | Cambridge County High School; Trinity College, Cambridge | Chemistry and mathematics | Tunny research Sept 1941–Jan 1942 |
| (Sir) F. Harry Hinsley | 1918 (21) | Queen Mary's School, Walsall (grammar); St John's College, Cambridge | History | Naval Section traffic analysis; Liaison officer between Naval Section and Admiralty; Anglo-American Intelligence Liaison 1942–1946; Assistant to director March 1944–June 1946 |

Table 2  Cryptanalysts, translators and researchers (arranged by family name)

| Name | Year (age) | Education | Background | Role |
|---|---|---|---|---|
| Alexander Aitken | 1895 (44) | Otago University, New Zealand; Edinburgh University | Mathematics, French, Latin Soldier WWI (commissioned) Lecturer in Mathematics, Edinburgh University | Foreign Office civilian working in Hut 6 |
| Charles Beckingham | 1914 (25) | Huntingdon Grammar School Queens' College Cambridge (state scholarship) | English; also Arabic cataloguer for British Museum Called up 1942, posted to Naval Intelligence Division (Admiralty) | Cryptanalyst |
| Ralph Bennett | 1911 (28) | Royal Liberty School, Romford (grammar) Magdalene College, Cambridge | Mediaeval history; also German | Hut 3, Intelligence report author |
| (Lord) Asa Briggs | 1921 (18) | Keighley Boys Grammar School Sidney Sussex, Cambridge University of London (external) | History, economics | Hut 6 cryptanalyst |
| John Cairncross | 1913 (26) | The Academy, Hamilton Glasgow University Sorbonne, Paris Trinity College, Cambridge | Modern languages Civil servant: Foreign Office from 1936; Treasury from Dec 1938; Private Secretary to Lord Hankey | Hut 6 (according to Cairncross – but probably Hut 3) Translator |
| Joan Clarke | 1917 (22) | Dulwich High School Newnham College, Cambridge | Mathematics | Hut 8 cryptanalyst |
| Alec Dakin | 1912 (28) | Grammar school (Yorkshire) Oxford University | Ancient languages, Egyptology | Translator, sorter – Hut 4 |
| Harry Golombek | 1911 (28) | Wilson's Grammar School, Camberwell King's College, London (did not complete degree) | Languages, mathematics Member of the British chess team Royal Artillery 1940–1942 | Hut 8 cryptanalyst |
| Philip Hall | 1904 (35) | King's College, Cambridge | Mathematics; also Italian, German Fellow in Mathematics, King's College Cambridge | Italian Section Japanese Section |

| Name | Year (Age) | Education | Background | Role |
|---|---|---|---|---|
| Leonard James Hooper | 1914 (25) | Alleyn's School, Dulwich; Worcester College, Oxford | Modern history | Cryptanalyst Italian Air Section; Cryptanalyst Japanese Air Section |
| William Millward | Not known | Oxford University | German with French Schoolteacher, Dulwich College RAF intelligence officer Aug 1941 | Air intelligence translator and analyst |
| Mavis Batey (née Lever) | 1921 (18) | University College, London; University of Zurich | Languages (German) | Cryptanalyst working under Dillwyn Knox. |
| Derek Taunt | 1917 (22) | Enfield Grammar School (City of London School); Jesus College, Cambridge | Pure mathematics Ordnance Board, Chislehurst | Hut 6 Control Section (comm. Y Service) Hut 6 watch (cryptanalysis) |
| Edward Thomas | 1918 (21) | Grammar schools in Portsmouth and Guildford; King's College, London | Languages Royal Navy intelligence officer Head of direction finding station – Iceland | Hut 4 Feb. 1942 Hut 3N (Hut 3 Naval Section) |
| Joan Thirsk (neé. Watkins) | 1921 (18) | Camden School; Westfield College, London | German scholarship to Switzerland ATS training | ATS – Fusion Room – Hut 6 |
| Charles Wynn-Williams | 1903 (36) | University College of North Wales, Bangor; Trinity College, Cambridge | Physics Lecturer in physics, Imperial College London, from 1935 | Bombe development 'Heath Robinson' machine development Colossus development |
| Irene Young | 1919 (20) | Esdale School; Edinburgh University | Not known | Translator |
| Beryll Lawry | Not known | University | French and German | Translator Hut 7 |
| Gordon Preston | 1925 (14) | Oxford University | Mathematics | Cryptanalyst, worked on Colossus |

Table 3  Lower-grade staff

| Name | | Education | Background | Role |
|---|---|---|---|---|
| Anne Lewis-Smith | Not known | College at Bristol | Not known | WRNS – Bombe operator |
| Mary J. Stewart | Not known | Boarding school | Did not do maths | WRNS – Bombe operator |
| Jeanne Bisgood | Not known | Boarding school | History | WRNS – machine operator |
| Ellen Spark | Not known | Not stated, though did have expectation to study history and economics at University of St Andrews | Economic, history, French | WRNS – Bombe operator |
| Diana Payne | Not known | No information provided | Clerk Ministry of Information | WRNS – Bombe operator |
| Ruth Bourne | Not known | University but did not finish | Not known | WRNS – Bombe operator |
| Alice Wolynskyj | Not known | Grammar school | Not known | WRNS – Bombe operator |
| Gwendoline Page | Not known | Grammar school | Not known | WRNS – Bombe operator |
| Barbara Moor | Not known | Grammar school | Not known | WRNS – Bombe operator |
| Mavis Faunch | Not known | Not known | Lettering artist for printing firm | Created labels for maps and diagrams for Hut 3 |
| Imogene Ryan | Not known | University of London | Read languages | WRNS at BP from 1943 |
| Vivienne Alford | Not known | Not known | Linguist and photographer | Kept indexes in the Naval Section |
| Rosemary Morton | Not known | Not known | Spoke German | WRNS – translated captured German documents |
| Pat Harrowing | Not known | Not known | Had lived in Hungry and had learned German. | WRNS – collated material for 'Naval Headlines' (intelligence synopsises created weekly for Winston Churchill) |

*Table 4* Other staff

| Mimi Gallilee | Not known | Not known | School girl; her mother was a Bletchley Park employee | Girl messenger |
|---|---|---|---|---|

## Note on Appendix 1 sources

The source material for the biographical data in the above tables comes from a variety of sources. The table for senior staff and managerial staff is drawn from a publication created by the Bletchley Park Trust, *The Bletchley Park War: Some Outstanding Individuals* (2006) by Brian Oakley.

The material from the second table is from a wider range of sources. The primary source of data is drawn from the short biographies written by James Thirsk in Thirsk, *Bletchley Park: An Inmate's Story* (Bromley, 2008), pp. 113–187. There are seven exceptions to this. First, the biographical information for Lord Asa Briggs was drawn from his wartime memoir: Asa Briggs, *Secret Days: Code-breaking in Bletchley Park* (London, 2011). The material relating to John Cairncross was drawn from his autobiography: John Cairncross, *Enigma Spy: An Autobiography – The Story of the Man Who Changed the Course of World War Two* (London, 1997). The biographical data for Alec Dakin, William Millward and Joan Murray was drawn from their respective chapters of reminisces in F. H. Hinsley and Alan Stripp (eds.), *Codebreakers: The Inside Story of Bletchley Park* (Oxford, 1993, 1994). The biographical information on Beryl Lawry and Gordon Preston was taken from the transcripts from oral history interviews between Lawry and Preston and volunteers of the Bletchley Park Trust. The two transcripts in question are from Dave Whitchurch (ed.), *Other People's Stories*, vol. 2 (2001). The volumes of these transcriptions are held by the Bletchley Park Trust Archive at Bletchley Park. Finally, Irene McPearson also contributed an interview to the Bletchley Park Trust, in Box 1 of Taped Miscellaneous Interviews. In addition to appearing within James Thirsk's list of biographies, Joan Thirsk was interviewed as part of this project, as was James Thirsk. James Thirsk's war memoir, *Bletchley Park: An Inmate's Story* (Bromley, 2008), also contributed to the biographical details above.

The third table containing the biographical details of lower-grade staff members also has a wide variety of sources. The biographical details of Imogene Ryan, Vivienne Alford and Pat Harrowing are drawn from reminiscences found in the Collection of Private Papers of M. W. Ackroyd, Imperial War Museum Archive, 91/4/1, no. 3; no. 6; no. 9. The details of Mary J. Stewart come from autobiographical articles in Hugh Skillen (ed.), *The Enigma Symposium: 1994* (London, 1994) (no page number). The details of Ellen Spark come from autobiographical articles in Hugh Skillen (ed.) *The Enigma Symposium: 1997* (London, 1997), pp. 88–93. The details of Diana Payne and further information by Vivienne Alford were taken from their respective autobiographical articles in F. H. Hinsley and Alan Stripp (eds), *Codebreakers: The Inside Story of Bletchley*

182  *Appendices*

*Park* (Oxford, 1993, 1994), pp. 132–138, 68–70. Ruth Bourne, Alice Wolynskyj, Gwendoline Page and Barbara Moor were interviewed as part of this project. The details of Mavis Faunch were drawn from the transcript of an interview she conducted with a volunteer from the Bletchley Park Trust. The transcript is in Dave Whitchurch (ed), *Other People's Stories*, vol. 1 (2000), pp. 39–40, held at the Bletchley Park Trust Archive.

Mimi Gallilee's details were drawn from the transcript of an interview she conducted with a volunteer from the Bletchley Park Trust. The transcript is in Dave Whitchurch (ed), *Other People's Stories*, vol. 2 (2001), pp. 55–57, held at the Bletchley Park Trust Archive. Biographical details for Anne Lewis-Smith were drawn from Anne Lewis-Smith, *Off Duty! Bletchley Part Outstation – Gayhurst Manor WW2* (Newport, 2006), p. 1. Jeanne Bisgood's biography appears in 'In Conversation...Jeanne Bisgood', in Peter Hickling (ed.), *No Better Place: A Celebration of Parkstone Golf Club 1909–2009* (Parkstone, 2009), pp. 66–69.

## Appendix 2  List and Location of Veterans' Wartime Recollections

| Veteran | Source |
| --- | --- |
| Vivienne Alford | Collection of Private Papers of M. W. Ackroyd, 91/4/1, no. 6, Imperial War Museum Archive |
|  | 'Naval Section VI', in F. H. Hinsley and Alan Stripp (eds), *Codebreakers: The Inside Story of Bletchley Park* (Oxford, 1993, 1994) |
| Joan Allen | Dave Whitchurch (ed.), *Other People's Stories*, vol. 3, Bletchley Park Trust Archive, 2001 |
|  | Interview, 22 July 2001, M-489–011, Side-B, Bletchley Park Trust Archive |
| Anonymous | Dave Whitchurch (ed.), *Other Peoples Stories*, vol. 3, Bletchley Park Trust Archive, 2001 |
| Bob Baker | Dave Whitchurch (ed.), *Other People's Stories*, vol. 3, Bletchley Park Trust Archive, 2001 |
| Louise Barrie | Gwendoline Page (ed.), *We Kept the Secret: Now it Can be Told – Some Memories of Pembroke V Wrens* (Wymondham, 2002) |
| Mavis Batey | *Dilly: The Man Who Broke Enigmas* (London, 2009) |
| Jeanne Bisgood | 'In Conversation...Jeanne Bisgood', in Peter Hickling (ed.), *No Better Place: A Celebration of Parkstone Golf Club 1909–2009* (Parkstone, 2009). |
| Gwen Blane | 'Outside the Gates', in Cook (ed.), *Bletchley Voices: Recollections of Local People* (Stroud, 1998) |
| Ruth Bourne | Interview with Christopher Smith |
| Asa Briggs | *Secret Days: Code-Breaking in Bletchley Park* (London, 2011) |
| John Cairncross | *The Enigma Spy: An Autobiography The Story of the Man Who Changed the Course of World War Two* (London, 1997) |
| Peter Calvocoressi | 'Interview with Peter Calvocoressi', *The Historian*, 55(2) (Winter, 1993), pp. 235–252 |
|  | *Top Secret Ultra: the Full Story of Ultra and its Impact on World War II* (London, 1981) |
| Marjory Campbell | Dave Whitchurch (ed.), *Other People's Stories*, vol. 4, Bletchley Park Trust Archive, 2002 |
| Mavis Cannon | Dave Whitchurch (ed.), *Other People's Stories*, vol. 4, Bletchley Park Trust Archive, 2002 |
| Margaret Chester | Dave Whitchurch (ed.), *Other People's Stories*, vol. 6, Bletchley Park Trust Archive, 2002 |
| Anne Chetwin-Stapleton | Dave Whitchurch (ed.), *Other People's Stories*, vol. 3, Bletchley Park Trust Archive, 2001 |
| Phylis Coles | Dave Whitchurch (ed.), *Other Peoples Stories*, vol. 5, Bletchley Park Trust Archive, 2002 |
| Joan Collins | Dave Whitchurch (ed.), *Other People's Stories*, vol. 2, Bletchley Park Trust Archive, 2001 |
| Collette Cooke | Dave Whitchurch (ed.), *Other People's Stories*, vol. 3, Bletchley Park Trust Archive, 2001 |

*Continued*

| Veteran | Source |
|---|---|
| John Croft | Dave Whitchurch (ed.), *Other People's Stories*, vol. 2, Bletchley Park Trust Archive, 2001 |
| Alec Dakin | 'Reminiscences of GCHQ and GCB 1942–45', *Intelligence and National Security*, 13(4) (Winter, 1998), pp. 133–143 |
| | 'The Z Watch in Hut 4, Part 1', in F. H. Hinsley and Alan Stripp (eds), *Codebreakers: The Inside Story of Bletchley Park* (Oxford, 1993, 1994) |
| Jenny Davies | 'A W.R.N.S. Life Codebreaking At Stanmore', *BBC WW2 People's Stories: An Archive of World War Two Memories – Written by the Public, Gathered by the BBC*, Article ID: A5496302, http://www.bbc.co.uk/history/ww2peopleswar/stories/02/a5496302.shtml (accessed 1 December 2009) |
| June Douglas | Dave Whitchurch (ed.), *Other People's Stories*, vol. 1, Bletchley Park Trust Archive, 2000 |
| Joy Ettridge | 'Hut 6, Bletchley Park', *BBC WW2 People's Stories: An Archive of World War Two Memories – Written by the Public, Gathered by the BBC*, Article ID: a4163942, http://www.bbc.co.uk/ww2peopleswar/stories/42/a4163942.shtml (accessed 27 October 2009) |
| Walter Eytan | 'The Z Watch in Hut 4, Part 1', in F. H. Hinsley and Alan Stripp (eds), *Codebreakers: The Inside Story of Bletchley Park* (Oxford, 1993, 1994) |
| Bess Farrow | Dave Whitchurch (ed.), *Other People's Stories*, vol. 3, Bletchley Park Trust Archive, 2001 |
| Mavis Faunch | Dave Whitchurch (ed.), *Other People's Stories*, vol. 1, Bletchley Park Trust Archive, 2000 |
| Muriel Garrilley | Dave Whitchurch (ed.), *Other People's Stories*, vol. 2, Bletchley Park Trust Archive, 2001 |
| Ron Gibbons | Dave Whitchurch (ed.), *Other People's Stories*, vol. 3, Bletchley Park Trust Archive, 2001 |
| Raymond John Goodman | Dave Whitchurch (ed.), *Other People's Stories*, vol. 4, Bletchley Park Trust Archive, 2002 |
| Ann Graham | Dave Whitchurch (ed.), *Other People's Stories*, vol. 2, Bletchley Park Trust Archive, 2001 |
| Pat Harrowing | Collection of Private Papers of M. W. Ackroyd, 91/4/1, Imperial War Museum Archive |
| Gil Hayward | 'Operation Tunny', in F. H. Hinsley and Alan Stripp (eds), *Codebreakers: The Inside Story of Bletchley Park* (Oxford, 1993, 1994) |
| Betty Hill | Dave Whitchurch (ed.), *Other People's Stories*, vol. 5, Bletchley Park Trust Archive, 2002 |
| F. H. Hinsley | 'Bletchley Park, the Admiralty, and the Naval Enigma', in F. H. Hinsley and Alan Stripp (eds), *Codebreakers: The Inside Story of Bletchley Park* (Oxford, 1993, 1994) |
| James Hogarth | *An Extraordinary Mixture: Bletchley Park in Wartime* (Glasgow, 2008) |
| Shelia Lancaster | Dave Whitchurch (ed.), *Other People's Stories*, vol. 1, Bletchley Park Trust Archive, 2000 |
| Beryll Lawry | Dave Whitchurch (ed.), *Other People's Stories*, vol. 2, Bletchley Park Trust Archive, 2001 |

| Pauline Lee | Dave Whitchurch (ed.), *Other People's Stories*, vol. 4, Bletchley Park Trust Archive, 2002 |
| Anne Lewis-Smith | *Off Duty! Bletchley Park Outstation – Gayhurst Manor WW2* (Newport, 2006) |
| Doreen G. Luke | *My Road to Bletchley Park: Britain's Best Kept Secret WWII Communications Centre* (Bodmin, 1998) |
| Joan Marr | Dave Whitchurch (ed.), *Other People's Stories*, vol. 1, Bletchley Park Trust Archive, 2000 |
| Margaret Martin | Dave Whitchurch (ed.), *Other People's Stories*, vol. 4, Bletchley Park Trust Archive, 2002 |
| Irene McPearson | Box 1 of Taped Miscellaneous Interviews, Bletchley Park Trust Archive |
| William Millward | 'Life In and Out of Hut 3', in Hinsley and Stripp (eds), *Codebreakers: the Inside Story of Bletchley Park* (Oxford, 1993, 1994) |
| Barbara Moor | Interview with Christopher Smith |
| Ewan Montagu | *Beyond Top Secret U* (London, 1977) |
| Rosemary Morton | Collection of Private Papers of M. W. Ackroyd, 91/4/1, no. 9, Imperial War Museum Archive |
| Wendy Munro | Dave Whitchurch (ed.), *Other People's Stories*, vol. 4, Bletchley Park Trust Archive, 2002 |
| Joan Murray | 'Hut 8 and Naval Enigma, Part 1', in F. H. Hinsley and Alan Stripp (eds), *Codebreakers: The Inside Story of Bletchley Park* (Oxford, 1993, 1994) |
| Diana Neil | Dave Whitchurch (ed.), *Other People's Stories*, vol. 4, Bletchley Park Trust Archive, 2002 |
| Rolf Noskwith | 'Hut 8 From the Inside', in Michael Smith and Ralph Erskine (eds), *Action this Day* (London, 2001) |
| | 'Hut 8 and Naval Enigma: Part 2', in F. H. Hinsley and Alan Stripp (eds), *Codebreakers: The Inside Story of Bletchley Park* (Oxford, 1993, 1994) |
| Pamela O'Donahue | Dave Whitchurch (ed.), *Other People's Stories*, vol. 4, Bletchley Park Trust Archive, 2002 |
| Gwendoline Page | Interview with Christopher Smith |
| Mary Zelie Pain | Interview on 17 January 1989, 10595/3, IWM Sound Archive |
| Diana Payne | 'The Bombes' in F. H. Hinsley and Alan Stripp (eds), *Codebreakers: The Inside Story of Bletchley Park* (Oxford, 1993, 1994) |
| Elizabeth Laura Persival | Dave Whitchurch (ed.), *Other People's Stories*, vol. 2, Bletchley Park Trust Archive, 2001 |
| Gordon Preston | Dave Whitchurch (ed.), *Other People's Stories*, vol. 2, Bletchley Park Trust Archive, 2001 |
| Annie Sylvia Pulley | 'W.R.N.S. Breaking the Enigma Code. Bletchley Park', *BBC WW2 People's Stories: An Archive of World War Two Memories – Written by the Public, Gathered by the BBC*, Article ID: A5804499, http://www.bbc.co.uk/history/ww2peopleswar/stories/99/a5804499.shtml (accessed 1 December 2009) |
| Mary Rae | Dave Whitchurch (ed.), *Other People's Stories*, vol. 2, Bletchley Park Trust Archive, 2001 |
| Beryl Robertson | Dave Whitchurch (ed.), *Other People's Stories*, vol. 1, Bletchley Park Trust Archive, 2000 |

*Continued*

| Veteran | Source |
|---|---|
| Imogene Ryan | Collection of Private Papers of M. W. Ackroyd, 91/4/1, no. 3; no. 6; no. 9, Imperial War Museum Archive |
| Kay Sheargold | 'Mrs Kay Sheargold to Mr Eric Rhodes, 21/10/82', Eric Rhodes Papers, Misc. 2827, Misc. Box 190, Original Research Correspondence, IWM. |
| Don Smith | Dave Whitchurch (ed.), *Other People's Stories*, vol. 3, Bletchley Park Trust Archive, 2001 |
| Ellen Spark | Hugh Skillen (ed.), *The Enigma Symposium: 1997* (London, 1997) |
| Mary J. Stewart | Hugh Skillen (ed.), *The Enigma Symposium: 1994* (London, 1994) |
| H. L. Swatton | Dave Whitchurch (ed.), *Other People's Stories*, vol. 3, Bletchley Park Trust Archive, 2001 |
| Derek Taunt | 'Hut 6: 1941–1945', in F. H. Hinsley and Alan Stripp (eds), *Codebreakers: The Inside Story of Bletchley Park* (Oxford, 1993, 1994) |
| | 'Hut 6 From the Inside', in Michael Smith and Ralph Erskine (eds), *Action This Day* (London, 2001) |
| James Thirsk | Interview with Christopher Smith |
| Joan Thirsk | Interview with Christopher Smith |
| Edward Thomas | 'A Naval Officer in Hut 3', in F. H. Hinsley and Alan Stripp (eds), *Codebreakers: The Inside Story of Bletchley Park* (Oxford, 1993, 1994) |
| Jean Valentine | Dave Whitchurch, *Other People's Stories*, vol. 3, Bletchley Park Trust Archive, 2001 |
| Bob Vicary | Dave Whitchurch (ed.), *Other People's Stories*, vol. 3, Bletchley Park Trust Archive, 2002 |
| Gwen Watkins | *Cracking the Luftwaffe Codes: The Secrets of Bletchley Park* (London, 2006) |
| Bob Watson | 'How the Bletchley Park Buildings Took Shape', in F. H. Hinsley and Alan Stripp (eds), *Codebreakers: The Inside Story of Bletchley Park* (Oxford, 1993, 1994) |
| Gordon Welchman | *The Hut Six Story* (London, 1986) |
| Patrick Wilkinson | 'Italian Naval Decrypts', in F. H. Hinsley and Alan Stripp (eds), *Codebreakers: The Inside Story of Bletchley Park* (Oxford, 1993, 1994) |
| F. W. Winterbotham | *The Ultra Secret: The Inside Story of Operation Ultra, Bletchley Park and Enigma* (London, 2000) |
| Ann Witherbird | Dave Whitchurch (ed.) *Other People's Stories*, vol. 2, Bletchley Park Trust Archive, 2001 |
| Arthur Witherbird | Dave Whitchurch (ed.) *Other People's Stories*, vol. 2, Bletchley Park Trust Archive, 2001 |
| Alice Wolyinskj | Interview with Christopher Smith |
| | Unpublished personal recollections provided to Christopher Smith |
| Irene Young | *Enigma Variations: Love, War and Bletchley Park* (Edinburgh, 1990) |

# Appendix 3  G.C. & C.S. Organisation – March 1944

Monica Zambia, *A History of British SIGINT, 1914–1945, Vol. III Appendices*, p. 811, HW 43/3, TNA

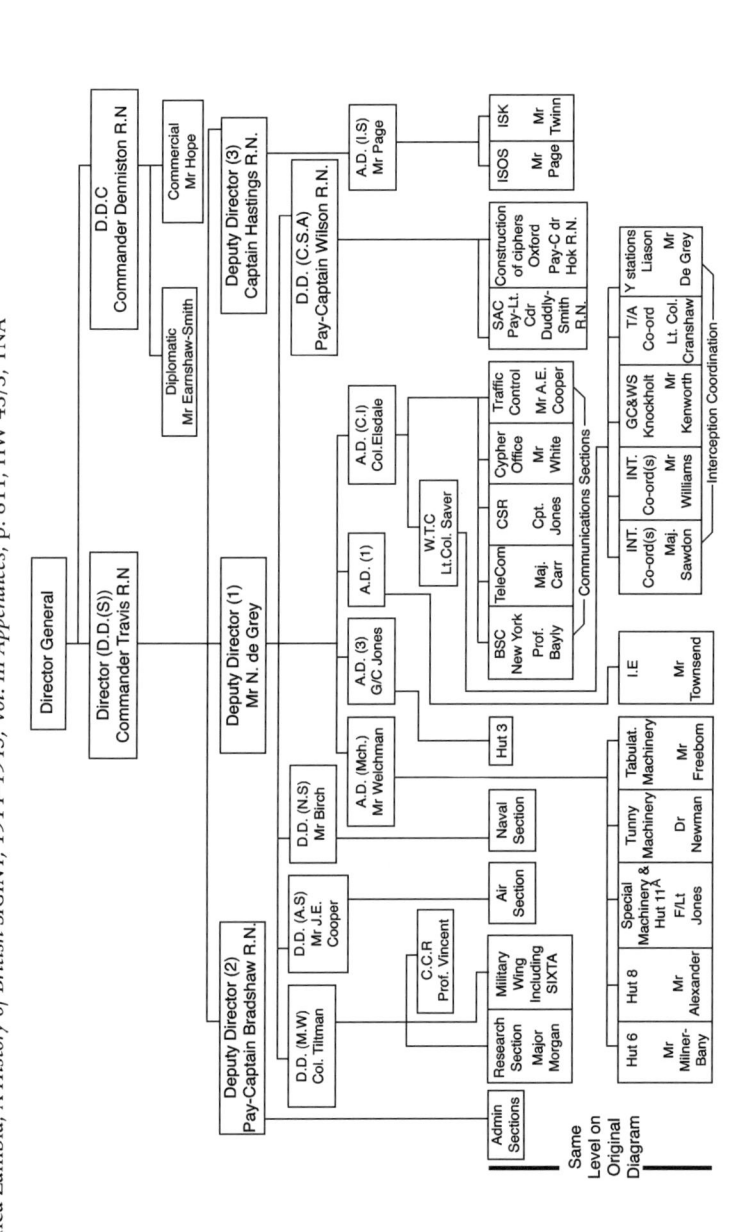

- Director General
  - Director (D.D.(S)) Commander Travis R.N
    - D.D.C Commander Denniston R.N
      - Diplomatic Mr Earnshaw-Smith
      - Commercial Mr Hope
    - Deputy Director (3) Captain Hastings R.N.
      - D.D. (C.S.A) Pay-Captain Wilson R.N.
        - SAC Pay-Lt. Cdr Duddly-Smith R.N.
        - Construction of ciphers Oxford Pay-C dr Hok R.N.
      - A.D. (I.S) Mr Page
        - ISOS Mr Page
        - ISK Mr Twinn
    - Deputy Director (1) Mr N. de Grey
      - A.D. (C.I) Col. Eisdale
        - TeleCom Maj. Carr
        - CSR Cpt. Jones
        - Cypher Office Mr White
        - Traffic Control Mr A.E. Cooper
      - A.D. (1)
        - W.T.C Lt.Col. Saver
      - A.D. (3) G/C Jones
        - BSC New York Prof. Bayly
      - A.D. (Mch.) Mr Weichman
        - Hut 3
      - I.E Mr Townsend
      - INT. Co-ord(s) Maj. Sawdon
      - INT. Co-ord(s) Mr Williams
      - GC&WS Knockholt Mr Kenworth
      - T/A Co-ord Lt. Col. Cranshaw
      - Y stations Liason Mr De Grey
    - Deputy Director (2) Pay-Captain Bradshaw R.N.
      - D.D. (M.W) Col. Tiltman
        - Research Section Major Morgan
      - D.D. (A.S) Mr J.E. Cooper
        - Military Wing Including SIXTA
        - Air Section
      - D.D. (N.S) Mr Birch
        - Naval Section
      - C.C.R Prof. Vincent
      - Admin Sections
      - Hut 6 Mr Milner-Bany
      - Hut 8 Mr Alexander
      - Special Machinery & Hut 11ᴬ F/Lt Jones
      - Tunny Machinery Dr Newman
      - Tabulat. Machinery Mr Freebom

Same Level on Original Diagram

Interception Coordination — Communications Sections

# Glossary

| | |
|---|---|
| Abwehr | The German intelligence service |
| AD(1) | Assistant Director 1: Head of Intelligence Exchange Sections |
| AD(3) | Assistant Director 3: Head of Hut 3 |
| AD(A) | Assistant Director (Administration): Assistant Director in charge of administration from 1942 to 1944 (Pay-Captain, Commander Bradshaw) |
| AD(CI) | Assistant Director (Communications and Interception): Chief of GC&CS's various Communications Sections |
| AD(IS) | Acting Director (Intelligence School): Head of GC&CS's Intelligence Sections (the two sections which dealt with Abwehr traffic) |
| AD(Mech) | Acting Director (Mechanisation): Head of GC&CS's Machine Sections (Gordon Welchman) |
| AD(O) | Assistant Director (Overseas): GC&CS's liaison with overseas allied units, and the Secret Intelligence Service, 1941–1944 (Captain Hastings) |
| AD(S) | Assistant Director (Service): Second in command at Bletchley Park, 1942 to 1944 (Nigel de Grey) |
| ATS | Auxiliary Territorial Service: the women's branch of the British Army |
| Banburismus | A cryptanalytic process |
| Bletchley Park | The primary war station of GC&CS during the Second World War |
| Bombe | A machine designed to aid in the process of cryptanalysis |
| CCR | Cryptographic Coordination Records |
| Cipher | A system whereby individual letters, numbers or punctuation are rearranged or replaced with other letters, numbers or punctuation |
| Colossus | A machine designed to aid in the process of cryptanalysis |
| Commercial Section | The section which studied foreign commercial wireless traffic |
| CSR | Central Signals Registry |
| DD(1) | Deputy Director 1: Deputy head of GC&CS (Nigel de Grey) |
| DD(2) | Deputy Director 2: Deputy Director in charge of administration from 1944 on (Pay-Captain, Commander Bradshaw) |
| DD(3) | Deputy Director 3: GC&CS's liaison with overseas allied units, and the Secret Intelligence Service, from 1944 (Captain Hastings) |
| DD(AS) | Deputy Director (Air Service): Head of GC&CS's Air Sections (Josh Cooper) |

## Glossary

| | |
|---|---|
| DD(C) | Deputy Director (Civil): Head of GC&CS's Civil and Diplomatic Sections (Alistair Denniston from 1942) |
| DD(MW) | Deputy Director (Military Wing): Head of GC&CS's Military Sections (Brig. John Tiltman) |
| DD(S) | Deputy Director (Service): Head of GC&CS's Service Sections (Edward Travis from 1942) |
| Diplomatic Section | The section which studied foreign diplomatic wireless traffic |
| Director | Head of GC&CS (Alistair Denniston 1919–1942; Edward Travis 1942–1952) |
| Director General | Chief of the Secret Intelligence Service and GC&CS (Hugh Sinclair 1923–1939, followed by Stewart Menzies 1939–1952) |
| Enigma | An electrical cipher machine |
| Fish | The British codename for Axis teleprinter traffic transmitted by wireless |
| GC&CS | Government Code and Cypher School |
| GCHQ | Government Communications Headquarters |
| *Heer* | The German Army |
| Hollerith/Tabulating Section | The section tasked with collating, storing and sorting information derived from intercepted wireless traffic |
| Hollerith machine | Machines used to create, store and sort data onto punch cards |
| Hut 3 | The section tasked with translating and distributing German army and air force Enigma traffic |
| Hut 4 | The section tasked with translating and distributing German naval Enigma traffic |
| Hut 6 | The section tasked with the cryptanalysis of German army and air force Enigma traffic |
| Hut 8 | The section tasked with the cryptanalysis of German naval Enigma traffic |
| Hut 11 | The Bombe section |
| ISK | Intelligence/Illicit Service Knox: The Section that examined *Abwehr* Enigma traffic |
| ISOS | Intelligence/Illicit Service Oliver Strachey: The Section that examined *Abwehr* non-Enigma traffic |
| JMC | Joint Management Committee |
| *Luftwaffe* | The German air force |
| Military | Relating to land-based services – e.g., the *Wehrmacht* |
| PID | Political Intelligence Department: A branch of the Foreign Office which information on the conditions of various European nations |
| RAF | Royal Air Force |
| RN | Royal Navy |

# Glossary

| | |
|---|---|
| Robinson machine | A machine designed to aid in the process of cryptanalysis |
| SAC | Security of Allied Cyphers: the section tasked with advising the various arms of the British state on wireless traffic security |
| Service | Armed forces: Land, Sea, Air |
| SIS | Secret Intelligence Service |
| SOE | Secret Operations Executive: A clandestine British agency which operated behind enemy lines in occupied Europe |
| Traffic | Wireless messages |
| Traffic analysis | The analysis of the origin, call-sign and frequency of wireless traffic |
| Tunny | The British codename for the Lorenz teleprinter cipher machines |
| Type-x | A British electronic cipher machine |
| W/T | wireless telegraphy |
| WAAF | Women's Auxiliary Air Force: the women's branch of the RAF |
| *Wehrmacht* | The German armed forces |
| Wren | A member of the Women's Royal Naval Service |
| WRNS | Women's Royal Naval Service: the women's branch of the Royal Navy |
| WTC | Wireless Traffic Coordinator |
| Y Service | The organisation tasked with operating wireless interceptions |
| Y station | Wireless interception/direction finding station |

# Notes

## Introduction

1. These include, but are not limited to, *The Bletchley Circle*, ITV, World Productions (September 2012–January 2014); Robert Harris, *Enigma* (London, 1995); *Hut 33*, BBC Radio 4, BBC (July 2007–present); *Station X*, Channel 4, Darlow Smithson Productions (1999); *Enigma*, dir. Michael Apted, BVI, 2001; *The Imitation Game*, dir. Morten Tyldum, StudioCanal, 2009.
2. Bletchley Park is also sometimes referred to as 'Station X' because the site also housed the Secret Intelligence Service's (MI6) radio station ten.
3. F. H. Hinsley, 'The Influence of ULTRA in the Second World War', paper given to the Cambridge University Security Group Seminar, 19 October 1993, http://www.cix.co.uk/~klockstone/hinsley.htm (accessed 11 May 2015).
4. Kerry Johnson and John Gallehawk (eds), *Figuring it Out at Bletchley Park 1939–1945* (2007), pp. 3–14.
5. Named after the room in the Admiralty in which it had been first housed.
6. Frank Birch, *The Official History of Sigint*, John Jackson (ed.), vol. 1 (part 1) (Milton Keynes, 2004), p. 3. This work in an internal history of the agency conducted shortly after the Second World War and remained classified along with the agency's other records until long after the conclusion of the war. An edited version of this three-volume document has since been published in two parts, and this published edition is utilised frequently throughout this book.
7. Birch, *Official History of Sigint*, vol. 1.1, p. 7.
8. Simon Singh, *The Code Book: The Secret History of Codes and Code-Breaking* (London, 2000), p. 110.
9. Michael Smith, 'GC&CS and the First Cold War', in Michael Smith and Ralph Erskine (eds), *Action This Day* (London, 2001), p. 16.
10. Smith, 'GC&CS and the First Cold War', p. 16.
11. A. G. Denniston, 'The Government Code and Cypher School Between the Wars', in Christopher Andrew (ed.), *Codebreaking and Signals Intelligence* (London, 1986), p. 49.
12. Smith, 'GC&CS and the First Cold War', p. 17.
13. Smith, 'GC&CS and the First Cold War', p. 17.
14. Wesley Wark, *The Ultimate Enemy: British Intelligence and Nazi Germany 1933–1939* (Oxford, 1986), p. 18.
15. Birch, *Official History of Sigint*, vol. 1.1, p. 20.
16. For a detailed description of the technical details of the Enigma system see Singh, *The Code Book*, pp. 124–142.
17. Birch, *Official History of Sigint*, vol. 1.1, p. 20.
18. Michael Smith, *Station X: The Codebreakers of Bletchley Park* (London, 2004), p. 25.

19. Jerzy Różycki died in 1942 when the ship he was travelling on, the S. S. Lamoricière, sank in the Mediterranean Sea. Ronald Lewin, *Ultra Goes to War: The Secret Story* (London, 1978, 1980), p. 49 (note).
20. The influence of Ultra on the Second World War is a subject which has attracted considerable scholarly interest and it is beyond the scope of this book to provide more than a cursory discussion of this topic. For a rich scholarly bibliography outlining the vast literature dedicated to Ultra's impact on the various campaigns and battles of the Second World War, see Donald J. Sexton, *Signals Intelligence in World War II: A Research Guide* (Westport, CT, 1996).
21. Ralph Bennett, *Behind the Battle: Intelligence in the War With Germany, 1939–1945*, revised edition (London, 1994, 1999), pp. 60–61.
22. Peter Calvocoressi, *Top Secret Ultra: The Full Story of Ultra and its Impact on World War II* (London, 1980, 1981), p. 92.
23. F. H. Hinsley, E. E. Thomas, C. F. G. Ransom and R. C. Knight, *British Intelligence in the Second World War: Its Influence on Strategy and Operations*, vol. 2 (London, 1981), p. 169.
24. For details regarding Ultra and the war in the Atlantic, see David Kahn, *Seizing the Enigma: The Race to Break the German U-Boat Codes, 1939–1943* (London, 1996).
25. Bennett, *Behind the Battle*, p. xxiii.
26. F. W. Winterbotham, *The Ultra Secret: The Inside Story of Operation Ultra, Bletchley Park and Enigma* (London, 1974, 2000).
27. Władysław Kozaczuk, *Bitwa o tajemnice: Służby wywiadowcze Polski i Rzeszy Niemieckiej 1922–1939 (Secret Battle: The Intelligence Services of Poland and the German Reich, 1922–1939)* (Warsaw, 1967); Hugh Trevor-Roper, *The Philby Affair: Espionage, Treason and Secret Services* (London, 1968); Gustave Bertrand, *Enigma ou la plus grande énigme de la guerre 1939–1945 (Enigma or the Greatest Enigma of the War of 1939–1945)* (Paris, 1973).
28. David Hooper, *Official Secret: The Use and Abuse of the Act* (London, 1988), p. 250.
29. Memoirs include: Ewen Montagu, *Beyond Top Secret U* (London, 1977); Calvocoressi, *Top Secret Ultra*; Gordon Welchman, *The Hut Six Story: Breaking the Enigma Codes* (New York, NY, 1982). Histories include: Lewin, *Ultra Goes to War*; Hinsley et al., *British Intelligence in the Second World War*, 5 vols; Ralph Bennett, *Ultra in the West: The Normandy Campaign, 1944–45* (New York, NY, 1979); Nigel West, *GCHQ: The Secret Wireless War 1900–86* (London, 1986). Also important is Andrew Hodges' still definitive biography of the cryptanalyst Alan Turing: Andrew Hodges, *Alan Turing: The Enigma* (New York, NY, 1983). Important recent histories include Richard Aldrich, *GCHQ: The Uncensored Story of Britain's Most Secret Intelligence Agency* (London, 2010).
30. Irene Young, *Enigma Variations: Love, War and Bletchley Park* (Edinburgh, 1990); D. G. Luke, *My Road to Bletchley Park: Britain's Best Kept Secret WWII Communications Centre* (Bodmin, 1998). Important collections of autobiographical narratives, including contributions by low-grade staff, include: F. H. Hinsley and A. Stripp (eds), *The Codebreakers* (Oxford, 1993, 1994); Smith and Erskine (eds), *Action This Day* (London, 2001); Gwendoline Page (ed.), *We Kept the Secret: Now it can be Told – Some Memories of Pembroke V Wrens* (Wymondham, 2002).

31. Young, *Enigma Variations*, p. 11.
32. For examples see: Smith, *Station X*; Stephen Budiansky, *Battle of Wits: The Complete Story of Codebreaking in World War II* (London, 2000); Sinclair McKay, *The Secret Life of Bletchley Park: The History of the Wartime Codebreaking Centre and the Men and Women Who Worked There* (London, 2010).
33. Tessa Dunlop, *The Bletchley Girls: War, Secrecy, Love and Loss: The Women of Bletchley Park Tell Their Story* (London, 2015); Michael Smith, *The Debs of Bletchley Park: And Other Stories* (London, 2015).
34. There are some exceptions to this, including: Annie Burman, 'Gendering Decrytion – Decrypting Gender: The Gender Discourse of Labour at Bletchley Park 1939–1945' (Unpublished Masters' Dissertation: University of Uppsala, 2013); Christopher Smith, 'Operating Secret Machines: Military Women and the Intelligence Production Line, 1939–1945', in *Women's History Magazine*, issue 76 (Autumn 2014), pp. 30–36.
35. Johnson and Gallehawk, *Figuring it Out*, p. 9. This work is a compendium of statistical evidence compiled from the agency's weekly statistical returns.
36. Richard Titmuss, *Problems of Social Policy* (London, 1950), p. 508.
37. Arthur Marwick, *Britain in the Century of Total War* (London, 1968, 1970), p. 289.
38. Marwick, *Century of Total War*, pp. 289–290.
39. Arthur Marwick, *War and Social Change in the Twentieth Century: A Comparative Study of Britain, France, Germany, Russia and the United States* (Basingstoke, 1974), p. 16.
40. Marwick, *Century of Total War*, pp. 292–293.
41. Arthur Marwick, 'Introduction', in Arthur Marwick (ed.), *Total War and Social Change* (London, 1988), p. 17.
42. Penny Summerfield, 'The "levelling of class"', in Harold L. Smith (ed.), *War and Social Change: British Society in the Second World War* (Manchester, 1986), pp. 201–202.
43. Penny Summerfield, *Reconstructing Women's Wartime Lives: Discourse and Subjectivity in Oral Histories of the Second World War* (Manchester, 1996), pp. 98–99; p. 7.
44. Jon Agar, *The Government Machine: A Revolutionary History of the Computer* (London, 2003).
45. R. A. Ratcliff, *Delusions of Intelligence: Enigma, Ultra, and the End of Secure Ciphers* (Cambridge, 2006), pp. 102–105.
46. Ratcliff, *Delusions of Intelligence*, pp. 186–189.
47. Christopher Grey, *Decoding Organization: Bletchley Park, Codebreaking and Organization Studies* (Cambridge, 2012), p. 2.

# 1 The Organisation of the Government Code and Cypher School

1. J. D. Scott and R. Hughes, *The Administration of War Production* (London, 1955), p. 84.
2. William Hornby, *Factories and Plant* (London, 1958), p. 204.
3. Scott and Hughes, *Administration of War Production*, p. 83.
4. Hornby, *Factories and Plant*, pp. 285–286.

5. Hornby, *Factories and Plant*, pp. 285–296.
6. Michael Smith, 'The Government Code and Cypher School in the First Cold War', in Smith and Erskine, *Action This Day*, pp. 16–17.
7. Denniston was a gifted linguist. Having joined the Royal Navy in 1914, his knowledge of German made him an ideal candidate for intelligence work and he was posted to the Admiralty's cryptanalysis section – Room 40. At that time Room 40 was headed by Sir Alfred Ewing; upon Ewing's retirement in 1916, Dennison replaced him as the section's de facto head. When the decision to form GC&CS was taken, Denniston was named its commanding officer. See Robin Denniston, *Thirty Secret Years: A. G. Dennison's Work in Signals Intelligence 1914–1944* (Trowbridge, 2007), p. 12.
8. A. G. Denniston, 'The Government Code and Cypher School', in Andrew, *Codebreaking and Signals Intelligence*, p. 51.
9. Denniston, 'The Government Code and Cypher School', in Andrew, *Codebreaking and Signals Intelligence*, p. 52.
10. Denniston, 'The Government Code and Cypher School', in Andrew, *Codebreaking and Signals Intelligence*, pp. 52–53.
11. While seemingly a small number, this was in fact around the total wartime strength of Britain's cryptanalytic bureaus during the First World War. See Brian Oakley, *The Bletchley Park War: Some of the Outstanding Individuals* (Bletchley, 2006), p. 2.
12. Smith, *Station X*, p. 20. Smith suggests that Sinclair purchased the site with £7,500 of his own money, but recent research has cast doubt on this assumption. See Keith Jeffrey, *MI6: The History of the Secret Intelligence Service 1909–1949* (London, 2010), p. 319.
13. This proved to be an accurate supposition and over the entire course of the war only two bombs fell on Bletchley Park. These bombs, which struck the estate in November 1940, were not deliberately targeted at Bletchley, and instead appear to have been dropped by a German bomber with some remaining ordnance following a bombing run over Coventry. See S. McKay, *The Secret Life of Bletchley Park*, p. 119.
14. Linda Monckton, 'Bletchley Park, Buckinghamshire: The Architecture of the Government Code and Cypher School', *Post-Medieval Archaeology*, 40(2) (2006), p. 294. See also Grey, *Decoding Organization*, p. 33. My thanks to Christopher Grey who correctly pointed out to me, following a reading of an earlier draft of this book, that GC&CS did not select Bletchley Park because of its capacity for building work. As Professor Grey notes, GC&CS's officials had yet to conceive of the rapid expansion that would soon follow.
15. Bob Watson, 'How the Bletchley Park Buildings Took Shape', in Hinsley and Stripp, *Codebreakers*, p. 307.
16. Christopher Grey and Andrew Sturdy, 'The 1942 Reorganization of the Government Code & Cypher School', *Cryptologia*, 32(4) (2008), p. 318.
17. Grey, *Decoding Organization*, p. 33.
18. Nigel de Grey had been a key figure in British cryptanalysis since the First World War, and his most notable achievement in that war had been his work on the Zimmerman Telegram.
19. Cited in Grey and Sturdy, 'The 1942 Reorganization of GC & CS', *Cryptologia*, pp. 312–313.
20. Grey and Sturdy, 'The 1942 Reorganization of GC & CS', *Cryptologia*, p. 314.

21. F. Birch, *The Official History of British Sigint*, vol. 1:1, p. 90.
22. Birch, *The Official History of British Sigint*, vol.1:1, p. 12.
23. Birch, *The Official History of British Sigint*, vol. 1:1, p. 9.
24. Birch, *The Official History of British Sigint*, vol. 1:1, p. 12.
25. Birch, *The Official History of British Sigint*, vol. 1:1, p. 84.
26. Birch, *The Official History of British Sigint*, vol. 1:1, p. 33.
27. Birch, *The Official History of British Sigint*, vol. 1:1, p. 103.
28. Birch, *The Official History of British Sigint*, vol. 1:1, p. 44.
29. Bletchley Park Trust, *History of Bletchley Park Huts & Blocks 1939–1945*, Bletchley Park Trust Report No. 18, revised by A. Bonsall (Bletchley, 2009), p. 3.
30. Birch, *The Official History of British Sigint*, vol. 1:1, p. 87.
31. Birch, *The Official History of British Sigint*, vol. 1:1, p. 87.
32. Bletchley Park Trust, *History of Bletchley Park Huts & Blocks 1939–1945*, p. 3.
33. Birch, *The Official History of British Sigint*, vol. 1:1, p. 87.
34. Birch, *The Official History of British Sigint*, vol. 1:1, p. 87.
35. Birch, *The Official History of British Sigint*, vol. 1:1, pp. 41–42, 89. See also R. Ratcliff, *Delusions of Intelligence*, pp. 113–114.
36. Ratcliff, *Delusions of Intelligence*, pp. 113–114.
37. Bletchley Park Trust, *History of Bletchley Park Huts & Blocks 1939–1945*, pp. 3–4. Eric Jones would during the 1950s go on to become the head of GCHQ.
38. Birch, *The Official History of British Sigint*, vol. 1:1, p. 44.
39. Bletchley Park Trust, *History of Bletchley Park Huts & Blocks 1939–1945*, p. 4.
40. Smith, *Station X*, p. 26.
41. J. Agar, *The Government Machine*, p. 205.
42. Smith, *Station X*, p. 60.
43. Ratcliff, *Delusions of Intelligence*, p. 101; Grey, *Decoding Organization*, pp. 35, 45.
44. Colossus was a semi-programmable electronic computer – and the first of its kind. It arguably heralded the dawn of the computer technology. See Paul Gannon, *Colossus: Bletchley Park's Greatest Secret* (London, 2007), pp. xix–xx.
45. Smith, *Station X*, pp. 152–156.
46. Birch, *The Official History of British Sigint*, vol. 1:1, p. 85.
47. Birch, *The Official History of British Sigint*, vol. 1:1, p. 87.
48. The service sections reported to Denniston's deputy, Edward Travis.
49. Birch, *The Official History of British Sigint*, vol. 1:1, p. 33.
50. Birch, *The Official History of British Sigint*, vol. 2, p. 186.
51. Birch, *The Official History of British Sigint*, vol. 1:1, p. 30.
52. Ratcliff, *Delusions of Intelligence*, pp. 94–95.
53. Ratcliff, *Delusions of Intelligence*, pp. 94–95.
54. Bletchley Park Trust, *History of Bletchley Park Huts & Blocks 1939–1945*, p. 7.
55. Monckton, 'Bletchley Park, Buckinghamshire', p. 294.
56. Bletchley Park Trust, *History of Bletchley Park Huts & Blocks 1939–1945*, p. 5.
57. Monckton, 'Bletchley Park, Buckinghamshire', p. 295.
58. Watson, 'How the Bletchley Park Buildings Took Shape', p. 307.
59. Watson, 'How the Bletchley Park Buildings Took Shape', p. 307.
60. Bletchley Park Trust, *History of Bletchley Park Huts & Blocks 1939–1945*, p. 8.
61. Ted Enever, *Britain's Best Kept Secret: Ultra's Base at Bletchley Park* (Stroud, 1994), p. 42.
62. Bletchley Park Trust, *History of Bletchley Park Huts & Blocks 1939–1945*, p. 8.

63. Enever, *Britain's Best Kept Secret*, p. 43.
64. William Millward, 'Life In and Out of Hut 3', in Hinsley and Stripp, *Codebreakers*, p.19.
65. Bletchley Park Trust, *History of Bletchley Park Huts & Blocks 1939–1945*, pp. 8–9, 20.
66. Bletchley Park Trust, *History of Bletchley Park Huts & Blocks 1939–1945*, p. 10.
67. For details of these sections see Bletchley Park Trust, *History of Bletchley Park Huts & Blocks 1939–1945*, p. 10.
68. The sunray clinic provided staff members with the opportunity to undergo a course of treatment under an ultra-violet lamp. The agency was advised by its medical officer that a course of treatment would benefit the health of staff members. Commander Bradshaw, 'Sunray Clinic', AD(A) No. 254, 28 January 1944, HW 64/27, TNA.
69. Bletchley Park Trust, *History of Bletchley Park Huts & Blocks 1939–1945*, pp. 10–11.
70. Bletchley Park Trust, *History of Bletchley Park Huts & Blocks 1939–1945*, p. 11.
71. Birch, *The Official History of British Sigint 1914–1945*, vol. 1:1, p. 41.
72. G. Welchman, *The Hut Six Story: Breaking the Enigma Codes*.
73. Bletchley Park Trust, *History of Bletchley Park Huts & Blocks 1939–1945*, p. 11.
74. Bletchley Park Trust, *History of Bletchley Park Huts & Blocks 1939–1945*, pp. 18–19.
75. Monckton, 'Bletchley Park, Buckinghamshire', p. 296.
76. Monckton, 'Bletchley Park, Buckinghamshire', p. 296.
77. Oakley, *The Bletchley Park War*, p. 14.
78. Bletchley Park Trust, *History of Bletchley Park Huts & Blocks 1939–1945*, pp. 12, 19.
79. Bletchley Park Trust, *History of Bletchley Park Huts & Blocks 1939–1945*, pp. 9, 12–13.
80. David Kahn, *Seizing the Enigma: The Race to Break the German U-Boat Codes, 1939–1943*, p. 189.
81. Enever, *Britain's Best Kept Secret*, pp. 49–53.
82. Budiansky, *Battle of Wits: The Complete Story of Codebreaking in World War II*, p. 304.
83. Bletchley Park Trust, *History of Bletchley Park Huts & Blocks 1939–1945*, p. 16.
84. Enever, *Britain's Best Kept Secret*, pp. 70–71.
85. Enever, *Britain's Best Kept Secret*, p. 61.
86. Grey, *Decoding Organization*, pp. 234–240.
87. John Jackson (ed.), *The Secret War of Hut 3: The First Full Story of How Intelligence from Enigma Signals Decoded at Bletchley Park Was Used During World War Two* (Milton Keynes, 2002), p. 2. This work is an edited reproduction of the internal history of Hut 3 produced by GCHQ immediately after the Second World War (and abridged and amended to include additional quotations from Hut 3 veterans).
88. Quoted in Smith, *Station X*, p. 144.
89. Denniston quoted in Christopher Grey and Andrew Sturdy, 'The 1942 Reorganization of the Government Code and Cypher School', Paper presented to the Oxford Intelligence Group, Nuffield College Oxford, 7 June 2007, p. 20.

90. Denniston quoted in Grey and Sturdy, 'The 1942 Reorganization of the Government Code and Cypher School', Paper presented to the Oxford Intelligence Group, p. 20.
91. Welchman, *The Hut Six Story*, p. 126.
92. Welchman, *The Hut Six Story*, p. 127.
93. A. Hodges, *Alan Turing: The Enigma*, p. 204.
94. Birch, *The Official History of British Sigint*, vol. 2, p. 192.
95. Quoted in Budiansky, *Battle of Wits*, p. 158.
96. Budiansky, *Battle of Wits*, p. 203.
97. D. R. Nicoll, 'Jones, Sir Eric Malcolm (1907–1986)', rev. *Oxford Dictionary of National Biography*, http://www.oxforddnb.com/view/article/40175 (accessed 22 May 2012).
98. Grey and Sturdy quoting HW 14/145, TNA, p. 29; Christopher Grey and Andrew Sturdy, 'A Chaos that Worked: Organizing Bletchley Park', in *Public Policy and Administration*, 25(1) (2010), p. 57.
99. Phyllis Coles, 'Interview with Phyllis Coles', in Dave Whitchurch (ed.), *Other People's Stories*, vol. 5, Bletchley Park Trust Archive, 2002, p. 39.
100. Anon., 'Avis Ambler and other Bombe Operators', in Whitchurch, *Other People's Stories*, vol. 3, p. 19.
101. Budiansky, *Battle of Wits*, pp. 202–206.
102. Budiansky, *Battle of Wits*, pp. 202–206.
103. Quoted in Smith, *Station X*, p. 126.
104. Quoted in Grey, *Decoding Organization*, pp. 161–162.
105. Grey, *Decoding Organization*, pp. 161–163.
106. Johnson and Gallehawk, *Figuring it Out*, p. 7.
107. A. M. Turing, W. G. Welchman, C. H. O'D. Alexander, P. S. Milner-Barry to Winston Churchill, 21 October 1941, reproduced in Smith and Erskine, *Action This Day*, pp. ix–xii.
108. Birch, *The Official History of British Sigint*, vol. 1:1, p. 107.
109. Birch, *The Official History of British Sigint*, vol. 1:1, p. 107.
110. Birch, *The Official History of British Sigint*, vol. 1:1, p. 108.
111. Birch, *The Official History of British Sigint*, vol. 1:1, p. 108.
112. Birch, *The Official History of British Sigint*, vol. 2, pp. 54–56.
113. Birch, *The Official History of British Sigint*, vol. 2, pp. 54–56.
114. Johnson and Gallehawk, *Figuring it Out*, p. 10.
115. As a side note, it is worth noting that, in retrospect, it appears that despite the serious problems that remained under his leadership, the manner in which Dennison was side-lined, and eventually replaced, was clearly unfair and failed to adequately recognise the magnitude of the problems he overcame and the tight-rope of competing interests that his leadership walked.
116. Birch, *The Official History of British Sigint*, vol. 1:1, p. 90.

## 2  Recruitment at GC&CS: 1919–1945

1. Paul Kennedy, *The Realities Behind Diplomacy* (London, 1981), p. 230.
2. Birch, *The Official History of British Sigint*, vol. 1:1, pp. 3–7.
3. Smith, 'The Government Code and Cypher School in the First Cold War', in Smith and Erskine, *Action This Day*, pp. 16–17.

## 198  Notes

4. Calvocoressi, *Top Secret Ultra* p. 11.
5. Calvocoressi, *Top Secret Ultra*, p. 11.
6. Calvocoressi, *Top Secret Ultra*, p. 11.
7. Calvocoressi, *Top Secret Ultra*, p. 12.
8. Peter Calvocoressi in Roger Adelson, 'Interview with Peter Calvocoressi', *The Historian*, 55(2) (Winter, 1993), pp. 236–237.
9. Calvocoressi in Adelson, 'Interview with Peter Calvocoressi', p. 238.
10. Calvocoressi in Adelson, 'Interview with Peter Calvocoressi', p. 241; Calvocoressi, *Top Secret Ultra*, p. 7.
11. Calvocoressi in Adelson, 'Interview with Peter Calvocoressi', p. 242.
12. Calvocoressi, *Top Secret Ultra*, p. 8.
13. Calvocoressi, *Top Secret Ultra*, pp. 8–9.
14. Welchman, *The Hut Six Story*, p. 159.
15. Brian Oakley, *The Bletchley Park War: Some Outstanding Individuals – Edition 2.2* (Bletchley, 2006).
16. For a complete list of individuals and sources see Appendix 1.
17. Oakley, *The Bletchley Park War*, pp. iv–vii.
18. Oakley, *The Bletchley Park War*, pp. 6–7; see also D. R. Nicoll, 'Travis, Sir Edward Wilfrid Harry (1888–1956)', rev. *Oxford Dictionary of National Biography*, http://www.oxforddnb.com/view/article/61098 (accessed 28 March 2011).
19. It is necessary to note that many of the 'Chiefs' listed above started as 'Indians' and as the agency expanded went on to command sections or subsections of their own. For further details see Appendix 1.
20. David Edgerton, *Warfare State: Britain, 1920–1970* (Cambridge, 2006), pp. 132–133.
21. Ross McKibbin, *Classes and Cultures: England 1918–1951* (Oxford, 1998), p. 249.
22. David Kahn, *The Codebreakers: Abridged Version* (London, 1974), pp.129–139.
23. Christopher Andrew, *Secret Service: The Making of the British Intelligence Community* (Sevenoaks, 1985, 1986), p.150.
24. Christopher Andrew, 'Bletchley Park in Pre-War Perspective', in Erskine and Smith, *Action This Day*, p. 5.
25. Denniston, 'The Government Code and Cypher School Between the Wars', in Andrew, *Codebreaking and Signals Intelligence*, p. 52.
26. R. Lewin, *Ultra Goes To War: The Secret Story*, p. 52.
27. E. I. Carlyle, 'Ewing, Sir (James) Alfred (1855–1935)', rev. *Oxford Dictionary of National Biography* (Oxford, 2004), http://www.oxforddnb.com/view/article/33058 (accessed 16 December 2014).
28. Denniston, 'The Government Code and Cypher School Between the Wars', in Andrew, *Codebreaking and Signals Intelligence*, p. 52.
29. Tony Comer, Public Lecture, 'The Development of GCHQ and What it Cost', Department of International Politics, Aberystwyth University, 7 March 2011.
30. Richard Langhorne, 'Hinsley, Sir (Francis) Harry (1918–1998)', rev. *Oxford Dictionary of National Biography*, http://www.oxforddnb.com/view/article/69418 (accessed 28 March 2011).
31. F. H. Hinsley, 'Bletchley Park, the Admiralty, and the Naval Enigma', in Hinsley and Stripp, *Codebreakers*, p. 77.
32. T. E. B. Howarth, *Cambridge Between Two Wars* (London, 1978), p. 240.

## Notes 199

33. Patrick Wilkinson, 'Italian Naval Decrypts', in Hinsley and Stripp, *Codebreakers*, p. 61.
34. Denniston to Mr Crawford, 9 February 1937, HW 72/9, TNA.
35. Denniston to Mr Peters, 26 April 1932, HW 72/9, TNA.
36. Denniston to C. E. D. Peters, 4 October 1935, HW 72/9, TNA.
37. Gil Hayward, 'Operation Tunny', in Hinsley and Stripp, *Codebreakers*, p. 182.
38. Walter Eytan, 'The Z Watch in Hut 4, Part 1', in Hinsley and Stripp, *Codebreakers*, p. 57.
39. Birch, *Official History of Sigint*, vol. 2, p. 82.
40. I. Young, *Enigma Variations: Love, War and Bletchley Park*, p. 77.
41. Ratcliff, *Delusions of Intelligence*, p. 79.
42. Birch, *Official History of Sigint*, vol. 2, p. 82.
43. Frank Birch to Unknown Recipient, 'Details of Requirements', 19 August 1942, HW 63/73, TNA.
44. Kahn, *Codebreakers*, pp. 81–82.
45. Christopher Andrew, 'F. H. Hinsley and the Cambridge Moles: Two Patterns of Intelligence Recruitment', in Richard Langhorne (ed.), *Diplomacy and Intelligence During the Second World War* (Cambridge, 1985), p. 35.
46. Joan Murray, 'Hut 8 and the Naval Enigma, Part 1', in Hinsley and Stripp, *Codebreakers*, p. 113.
47. Mavis Batey, 'Knox, (Alfred) Dillwyn (1884–1943)', rev. *Oxford Dictionary of National Biography* (Oxford, 2004); online edn, Oct 2006, http://www.oxforddnb.com/view/article/37641 (accessed 28 March 2011).
48. Mavis Batey, *Dilly: The Man Who Broke Enigmas* (London, 2009), p. 20.
49. Andrew, 'F. H. Hinsley and the Cambridge Moles', in Langhorne, *Diplomacy and Intelligence*, p. 35.
50. Andrew, 'F. H. Hinsley and the Cambridge Moles', in Langhorne, *Diplomacy and Intelligence*, p. 35.
51. Andrew, 'F. H. Hinsley and the Cambridge Moles', in Langhorne, *Diplomacy and Intelligence*, p. 35.
52. Andrew, 'F. H. Hinsley and the Cambridge Moles', in Langhorne, *Diplomacy and Intelligence*, p. 35.
53. E. R. P. Vincent quoted in Andrew, *Secret Service*, p. 634.
54. Quoted in Smith, *Station X*, p. 68.
55. Hodges, *Turing*, p. 49.
56. Andrew, *Secret Service*, pp. 633–634.
57. Alistair Denniston to C. E. D. Peters, 26 April, 1932, HW 72/9, TNA.
58. Denniston to E. A. Greswell, 25 February 1938, HW 72/9, TNA.
59. AD(A) [Cmdr. Bradshaw] to H. S. Hoff, 23 May 1943, Ref. No 563, HW 64/73, TNA.
60. Monica Zambia, *A History of British SIGINT, 1914–1945, Vol. III Appendices*, HW 43/3, TNA, p. 811.
61. Grey, *Decoding Organization*, p. 159.
62. 'Numbers of Graduates of the University of Cambridge', *Davis Archive of Female Mathematicians*, http://www-history.mcs.st-and.ac.uk/history/Davis/Indexes/yCambridge.html (accessed 26 February 2015).
63. Denniston to T. J. Wilson, 16 May 1938, HW 72/9, TNA.
64. 'Establishment of GC&CS', HW 72/1, TNA.

## 200 Notes

65. Original emphasis on 'must'.
66. Anon. to Miss. Moore, 'No. 4930', 12 November 1942, HW 64/73, TNA.
67. A. W. Kearn, 'Appointments in the Foreign Office', Ministry of Labour, 29 April 1943, HW 64/73, TNA.
68. Nesca Robb, 'Wastage of Women', 21 June 1940, in Fiona Glass and Philip Marsden-Smedley (eds), *Articles of War: The Spectator Book of World War II* (London, 1989), p. 111.
69. AD(A) [Cmdr. Bradshaw] to H. S. Hoff, 6 August 1943, Ref. No. 1897, HW 64/73, TNA.
70. Memo to Commander Bradshaw, 19 August 1942, HW 64/73, TNA.
71. Commander Bradshaw, 'Civil Service War Bonus', 5 December 1944, HW 64/61, TNA.
72. Birch, *Official History of Sigint*, vol. 2, p. 80.
73. O. V. Guy to Alistair Denniston, 25 June 1932, HW 72/9, TNA; Denniston to O. V. Guy, 27 June 1932, HW 72/9, TNA.
74. Denniston to Crawford, 9 February 1937, HW 72/9, TNA.
75. Grey, *Decoding Organization*, p. 137.
76. Calvocoressi, *Top Secret Ultra*, p. 16.
77. Andrew, 'F. H. Hinsley and the Cambridge Moles', in Langhorne, *Diplomacy and Intelligence*, p. 32.
78. Thomas J. Price, 'Spy Stories, Espionage and the Public in the Twentieth Century', *Journal of Popular Culture*, 30(3) (Winter, 1996), p. 85; Phillip Knightley, *The Second Oldest Profession* (New York, 1988), p. 122.
79. Cited in Andrew, 'F. H. Hinsley and the Cambridge Moles', in Langhorne, *Diplomacy and Intelligence*, p. 31.
80. The Cambridge Five were Soviet moles, all of whom were educated at Cambridge University, who infiltrated the British intelligence community during the 1930s and 1940s. They were Kim Philby, Donald Maclean, Guy Burgess, Anthony Blunt and John Cairncross.
81. F. W. Winterbotham, 'Recording of interview of Group Captain F. W. Winterbotham RAF, On Sydney Radio in February 1977: Recorded by Dr. Kenneth McConnell', in Whitchurch, *Other People's Stories*, vol. 1, p. 11.
82. Andrew, 'F. H. Hinsley and the Cambridge Moles', in Langhorne, *Diplomacy and Intelligence*, p. 31.
83. Andrew, 'F. H. Hinsley and the Cambridge Moles', in Langhorne, *Diplomacy and Intelligence*, p. 31.
84. Andrew, 'F. H. Hinsley and the Cambridge Moles', in Langhorne, *Diplomacy and Intelligence*, p. 30.
85. Peter Mandler, *The English National Character: The History of an Idea from Edmund Burke to Tony Blair* (London, 2006), p. 167.
86. Calvocoressi, *Top Secret Ultra*, pp. 62–79, 60.
87. Penny Summerfield, '"She Wants a Gun not a Dishcloth!": Gender, Service and Citizenship in Britain in the Second World War', in Gerard J. DeGroot and Corinna Peniston-Bird (eds), *A Soldier and a Woman: Sexual Integration in the Military* (Harlow, 2000), p. 119.
88. H. L. Swatton, 'Mr H. L. Swatton', in Whitchurch, *Other People's Stories*, vol. 3, p. 34.
89. Don Smith, 'Don Smith – Bombe Engineer', in Whitchurch, *Other People's Stories*, vol. 3, p. 11.

90. Smith, 'Don Smith – Bombe Engineer', in Whitchurch, *Other People's Stories*, vol. 3, p. 11.
91. Thirsk, *Bletchley Park*, pp. 17–18.
92. Swatton, 'Mr H. L. Swatton', in Whitchurch, *Other People's Stories*, vol. 3, p. 34.
93. Millward, 'Life In and Out of Hut 3', in Hinsley and Stripp, *Codebreakers*, p. 18.
94. Cairncross, *Enigma Spy*, p. 96.
95. Johnson and Gallehawk, *Figuring it Out*, pp. 124–127.
96. Johnson and Gallehawk, *Figuring it Out*, p. 16.
97. Watson, 'How the Bletchley Park Buildings Took Shape', in Hinsley and Stripp, *Codebreakers*, pp. 306–310.
98. Muriel Garrilly, 'Interview with Muriel (Mimi) Garrilly – Girl Messenger', in Whitchurch, *Other People's Stories*, vol. 2, p. 55. In the document, the name of the interviewee is given as Muriel Garrilly – however, in all likelihood, this is an error, and the interviewee is Mimi Gallilee. My thanks go to Professor Christopher Grey for making note of this point.
99. Johnson and Gallehawk, *Figuring it Out*, p. 16.
100. For examples see Phyllis Coles, in Whitchurch, *Other People's Stories*, vol. 5, p. 39; Betty Hill, in Whitchurch, *Other People's Stories*, vol. 5, p. 44.
101. Quoted in Grey, *Decoding Organization*, p. 137.
102. Grey, *Decoding Organization*, p. 137.
103. James Hogarth, *An Extraordinary Mixture: Bletchley Park in Wartime* (Glasgow, 2008), p. 26.
104. Grey, *Decoding Organization*, p. 137.
105. A. M. Turing, W. G. Welchman, C. H, O'. D. Alexander and P. S. Milner-Barry to Prime Minister, 21 October 1941, in Smith and Erskine, *Action This Day*, pp. ix–xii.
106. Birch, *The Official History of Sigint*, p. 97.
107. Johnson and Gallehawk, *Figuring it Out*, pp. 42–50.
108. Jean Valentine, in Whitchurch, *Other People's Stories*, vol. 3, p. 13.
109. For example, Anne Chetwin-Stapleton notes that other than a secretarial course she 'hadn't much experience of anything'. Anne Chetwin-Stapleton, in Whitchurch, *Other People's Stories*, vol. 3, p. 29.
110. Collette Cooke, 'Bombe Operator', in Whitchurch, *Other People's Stories*, vol. 3, p. 25.
111. Payne, 'The Bombes', in Hinsley and Stripp, *Codebreakers*, p. 133.
112. Nigel de Grey, 'Memorandum', 17 August 1949, HW 50/50, TNA, p. 7.
113. Cooke, 'Bombe Operator', in Whitchurch, *Other People's Stories*, vol. 3, p. 25.
114. A two-volume work produced by the agency after the conclusion of the war on Tunny. See Gannon, *Colossus*; Smith, *Station X*, pp. 148–164.
115. Quoted in Gannon, *Colossus*, p. 344.
116. Gerard DeGroot, 'Lipstick on Her Nipples, Cordite in her Hair: Sex and Romance among British Service Women during the Second World War', in DeGroot and Peniston-Bird, *A Soldier and a Woman: Sexual Integration in the Military*, p. 109; a point echoed by Penny Summerfield: see Summerfield, *Reconstructing Women's Wartime Lives*, pp. 174–177.
117. Johnson and Gallehawk, *Figuring it Out*, p. 47.
118. Bess Farrow (nee Cooper) interview with Peter Wecombe, 22 January 2001, in Whitchurch, *Other People's Stories*, vol. 3, p. 27.

119. Barbara Moor, interview with Christopher Smith, 30 April 2010.
120. Gwendoline Page, interview with Christopher Smith, 29 April 2010.
121. Ruth Bourne, interview with Christopher Smith, 8 May 2010.
122. Alice Wolynskyj, unpublished personal recollections provided to Christopher Smith, 27 April 2010.
123. Joan Thirsk, interview with Christopher Smith, 28 April 2010.
124. Birch, *Official History of Sigint*, vol. 1:1, p. 58.
125. Derived from raw data compiled by Kerry Johnson and John Gallehawk. Johnson and Gallehawk, *Figuring it Out*, pp. 3–14. The data in Figure 2.1 and Table 2.1 do not include staff at outstations or from SIS. Johnson and Gallehawk, *Figuring it Out*, pp. 3–10.
126. Johnson and Gallehawk, *Figuring it Out*, p. 3.
127. John Jackson, 'Introduction', in Birch, *Official History of Sigint*, vol. 1:1, p. vi.
128. Johnson and Gallehawk, *Figuring it Out*, p. 170.
129. Denniston, 'The GC&CS between the Wars', in Andrew, *Codebreaking and Signals Intelligence*, p. 50.
130. Denniston, 'The GC&CS between the Wars', in Andrew, *Codebreaking and Signals Intelligence*, p. 53.
131. Denniston, 'The GC&CS between the Wars', in Andrew, *Codebreaking and Signals Intelligence*, p. 52.
132. Johnson and Gallehawk, *Figuring it Out*, p. 7.
133. Compiled from raw data compiled by Johnson and Gallehawk. Johnson and Gallehawk, *Figuring it Out*, pp. 7–10.
134. Birch, *Official History of Sigint*, vol. 1:2, p. 46.
135. Birch, *Official History of Sigint*, vol. 1:2, p. 109.
136. Johnson and Gallehawk, *Figuring it Out*, pp. 48–50.
137. Johnson and Gallehawk, *Figuring it Out*, p. 10.
138. [No author given, but certainly written by Denniston as confirmed in later documents within the file] to C.S.S. [Chief of the Secret Service], 'Pay of Cryptographers.', 13 August 1941, HW 64/67, TNA.
139. [No author given, but certainly written by Denniston as confirmed in later documents within the file] to C.S.S. [Chief of the Secret Service], 'Pay of Cryptographers', 13 August 1941, HW 64/67, TNA.
140. Birch, *Official History of Sigint*, vol. 2, p. 83.
141. [No author no date] Rates of Pay (For Provisional Assessment) for Mobile Women Serving with the Women's Forces, HW 64/67, TNA.
142. Sixteen universities in England, Scotland and Wales produced 279 graduates in mathematics in 1938. While Cambridge provided 95, the single largest contribution to this figure, this still only comprised a little over a third of the total mathematicians produced in the UK that year. 'The Davis Archive: Mathematical Women in the British Isles, 1878–1940', http://www-history.mcs.st-and.ac.uk/Davis/Indexes/statindex.html (accessed 26 February 2015).
143. Cambridge University was by no means unique in that respect. London produced 63 mathematics graduates in 1938, 39 of whom were male. Oxford University produced a further 33 mathematics graduates, 30 of whom were male. 'The Davis Archive: Mathematical Women in the British Isles, 1878–1940', http://www-history.mcs.st-and.ac.uk/Davis/Indexes/statindex.html (accessed 26 February 2015).

144. Summerfield, *Reconstructing Women's Wartime Lives*, p. 165.
145. Summerfield, *Reconstructing Women's Wartime Lives*, p. 165.
146. Mrs Mary Zelie Pain, interview on 17 January 1989, 10595/3, IWM Sound Archive.
147. Batey, *Dilly*.
148. Summerfield, 'Women, War and Social Change', p. 97.
149. Summerfield, 'Women, War and Social Change', p. 98.
150. Summerfield, 'Women, War and Social Change', p. 98.
151. Summerfield, *Reconstructing Women's Wartime Lives*, p. 7. See also H. M. D. Parker, *Manpower: A Study of War-time Policy and Administration* (London, 1957), p. 376.

## 3 On-Duty Life at the Government Code and Cypher School

1. F. W. Winterbotham, *The Ultra Secret: The Inside Story of Operation Ultra, Bletchley Park and Enigma*, p. ix.
2. *The Imitation Game*, dir. Morten Tyldum, StudioCanal, 2009.
3. The work of those involved in the Y Service, unlike their colleagues at Bletchley Park, has received comparatively little attention. Memoirs such as Aileen Clayton, *The Enemy is Listening: the Story of the Y Service* (London, 1988) and Joan Nicholls, *England Needs You: The Story of Beaumanor Y Station World War II* (Cheam, 2000) have been written, revealing some light on the topic. However, the topic has, for the most part, yet to be explored by historians.
4. Birch, *History of British Sigint*, vol. 2, p. 81.
5. Johnson and Gallehawk, *Figuring it Out*, p. 51.
6. Louis Kruh and C. A. Deavours, 'The Type-x Cryptograph', *Cryptologia*, 7(3) (April 1983), p. 145.
7. Joy Ettridge, 'Hut 6, Bletchley Park', Article ID: A4163942, http://www.bbc.co.uk/history/ww2peopleswar/stories/42/a4163942.shtml (accessed 4 January 2015).
8. TA was also known as W/T intelligence, W/T operational intelligence, and wireless network research; see Hinsley, et al., *British Intelligence in the Second World War*, vol. 1, p. 21 and footnote.
9. James Thirsk, *Bletchley Park: An Inmate's Story* (London, 2008), p. 49.
10. Asa Briggs, *Secret Days: Code-breaking in Bletchley Park* (London, 2011), pp. 93–94; Thirsk, *Bletchley Park*, pp. 47–50.
11. Gannon, *Colossus*, p. 326.
12. Such as Bombe machines.
13. Noskwith, 'Hut 8 From the Inside', in Smith and Erskine, *Action this Day*, p. 199.
14. Derek Taunt, 'Hut 6: 1941–1945', in Hinsley and Stripp, *Codebreakers*, p. 101.
15. Noskwith, 'Hut 8 From the Inside', in Smith and Erskine, *Action This Day*, p. 199.
16. For a description of such methods, see Frank Carter, 'Rodding'; 'Buttoning Up', in Batey, *Dilly*, pp. 174–205.

17. Unnamed cryptanalyst quoted in Marion Hill, *Bletchley Park People: Churchill's Geese That Never Cackled* (Stroud, 2004), p. 42.
18. Briggs, *Secret Days*, p. 82.
19. Grey, *Decoding Organization*, p. 189.
20. Grey, *Decoding Organization*, pp. 189–191.
21. Quoted in Grey, *Decoding Organization*, p. 189.
22. Welchman, *The Hut Six Story*, pp. 125–127.
23. Noskwith, 'Hut 8 From the Inside', in Smith and Erskine, *Action This Day*, p. 207.
24. McKay, *The Secret Life of Bletchley Park*, p. 166.
25. Briggs, *Secret Days*, p. 8.
26. Briggs, *Secret Days*, p. 107.
27. McKay, *The Secret Life of Bletchley Park*, p. 166.
28. Noskwith, 'Hut 8 From the Inside', in Smith and Erskine, *Action This Day*, p. 207.
29. Quoted in Budiansky, *Battle of Wits*, p. 282.
30. Quoted in Smith, *Station X*, p. 117.
31. McKay, *The Secret Life of Bletchley Park*, p. 88.
32. Welchman, *Hut Six Story*, p. 57.
33. Payne, 'The Bombes', in Hinsley and Stripp, *Codebreakers*, p. 134.
34. Payne, 'The Bombes', in Hinsley and Stripp, *Codebreakers*, p. 134.
35. Cooke, 'Bombe Operator', in Whitchurch, *Other People's Stories*, vol. 3, p. 25.
36. Payne, 'The Bombes', in Hinsley and Stripp, *Codebreakers*, p. 134.
37. Cooke, 'Bombe Operator', in Whitchurch, *Other People's Stories*, vol. 3, p. 25. Diana Payne on the other hand noted the shift system as being 'watches of four weeks' duration: 8 a.m. to 4 p.m. the first seven days, 4 p.m. to midnight the second week, midnight to 8 a.m. the third, and then three days of eight hours off alternatively, ending with a much-needed four days' leave.' Payne, 'The Bombes', in Hinsley and Stripp, *Codebreakers*, pp. 135–136.
38. Payne, 'The Bombes', in Hinsley and Stripp, *Codebreakers*, pp. 135–136.
39. Alice Wolnskyj, Personal Correspondence with Christopher Smith, 27 April 2010.
40. Farrow, 'Bombe Operator', in Whitchurch, *Other People's Stories*, vol. 3, p. 28.
41. Paul Fussell, *Wartime: Understanding and Behaviour in the Second World War* (Oxford, 1990), pp. 79–95.
42. Payne, 'The Bombes', in Hinsley and Stripp, *Codebreakers*, p. 134.
43. The codename applied to high-level German encrypted teleprinter traffic.
44. Nigel de Grey, 'Memorandum', 17 August 1949, HW 50/50, TNA, p. 7.
45. Summerfield, *Reconstructing Women's Wartime Lives*, pp. 133–135.
46. Cooke, 'Bombe Operator', in Whitchurch, *Other People's Stories*, vol. 3, p. 25.
47. Jenny Davies, 'A W.R.N.S. Life Codebreaking at Stanmore', BBC, 'WW2 People's War' Article ID: A5496302, http://www.bbc.co.uk/history/ww2peopleswar/stories/02/a5496302.shtml (accessed 1 December 2009).
48. Payne, 'The Bombes', in Hinsley and Stripp, *Codebreakers*, p. 136.
49. The Robinson machine was built to aid the cryptanalysis of 'Tunny'. Tunny was the codename given to *Wehrmacht* high-level teleprinter traffic enciphered by Lorenz SZ-40 and SZ-42 machines. The machine was named after the impossibly intricate and complex machinery dreamt up by the cartoonist William Heath Robinson (1872–1944).

50. For full discussions of the application and technical descriptions of the machines see Gannon, *Colossus*; Smith, *Station X*, pp. 148–164.
51. Gannon, *Colossus*, p. 345.
52. Smith, *Station X*, pp. 158–159.
53. McKay, *The Secret Life of Bletchley Park*, p. 265.
54. Gannon, *Colossus*, p. 343.
55. Summerfield, *Reconstructing Women's Wartime Lives*, p. 7.
56. General Report on Tunny, 279, quoted in Gannon, *Colossus*, pp. 287–288.
57. Dakin, 'The Z Watch in Hut 4', in Hinsley and Stripp, *Codebreakers*, p. 52.
58. Alford, 'Naval Section VI', in Hinsley and Stripp, *Codebreakers*, p. 69.
59. John Cairncross, *The Enigma Spy: An Autobiography – The Story of the Man Who Changed the Course of World War Two* (London, 1997), p. 97.
60. Cairncross, *Enigma Spy*, p. 97.
61. Rosemary Morton, Collection of Private Papers of M. W. Ackroyd, 91/4/1, no. 9, Imperial War Museum Archive.
62. Cairncross, *Enigma Spy*, p. 109.
63. Cairncross, *Enigma Spy*, p. 97.
64. Mrs Vivienne Alford, no. 6, 91/4/1, The papers of Mrs M. W. Ackroyd, Imperial War Museum.
65. Cairncross, *Enigma Spy*, p. 98.
66. Edward Thomas, 'A Naval Officer in Hut 3', in Hinsley and Stripp, *Codebreakers*, p. 45.
67. Thomas, 'A Naval Officer in Hut 3', in Hinsley and Stripp, *Codebreakers*, p. 45.
68. Ron Gibbons, in Whitchurch, *Other People's Stories*, vol. 3, pp. 22–24.
69. Gibbons, in Whitchurch, *Other People's Stories*, vol. 3, p. 24.
70. Martin, in Whitchurch, *Other People's Stories*, vol. 4, p. 46.
71. Coles, in Whitchurch, *Other People's Stories*, vol. 5, p. 39; Gibbons, in Whitchurch, *Other People's Stories*, vol. 3, p. 23.
72. Coles, in Whitchurch, *Other People's Stories*, vol. 5, p. 39.
73. Coles, in Whitchurch, *Other People's Stories*, vol. 5, p. 39.
74. Martin, in Whitchurch, *Other People's Stories*, vol. 4, p. 46.
75. Martin, in Whitchurch, *Other People's Stories*, vol. 4, p. 46.
76. Coles, in Whitchurch, *Other People's Stories*, vol. 5, p. 39.
77. Joan Allen, Interview, 22 July 2001, M-489-011, Side-B, Bletchley Park Trust Archive.
78. Hill, *Bletchley Park People*, pp. 69–70. See also McKay, *The Secret Life of Bletchley Park*, pp. 121–129.
79. Allen, Interview, 22 July 2001, M-489-011, Side-B, Bletchley Park Trust Archive.
80. Allen, Interview, 22 July 2001, M-489-011, Side-B, Bletchley Park Trust Archive.
81. Allen, Interview, 22 July 2001, M-489-011, Side-B, Bletchley Park Trust Archive.
82. Birch, *The Official History of British Sigint*, vol. 2, p. 103.
83. Budiansky, *Battle of Wits*, p. 123.
84. Mrs Mary Z. Pain interview with Conrad Wood, 10595/3, reel 2, 17 January 1989, IWM Sound Archive.
85. Mrs Mary Z. Pain, 10595/3, reel 2, 17 January 1989, IWM Sound Archive.

86. Swatton, in Whitchurch, *Other People's Stories*, vol. 3, p. 34.
87. Mrs Mary Z. Pain, 10595/3, reel 1, 17 January 1989, IWM Sound Archive.
88. Mrs Mary Z. Pain, 10595/3, reel 2, 17 January 1989, IWM Sound Archive. See also Swatton, in Whitchurch, *Other People's Stories 3*, p. 34.
89. Mrs Mary Z. Pain, 10595/3, reel 2, 17 January 1989, IWM Sound Archive.
90. Mrs Mary Z. Pain, 10595/3, reel 2, 17 January 1989, IWM Sound Archive.
91. Mrs Mary Z. Pain, 10595/3, reel 2, 17 January 1989, IWM Sound Archive. Mary Pain also noted that on one notable occasion the hut also suffered a rodent infestation.
92. Unknown author [illegible signature] to AD(A) [Commander Bradshaw] Ventilation in Block 'E', 10 September 1943, HW 64/62, TNA.
93. N. W. [Unknown] to Commander Bradshaw, 23 November 1943, HW 64/62, TNA.
94. Mrs Mary Z. Pain, 10595/3, reel 1, 17 January 1989, IWM Sound Archive. This individual may have been Mr A. White, head of Bletchley Park's Cypher Office, however, given that it appears that Type-x machines were employed in numerous sections of GC&CS, this is not possible to confirm.
95. Mrs Mary Z. Pain, 10595/3, reel 1, 17 January 1989, IWM Sound Archive.
96. Mrs Mary Z. Pain, 10595/3, reel 2, 17 January 1989, IWM Sound Archive.
97. Mrs Mary Z. Pain, 10595/3, reel 2, 17 January 1989, IWM Sound Archive.
98. Summerfield, *Reconstructing Women's Wartime Lives*, pp. 132, 167.
99. N. W. [Unknown] to Commander Bradshaw, 23 November 1943, HW 64/62, TNA.
100. Unknown author [illegible signature] to Commander Bradshaw, E Block, 16 December 1943, HW 64/62, TNA.
101. N. W. [Unknown] to Commander Bradshaw, 23 November 1943, HW 64/62, TNA.
102. Presumably either the actual BBC radio programme which played dance music and was designed for factory workers working long shifts, or a derivative of the same idea. Siân Nicholas, 'The Good Servant: The Origins and Development of BBC Listener Research 1936–1950' (2006), http://www.britishonlinearchives.co.uk/guides/9781851171248.php, (accessed 19 September 2012).
103. Captain Melrose to AD(A) [Commander Bradshaw], 9 November 1943, HW 64/62, TNA.
104. Captain Melrose to AD(A) [Commander Bradshaw], 9 November 1943, HW 64/62, TNA.
105. Grey, *Decoding Intelligence*, p. 192.
106. AD(S) [The document is signed under the title AD(S), however it does not appear to be the signature of Nigel de Grey who held that position] to ADA [Commander Bradshaw, without the usual brackets surrounding the 'A'], 13 October 1943, HW 64/62, TNA.
107. Mr White to Captain Melrose, 11 November 1943, HW 64/62, TNA.
108. Mrs Mary Z. Pain, 10595/3, reel 2, 17 January 1989, IWM Sound Archive.
109. Mrs Mary Z. Pain, 10595/3, reel 2, 17 January 1989, IWM Sound Archive.
110. Mrs Mary Z. Pain, 10595/3, reel 2, 17 January 1989, IWM Sound Archive.
111. Mrs Mary Z. Pain, 10595/3, reel 2, 17 January 1989, IWM Sound Archive.
112. The transcription places girl friend in inverted commas.
113. Bob Baker, in Whitchurch, *Other People's Stories*, vol. 3, p. 37.

114. Margaret Chester, in Whitchurch, *Other People's Stories*, vol. 6, p. 17.
115. Matt Cook, 'Queer Conflicts: Love, Sex and War 1914–1967', in Matt Cook (ed.), *A Gay History of Britain: Love and Sex Between Men Since the Middle Ages* (Oxford, 2007), p. 58.
116. For an example see McKay, *The Secret Life of Bletchley Park*, p. 7. See also Cairncross, *Enigma Spy*, p. 98.
117. See Ratcliff, *Delusions of Intelligence*, pp. 106–126; Mona De Witte, 'The Ultra Secret: Security of the British Codebreaking Operations in World War II' (Unpublished Master's Dissertation: Université Denis Diderot Paris 7, 2009).
118. Denniston, G.N/N, 25 October 1939, HW 64/16, TNA.
119. Denniston, 'Challenge by Sentries', 6 April 1940, HW 64/16, TNA.
120. [Unknown Author], Issue of Passes, 12 June 1940, HW 64/16, TNA.
121. Johnson and Gallehawk, *Figuring it Out*, pp. 15–16.
122. Faunch, in Whitchurch, *Other People's Stories*, vol. 1, p. 39.
123. June Douglas, 'Recording of Interview with Mrs. June Douglas', in Whitchurch, *Other People's Stories*, vol. 1, p. 47.
124. Denniston, Official Secrets Acts – 1911 and 1920, 30 June 1941, HW 64/16, TNA.
125. Travis, Security in GC&CS, 11 May 1942, HW 64/16, TNA.
126. AD(S) [Commander Travis], Confidential, 22 September 1943, HW 64/16, TNA.
127. AD(S) [Nigel de Grey], Confidential, 22 September 1943, HW 64/16, TNA; Denniston, All Heads of Sections, 7 January 1942, HW 64/16, TNA.
128. Commander Bradshaw, Security Films, 2 May 1944, HW 64/16, TNA; AD(A) [Bradshaw] Film 'Next of Kin', 2 August 1942, HW 64/16, TNA.
129. Travis, DD(S) Serial Order No. 21, 30 April 1942, HW 64/16, TNA.
130. For an example, see Travis, Indiscreet Talk, 9 September 1941, HW 64/16, TNA.
131. For examples, see Denniston, Careless talk, 24 August 1940, HW 64/16, TNA; Travis, Indiscreet Talk, 9 September 1941, HW 64/16, TNA; Denniston, All Heads of Sections, 7 January 1942, HW 64/16, TNA; Travis, Security in GC&CS, 11 May 1942, HW 64/16, TNA.
132. [No stated author], Secrecy, 28 June 1942, HW 64/16, TNA.
133. [No stated author], Secrecy, 28 June 1942, HW 64/16, TNA.
134. Travis, Indiscreet Talk, 9 September 1941, HW 64/16, TNA.
135. Quoted in McKay, *The Secret Life of Bletchley Park*, p. 224.
136. Quoted in McKay, *The Secret Life of Bletchley Park*, p. 219.
137. In some cases new staff were reportedly shown a pistol in their initial security briefing as a dire warning of what would occur if they broke their silence. Grey, *Decoding Organization*, p. 122.
138. H. Bragg to the Bletchley Park Trust, July 2001, in Whitchurch, *Other People's Stories 4*, p. 58.
139. For instance, Commander Bradshaw, Security, 16 August 1941, HW 64/16, TNA.
140. Senior Security Officer Hayward to DD(2) [Bradshaw], 8 May 1944, HW 64/16, TNA.
141. Cairncross, *Enigma Spy*, p. 104.
142. Mr White to Commander Bradshaw, 22 November 1943, HW 64/71, TNA.

208  Notes

143. C. James to Senior Security Officer Hayward, 12 July 1945, HW 64/71, TNA.
144. Senior Security Officer Hayward to AD(A) [Commander Bradshaw], 3 September 1943, HW 64/71, TNA.
145. Commander Bradshaw, Loss of Property from Bath House, 4 October 1944, HW 64/16, TNA.
146. DD(1) [Nigel de Grey] to DD(2) [Commander Bradshaw], 9 May 1944, HW 64/16, TNA.
147. The monotony and tedium of such work is a point worth particular emphasis, as Mavis Cannon, a teleprinter operator, recalled: 'I didn't like it here, I found it very boring.' Mavis Cannon, in Whitchurch, *Other People's Stories*, vol. 4, p. 19.
148. Birch, *Official History of Sigint*, vol. 2, p. 84.
149. Mary Rae, in Whitchurch, *Other People's Stories*, vol. 2, p. 28
150. Rae, in Whitchurch, *Other People's Stories*, vol. 2, p. 28
151. Birch, *Official History of Sigint*, vol. 2, p. 84.

## 4 The Administration of Off-Duty Life and Staff Welfare

1. McKay, *The Secret Life of Bletchley Park*, p. 33.
2. Denniston to The Director [Admiral Hugh Sinclair], 16 September 1939, HW 14/1, TNA. The suggestion was dropped until 1942 when the reorganisation of GC&CS did eventually see these sections return to London and the newly demoted Denniston sent with them.
3. Denniston to Menzies, 12 September 1939, HW 14/1, TNA.
4. Johnson & Gallehawk, *Figuring it Out*, p. 90.
5. John Taylor, *Bletchley and District at War: People and Places* (Copt Hewick, 2009), p. 12.
6. Johnson and Gallehawk, *Figuring it Out*, p. 3.
7. *Minute Book of the Bletchley Urban District Council: 1941–42*, 25 September 1941, DC 14/1/18, Centre for Buckinghamshire Studies, Aylesbury, p. 77.
8. Titmuss, *Problems of Social Policy*, p. 366.
9. Minutes of the Bletchley Urban District Council, 8 January 1942. Bletchley Urban District Council – Minute Book 1941–42 – DC 14/1/18, Centre for Buckinghamshire Studies, Aylesbury, p. 77.
10. Minutes of the Bletchley Urban District Council, 21 May 1943. Bletchley Urban District Council – Minute Book 1942–43 – DC 14/1/20, Centre for Buckinghamshire Studies, Aylesbury, p. 24. The description of Bletchley Park staff as being 'war workers' and 'civil servants' is interesting. It is an example of the effect of the blanket of secrecy surrounding the institution and local knowledge of the operation being undertaken.
11. Minutes of the Bletchley Urban District Council, 6 July 1943. Bletchley Urban District Council – Minute Book 1943–44 – DC 14/1/20, Centre for Buckinghamshire Studies, Aylesbury, p. 43.
12. Bletchley Park Trust, *History of Bletchley Park Huts & Blocks 1939–1945*, p. 22. See also Commander Bradshaw, 'Bath House', 15 May 1944, HW 64/62, TNA.
13. Personnel, 7 October 1945, HW 64/72, TNA.

14. This was together at a number of large sites as opposed to numerous billets among the local population.
15. Thirsk, *Bletchley Park*, p. 77.
16. *Minute Book of the Bletchley Urban District Council: 1943–44*, 11 May 1943, DC 14/1/20, Centre for Buckinghamshire Studies, Aylesbury, p. 21.
17. Thirsk, *Bletchley Park*, p. 77.
18. *Minute Book of the Bletchley Urban District Council: 1943–44*, 8 June 1943, DC 14/1/20, Centre for Buckinghamshire Studies, Aylesbury, p. 30.
19. Johnson and Gallehawk, *Figuring it Out*, endnote 57, p. 190.
20. Johnson and Gallehawk, *Figuring it Out*, pp. 91–94.
21. Johnson and Gallehawk, *Figuring it Out*, pp. 95–98.
22. H.C Griffith to DD(2) [Commander Bradshaw], 'Numbers billeted or accommodated by areas as at 29 April 1945', 2 May 1945, HW 64/44, TNA.
23. Angus Calder, *The People's War: Britain 1939–1945* (London, 1969, 1992), p. 35
24. Bletchley, being in Buckinghamshire, is not within any of the counties traditionally associated with the Midlands. However, Bletchley is in the north of Buckinghamshire close to the county border with Bedfordshire, a county associated with the Midlands. A considerable number of billets requisitioned for Bletchley Park staff were in Bedfordshire, including Bedford, Aspley Guise, the Woburn Estate and Amptill.
25. Parker, *Manpower*, p. 396.
26. Parker, *Manpower*, p. 396.
27. For instance see Thirsk, *Bletchley Park*, p. 39.
28. Parker, *Manpower*, pp. 399–406.
29. Denniston to Menzies, 12 September 1939, no. 2. HW 14/1, TNA.
30. Johnson and Gallehawk, *Figuring it Out*, p. 124.
31. Ann Graham, 'Ann Graham interview and her husband Arthur Witherbird', in Whitchurch, *Other People's Stories*, vol. 2, p. 59.
32. Johnson and Gallehawk, *Figuring it Out*, p. 122.
33. Johnson and Gallehawk, *Figuring it Out*, p. 127.
34. Parker, *Manpower*, p. 403.
35. Calder, *The People's War*, p. 318.
36. Parker, *Manpower*, p. 403. See also Summerfield, *Women Workers*, pp. 132–133.
37. Parker, *Manpower*, pp. 403–405.
38. Grey, *Decoding Organization*, p. 56.
39. Michael Smith asserts that the chef was recruited from the Savoy, Sinclair McKay on the other hand contends that he had previously been employed at the Ritz. See Smith, *Station X*, p. 29; McKay, *The Secret Life of Bletchley Park*, p. 142.
40. Smith, *Station X*, p. 29.
41. An often recounted story in Bletchley Park folklore is that the overwhelmed chef attempted to end his own life. Smith, *Station X*, p. 29; McKay, *The Secret Life of Bletchley Park*, p. 142. Both agree on the chef's suicide attempt. However, no firm evidence exists to support this apocryphal tale of bureaucratic tragedy.
42. McKay, *The Secret Life of Bletchley Park*, p. 142.
43. P. Stanley Sykes, 'Luncheons', 2 October 1939, HW 64/56, TNA.
44. For an example see, Alistair Dennistion, 'Lunch Money – G.C.&C.S.', 28 October 1939, HW 64/56, TNA.

45. [Unknown Author] C.A.O., 'Breakfast and Dinner', 24 April 1940, HW 64/56, TNA.
46. [Unknown Author] C.A.O., 'Breakfast and Dinner', 24 April 1940, HW 64/56, TNA.
47. A. G. Denniston, 'Meal Subscriptions', 23 November 1941, HW 64/56, TNA.
48. Unfortunately, staff numbers prior to March 1942 have proven fragmentary. However, in April 1941, the staff contingent was 842, by March 1942 that figure was in excess of 1,600. This places the probable total staff numbers in October 1941 at around 1,200–1,300 persons. See [Untitled Document], 23 June 1942, HW 64/70, TNA, and Johnson and Gallehawk, *Figuring it Out*, p. 7.
49. Alistair Denniston, 'Meals at the War Station', [day obscured] August 1940, HW 64/56, TNA. The cost of midnight supper was not listed.
50. J. M. C. [Joint Management Committee], 'Tea', J. M. C. No. 26, 4 January 1941, HW 64/56, TNA.
51. Edward Travis, 'Meals at the War Station', 25 May 1941, HW 64/56, TNA.
52. McKay, *The Secret Life of Bletchley Park*, p. 143.
53. Johnson and Gallehawk, *Figuring it Out*, p. 116.
54. Johnson and Gallehawk, *Figuring it Out*, p. 10.
55. Johnson and Gallehawk, *Figuring it Out*, pp. 118–119.
56. Commander Bradshaw, 'Cafeteria Meals', 12 December 1944, HW 64/56, TNA.
57. Cannon, 'Mavis Cannon Interview', in Whitchurch, *Other People's Stories*, vol. 4, p. 19.
58. Johnson and Gallehawk, *Figuring it Out*, p. 13.
59. Joint Management Committee, 'Time of Dinner and Supper', 23 October 1940, J.M.C No. 6, HW 64/56, TNA.
60. J.M.C., 'Dinner', 12 May 1941, J.M.C. No. 48, HW 64/56, TNA.
61. Commander Bradshaw, 'Cafeteria Meals', 12 December 1944, HW 64/56, TNA.
62. C.A.O. (Denniston?), 'Mess Committee', 5 October 1940, HW 64/56, TNA; Arthur Ward, 'Life in the Army – Chapter 28', *BBC WW2 People's War*, Article ID: a4769264, www.bbc.co.uk/history/ww2peopleswar/stories/64/a4769264.shtml (accessed 14 March 2012).
63. C.A.O. (Denniston?), 'Mess Committee', 5 October 1940, HW 64/56, TNA.
64. J.M.C., 'Mess Committee', 15 October 1940, J.M.C. No. 3, HW 64/56, TNA.
65. J.M.C., Untitled, 30 October 1940, J.M.C. No. 9, HW 64/56, TNA.
66. Alistair Denniston, 'Catering', 21 September 1941, HW 64/56, TNA.
67. Bletchley Park Trust, *History of Bletchley Park Huts & Blocks*, p. 33.
68. Alistair Denniston, 'Catering', 21 September 1941, HW 64/56, TNA.
69. Alistair Denniston, 'Catering', 21 September 1941, HW 64/56, TNA.
70. Commander Bradshaw, 'Sandwich Lunches', 12 March 1942, HW 64/56, TNA.
71. Alistair Denniston, 'Catering', 21 September 1941, HW 64/56, TNA.
72. Alistair Denniston, 'Catering', 21 September 1941, HW 64/56, TNA.
73. A. G. Denniston, 'Morning and Afternoon Tea', 3 February 1941, HW 64/56, TNA.
74. C.A.O., 'Morning and Afternoon Tea', 10 February 1940, HW 64/56, TNA.
75. W. H. W. Ridley, 'Loss of Mess Traps', 5 August 1940, HW 64/56, TNA.
76. W. H. W. Ridley, 'Loss of Mess Traps', 5 August 1940, HW 64/56, TNA.
77. Alistair Denniston, 'Service Crockery, etc.', 1 January 1942, HW 64/56, TNA.
78. Commander Bradshaw, 'Cafeteria', 18 April 1944, B/P G.O., No. 42, HW 64/56, TNA.

Notes 211

79. Commander Bradshaw, 'Cafeteria Meals', 12 December 1944, B/P G.O., No. 138, HW 64/56, TNA., p. 3.
80. W. H. Ridley, 'Morning Tea', 28 June 1940, HW 64/56, TNA.
81. Commander Bradshaw, 'Afternoon Tea', 20 May 1942, HW 64/56, TNA.
82. Commander Bradshaw, 'Autoticket Machines', 5 May 1942, HW 64/56, TNA. It is interesting that considerable effort was made to ensure that tea was in constant supply while other commodities, such as soup, were expendable if only temporarily. This is perhaps unsurprising given the cultural status of tea in 1940s Britain, which George Orwell described as 'one of the main stays of civilization in this country'. George Orwell, 'A Nice Cup Of Tea', in Sonia Brownell Orwell and Ian Angus (eds), *As I Please: The Collected Essays, Journalism and Letters of George Orwell*, vol. 3, 1943–45 (Boston, 1968, 2000), p. 40.
83. Johnson and Gallehawk, *Figuring it Out*, pp. 77–80.
84. For instance, see Transport Officer [illegible signature] to AD(A) [Commander Bradshaw], 3 December 1943, HW 64/35, TNA.
85. Calder, *People's War*, p. 63.
86. Bletchley Park Trust, *History of Bletchley Park Huts & Blocks 1939–1945*, p. 8.
87. [Signature illegible] Unknown Squadron Leader, to DD(S) [Commander Edward Travis], 24 June 1942, HW 64/27, TNA.
88. Commander Bradshaw, 'Sick Bay, Bletchley Park', 2 May 1942, HW 64/27, TNA.
89. [Unknown author (Captain), signature illegible] to Commander Bradshaw, 'Medical Arrangements at B.P.', 7 August 1942, HW 64/27, TNA.
90. Johnson and Gallehawk, *Figuring it Out*, pp. 178–179.
91. AD(A) [Paymaster Commander A. R. Bradshaw, with signature] to DD(S) [Commander Edward Travis], Superintendent Matron, 11 March 1943, HW 64/27, TNA.
92. AD Bradhsaw, 'Sickbay, Bletchley Park', 2 May 1942, HW 64/27, TNA.
93. F. B. [Presumably Frank Birch, head of Hut 4] to AD(A) [Commander Bradshaw], 21 November 1943, HW 64/27, TNA.
94. Commander Bradshaw, 'Sun-Ray Clinic', 28 January 1944, HW 64/27, TNA.

## 5 Off-Duty Life: Staff Experience

1. Phoebe Senyard, quoted in Smith, *Station X*, p. 5.
2. Alistair Denniston, 'Catering', 21 September 1941, HW 64/56, TNA. Food rationing began in January 1940, initially placing controls on bacon, butter and sugar, and further controls were added over the course of the war.
3. Beryl Robertson, 'Interview', interviewed by Peter Wescombe, 9 January 2000, in Whitchurch, *Other People's Stories*, vol. 1, p. 14.
4. McPearson, in Whitchurch, *Other People's Stories*, vol. 3, p. 16.
5. Quoted in McKay, *The Secret Life of Bletchley Park*, p. 143.
6. [Anonymous author], 'Memorandum.' [no date given, but attached to Minutes dated 30 May 1942], HW 64/70, TNA.
7. Kay Sheargold, 'Mrs. Kay Sheargold to Mr. Eric Rhodes, 21/10/82', Eric Rhodes Papers, Misc. 2827, Misc. Box 190, Original Research Correspondence, IWM.
8. Shelia Lancaster, 'Shelia Lancaster', in Whitchurch, *Other People's Stories*, vol. 1, p. 43.

9. Thirsk, *Bletchley Park*, p. 23.
10. Quoted in McKay, *The Secret Life of Bletchley Park*, p. 143.
11. Gwen Watkins, *Cracking the Luftwaffe Codes: The Secrets of Bletchley Park* (London, 2006), pp. 217–223; Robert Harris, *Enigma* (London, 1995).
12. Watkins, *Cracking the Luftwaffe Codes*, pp. 221–222.
13. John Croft, 'John Croft Interview', in Whitchurch, *Other People's Stories*, vol. 2, p. 43.
14. John Croft, 'Reminiscences of GCHQ and GCB 1942–45', *Intelligence and National Security*, 13(4) (Winter, 1998), p. 136.
15. Louise Barrie, 'Louise Barrie (nee Gabriel)', in Page, *We Kept the Secret*, p. 12.
16. Welchman, *Hut Six Story*, pp. 185–186.
17. Young, *Enigma Variations*, p. 79.
18. Quoted in McKay, *The Secret Life of Bletchley Park*, p. 60.
19. Quoted in Hill, *Bletchley Park People*, p. 110.
20. McKay, *The Secret Life of Bletchley Park*, p. 60.
21. Quoted in Hill, *Bletchley Park People*, p. 109.
22. Thirsk, *Bletchley Park*, p. 39.
23. Quoted in Hill, *Bletchley Park People*, p. 109.
24. Quoted in Hill, *Bletchley Park People*, p. 109.
25. Hill, *Bletchley Park People*, p. 106.
26. Quoted in Michael Paterson, *Voices of the Code Breakers: Personal Accounts of the Secret Heroes of World War II* (Cincinnati, OH, 2008), p. 70.
27. Felicity Ashbee, quoted in Paterson, *Voices of the Code Breakers*, pp. 75–76.
28. [Anonymous author], 'Memorandum.' [no date given, but attached to Minutes dated 30 May 1942], HW 64/70, TNA.
29. M. P. Vivian to DCSS [Deputy Chief of the Secret Service, Valentine Vivian] 'Minutes', 30 May 1942, HW 64/70, TNA.
30. June Douglas, in Whitchurch, *Other People's Stories*, vol. 2, p. 48.
31. Thirsk, *Bletchley Park*, p. 40. The mention of eggs raises some questions given that they were subject to rationing. However, despite the controls they were often easily available either through the black market or from small-scale home producers who were exempt from the controls. See Ina Zweiniger-Bargielowska, *Austerity in Britain: Rationing, Controls and Consumption 1939–1945* (Oxford, 2000), p. 173. Bletchley was also home to a significant number of farm labourers, so eggs may have been easier to come by. A Vision of Britain Through Time, 'Bletchley UD, 1931 Census of England and Wales, Occupational Tables, Table 17: "Occupations (condensed list) of Males and Females, showing also the total Operatives and the Total Out of Work"', http://www.visionofbritain.org.uk/census/table_page.jsp?tab_id=EW1931OCC_M17 (accessed 19 March 2012).
32. Lawry, in Whitchurch, *Other People's Stories*, vol. 2, p. 44.
33. McPearson, in Whitchurch, *Other People's Stories*, vol. 3, p. 16.
34. Mrs L. P. Holliday, quoted in Paterson, *Voices of the Code Breakers*, p. 75.
35. Elizabeth Laura Persival, in Whitchurch, *Other People's Stories*, vol. 2, p. 32.
36. M. P. Vivian to DCSS [Deputy Chief of the Secret Service, Valentine Vivian] 'Minutes', 30 May 1942, HW 64/70, TNA.
37. Thirsk, *Bletchley Park*, p. 78.
38. Thirsk, *Bletchley Park*, p. 78.
39. Lewis-Smith, *Off Duty!*, p. 15.
40. Lewis-Smith, *Off Duty!*, p. 19.

Notes 213

41. Thirsk, *Bletchley Park*, p. 99.
42. D. G. Luke, *My Road to Bletchley Park: Britain's Best Kept Secret WWII Communications Centre*, p. 26.
43. Paterson, *Voices of the Code Breakers*, p. 91.
44. Briggs, *Secret Days*, p. 119.
45. Lewis-Smith, *Off Duty!*, p. 25.
46. Robertson, 'Interview', in Whitchurch, *Other People's Stories*, vol. 1, p. 14.
47. Faunch, 'Interview', in Whitchurch, *Other People's Stories*, vol. 1, p. 40.
48. Joe Moran, *On Roads: A Hidden History* (London, 2009), p. 139.
49. Moran, *On Roads*, p. 139.
50. 'Bletchley Park Recreational Club', 5 June 1941, No. 12, HW 14/16, TNA.
51. Bletchley Park Trust, *History of Bletchley Park Huts & Blocks 1939–1945*, p. 8.
52. 'Bletchley Park Recreational Club', 5 June 1941, No. 12, HW 14/16, TNA.
53. Johnson and Gallehawk, *Figuring it Out*, p. 3.
54. 'Bletchley Park Recreational Club', 5 June 1941, No. 12, HW 14/16, TNA.
55. 'Bletchley Park Recreational Club', 5 June 1941, No. 12, HW 14/16, TNA.
56. 'Bletchley Park Recreational Club', 5 June 1941, No. 12, HW 14/16, TNA.
57. Bletchley Park Trust, *History of Bletchley Park Huts & Blocks 1939–1945*, p. 33.
58. Bletchley Park Trust, *History of Bletchley Park Huts & Blocks 1939–1945*, p. 33.
59. Bletchley Park Trust, *History of Bletchley Park Huts & Blocks 1939–1945*, p. 8. See also Lancaster, in Whitchurch, *Other People's Stories*, vol. 1, pp. 43–44.
60. McKay, *The Secret Life of Bletchley Park*, p. 146.
61. McKay, *The Secret Life of Bletchley Park*, p. 245–255.
62. McKay, *The Secret Life of Bletchley Park*, p. 245.
63. Lawry, in Whitchurch, *Other People's Stories*, vol. 2, p. 43; Garrilly, in Whitchurch, *Other People's Stories*, vol. 2, p. 55.
64. McKay, *The Secret Life of Bletchley Park*, p. 246.
65. Wendy Munro, 'Interview', in Whitchurch, *Other People's Stories*, vol. 4, p. 49.
66. Quoted in Paterson, *Voices of the Code Breakers*, p. 90.
67. Luke, *My Road to Bletchley Park*, p. 25.
68. Alan McGowan, 'Codebreakers at Bletchley: Scottish Players at Bletchley', in *Scottish Chess*, 198 (June 2005), http://www.chessscotland.com/history/CodebreakersBletchley.htm (accessed 6 March 2012).
69. *Next of Kin* was an Ealing film made in 1942, starring, among others, Mervyn Johns and Basil Sydney. One of its main themes was the dangers of 'careless talk'.
70. [No name given, though probably Stuart Menzies given later correspondence in file] to Herbert Brittain, 15 October 1942, HW 64/47, TNA.
71. Bletchley Park Trust, *History of Bletchley Park Huts & Blocks 1939–1945*, p. 34.
72. Given the selection of *Next of Kin*, propaganda films that had a clear work- or security-related message.
73. Commander Bradshaw, 'Assembly Hall', 25 August 1943, HW 64/47, TNA.
74. Commander Bradshaw, 'Assembly Hall', 25 August 1943, HW 64/47, TNA.
75. Prof. E. R. Vincent to Mr Denny, 'B.P. Recreational Club', 12 September 1944, HW 64/47, TNA. Sadly, no record of which stars performed at Bletchley Park appears to have survived.
76. Malcolm Muggeridge, *Chronicles of Wasted Time, Volume Two: The Informal Grove* (London, 1973), p. 129.

77. McKay, *The Secret Life of Bletchley Park*, p. 32.
78. Bletchley Park Trust, *History of Bletchley Park Huts & Blocks 1939–1945*, p. 33.
79. Jeanne Bisgood, a Wren posted to Bletchley Park's Stanmore outstation, and a successful golfer who played for the English amateur team in 1949, recalled playing at the Stanmore Golf Club during the war. Bisgood, in Peter Hickling (ed.), *No Better Place: A Celebration of Parkstone Golf Club 1909–2009* (Parkstone, 2009), p. 67.
79. Bletchley Park Trust, *History of Bletchley Park Huts & Blocks 1939–1945*, p. 33.
80. McKibbin, *Classes and Cultures*, pp. 359–361.
81. McKay, *The Secret Life of Bletchley Park*, p. 33.
82. McKay, *The Secret Life of Bletchley Park*, p. 33.
83. Munro, in Whitchurch, *Other People's Stories*, vol. 4, p. 48.
84. Munro, in Whitchurch, *Other People's Stories*, vol. 4, p. 48.
85. Croft, in Whitchurch, *Other People's Stories*, vol. 2, p. 43.
86. Marjory Campbell, 'Interview', in Whitchurch, *Other People's Stories*, vol. 4, p. 51.
87. Munro, in Whitchurch, *Other People's Stories*, vol. 4, p. 48.
88. Persival, in Whitchurch, *Other People's Stories*, vol. 2, pp. 32–33.
89. For example, see Pauline Lee, 'Interview', in Whitchurch, *Other People's Stories*, vol. 4, p. 30.
90. Paterson, *The Voices of the Code Breakers*, p. 91.
91. Briggs, *Secret Days*, p. 119.
92. Lancaster, in Whitchurch, *Other People's Stories*, vol. 1, pp. 43–44.
93. Briggs, *Secret Days*, p. 118.
94. Penny Summerfield and Corinna Peniston-Bird, *Contesting Home Defence: Men, Women and the Home Guard in the Second World War* (Manchester, 2007), p. 132.
95. Alice Wolynskyj, personal correspondence to Christopher Smith, 27 April 2010.
96. Lancaster, in Whitchurch, *Other People's Stories*, vol. 1, p. 43.
97. Joan Marr, 'Interview', in Whitchurch, *Other People's Stories*, vol. 1, p. 46.
98. Douglas, in Whitchurch, *Other People's Stories*, vol. 1, p. 47.
99. Joan Collins, 'Interview', November 11 2000, in Whitchurch, *Other People's Stories*, vol. 2, p. 27.
100. Thirsk, *Bletchley Park*, p. 59.
101. Ann Witherbird, Arthur Witherbird, 'Ann Graham and her Husband Arthur Witherbird', August 2000, in Whitchurch, *Other People's Stories*, vol. 2, p. 58.
102. Gorley Putt quoted in Margaret Drabble, *Angus Wilson: A Biography* (London, 1995), p. 105.
103. Oliver Lawn quoted in McKay, *The Secret Life of Bletchley Park*, p. 196.
104. McKay, *The Secret Life of Bletchley Park*, p. 198.
105. McKay, *The Secret Life of Bletchley Park*, p. 196.
106. McKay, *The Secret Life of Bletchley Park*, p. 201.
107. Cannon, 'Interview', Whitchurch, *Other People's Stories*, vol. 4, p. 19.
108. Quoted in McKay, *The Secret Life of Bletchley Park*, p. 200.
109. Quoted in Hill, *Bletchley Park People*, p. 117.
110. McKay, *The Secret Life of Bletchley Park*, p. 200.

111. B. Brister to AD(A) [Commander Bradshaw], 'Report on Miss M. Dalley – Block A (Naval)', 6 March 1943, HW 64/27, TNA.
112. [No Author Given], 'Copy of Docket X.1054 dated 26 January 1944 – Unmarried Women: Maternity Leave.', dated 22 January 1944, received 26 January 1944, Initialled by M. V. M. [Unknown] 27 January 1944, and T. J. W. [Unknown] 1 February 1944, HW 64/67, TNA.
113. Mr Holloway to Establishment Officer, 'Copy of Docket X.9018 dated 4 September, 1943 – Unmarried Women: Maternity Leave.', Initialled by M. V. M. [Unknown] 7 September 1943, and T. J. W. [Unknown] 7 September 1943, HW 64/67, TNA.
114. Anne Lewis-Smith, *Off Duty! Bletchley Park Outstation – Gayhurst Manor WW2* (Newport, 2006), p. 21.
115. DeGroot, 'Lipstick on Her Nipples, Cordite in her Hair: Sex and Romance among British Service Women during the Second World War', in DeGroot and Peniston-Bird, *A Soldier and a Woman*, pp. 117–118.
116. Adrian Bingham, *Gender, Modernity, and the Popular Press in Inter-War Britain* (Oxford, 2004), pp. 177–178; Calder, *The People's War*, p. 313.
117. DeGroot, 'Sex and Romance among British Servicewomen', in DeGroot and Peniston-Bird, *A Soldier and a Woman*, p. 100.
118. Col. L. W. Harrison, 'The War Disease', *The Spectator*, 11 June 1943, in Glass and Marsden-Smedley, *Articles of War*, p. 266.
119. Quoted in Birch, *Official History of Sigint*, vol. 2, pp. 83–84.
120. Mass Observation, *War Factory* (London, 1943), pp. 83–84.
121. Briggs, *Secret Days*, p. 119. For a non-Bletchley example, see Len England, 'Report on Cinema Queue', in Jeffrey Richards and Dorothy Sheridan (eds), *Mass-Observation at the Movies* (London, 1987), p. 189.
122. Siân Nicholas, *Echo of War: Home Front Propaganda and the Wartime BBC, 1939–45* (Manchester, 1996), p. 71.
123. For instance, see Mass Observation, *War Factory*, p. 82.
124. For instance, see Mass Observation, *War Factory*, pp. 80–81.
125. McKay, *The Secret Life of Bletchley Park*, p. 146.
126. Zweiniger-Bargielowska, *Austerity in Britain*, p. 44.
127. McKay, *The Secret Life of Bletchley Park*, p. 64.

# 6 Bletchley Park and Its Impact on the Local Community

1. The nature of telecommunication technology at that time meant that signals passed along the system required regular amplification at a distance of approximately every 45 miles. Repeater stations were built to fill that purpose. John A. Taylor, *Bletchley Park's Secret Sisters: Psychological Warfare in World War II* (Dunstable, 2005), p. xiii.
2. Robert Cook, *Bletchley: Past & Present* (Stroud, 2004), p. 4.
3. A vision of Britain Through Time, 'Bletchley UD, 1931 Census of England and Wales, Occupational Tables, Table 17: "Occupations (condensed list) of males and females, showing also the total Operatives and the Total Out of Work"', http://www.visionofbritain.org.uk/census/table_page.jsp?tab_id=EW1931OCC_M17 (accessed 16 June 2015).
4. Ron Hellier interviewed by Christopher Smith, 21 January 2011.

5. A Vision of Britain Through Time, 'Bletchley UD, 1931 Census of England and Wales, Occupational Tables, Table 17: "Occupations (condensed list) of Males and Females, showing also the total Operatives and the Total Out of Work"', http://www.visionofbritain.org.uk/census/table_page.jsp?tab_id=EW1931OCC_M17 (accessed 16 June 2015).
6. Cook, *Bletchley*, p. 4.
7. *North Bucks Times and County Observer*, 7 June 1938, Milton Keynes Library, p. 4.
8. *North Bucks Times and County Observer*, 7 June 1938, Milton Keynes Library, p. 4.
9. *North Bucks Times and County Observer*, 28 June 1938, Milton Keynes Library, p. 4.
10. *The Bucks Standard*, 4 June 1938, Milton Keynes Library, p. 3.
11. D. C. Low, *The History of Bletchley Park and the Mansion* (Great Missenden, 1965), p. 11.
12. Ivy Fisher, *Old Bletchley Remembered* (Milton Keynes, 1979), p. 24.
13. *Minute Book of the Bletchley Urban District Council: 1941–42*, 6 June 1940, DC 14/1/17, p. 22. While the *Minute Books of the Bletchley Urban District Council* do make some reference to Bletchley Park's activities, typically regarding planning and billeting issues, these total fewer than 20 entries over the entire course of the war.
14. McKay, *The Secret Life of Bletchley Park*, p. 33.
15. Welchman, *The Hut Six Story*, p. 31.
16. *Minute Book of the Bletchley Urban District Council: 1943–1944*, 11 May 1943, DC 14/1/20, p. 21.
17. *Minute Book of the Bletchley Urban District Council: 1943–1944*, 8 June 1943, DC 14/1/20, p. 30.
18. *Minute Book of the Bletchley Urban District Council: 1943–1944*, 8 June 1943, DC 14/1/20, p. 30. The minutes contain no reference to opposition to this planned adjustment to the local footpath.
19. Johnson and Gallehawk, *Figuring it Out*, p. 126.
20. Johnson and Gallehawk, *Figuring it Out*, pp. 125–127.
21. Grey, *Decoding Organization*, p. 56.
22. Thirsk, *Bletchley Park*, p. 108.
23. Ron Hellier interviewed by Chrisopher Smith, 21 January 2011.
24. Watson, 'How the Bletchley Park Buildings Took Shape', in Hinsley and Stripp, *Codebreakers*, p. 306.
25. Unknown Naval Lieutenant [Signature unreadable] to Mr Denny, 11 September 1943, HW 64/47, TNA.
26. Mr A. D. White to Commander Bradshaw, 23/11/1943, HW 64/71, TNA.
27. As also noted earlier, this resulted in the Urban District Council considering prosecuting intransigent residents. *Minute Book of the Bletchley Urban District Council: 1943–1944*, 6 July 1943, DC 14/1/20, p. 34.
28. Bletchley Park Trust, *History of Bletchley Park Huts & Blocks 1939–1945*, reproduction of documents produced by the Government Communications Headquarters now stored at the National Archives, Kew, p. 21. Andrew Hodges' biography of Alan Turing provides a lengthy anecdote regarding a short-lived spell by Turing in the Home Guard. Hodges, *Alan Turing*, p. 232. It remains unclear whether this unit included non-Bletchley Park staff.

## Notes 217

29. Mr Sherwood to Commander Bradshaw, 20 December 1943, HW 64/47, TNA.
30. AD(A) [Commander Bradshaw] to Mr Sherwood, 22 December 1943, HW 64/47, TNA.
31. Ron Hellier interviewed by Christopher Smith, 21 January 2011.
32. Ron Hellier interviewed by Christopher Smith, 21 January 2011.
33. Ron Hellier interviewed by Christopher Smith, 21 January 2011.
34. Thirsk, *Bletchley Park*, p. 55. Jimmy reported the incident to the Bletchley Park security staff; the report compiled still exists within the agency's archives housed at the National Archives. A. W. Nicholson to Mr Hayward, 30 August 1943, HW 64/71, TNA.
35. [Unknown Author] to Col. V. P. T. Vivian, 30 May 1943, HW 68/8, TNA.
36. De Witte, *The Ultra Secret*, p. 24.
37. [Unknown Author] to Col. V. P. T. Vivian, 30 May 1943, HW 68/8, TNA.
38. Wren J. Marcel to Flight Lieutenant Jones, 6 March 1943, HW 62/8, TNA.
39. V. Vivian to Nigel de Grey, 22 March 1943, HW 62/8, TNA.
40. Nigel de Grey to Col. V. Vivian, 18 May 1943, HW 62/8, TNA.
41. Monagu, *Beyond Top Secret U*, p. 46.
42. Nigel de Grey to Col. V. Vivian, 18 May 1943, HW 62/8, TNA.
43. Nigel de Grey to Col. V. Vivian, 18 May 1943, HW 62/8, TNA.
44. Ron Staniford, 'Conscientious Objector', in Robert Cook (ed.), *Bletchley Voices: Recollections of Local People* (Stroud, 1998), p. 93.
45. Ron Hellier interviewed by Christopher Smith, 21 January 2011.
46. Ron Hellier interviewed by Christopher Smith, 21 January 2011.
47. Ron Hellier interviewed by Christopher Smith, 21 January 2011. Ron also recalled that the building workers employed on the site used to drink at one of the local pubs and that the pub gained a reputation for being rough. Ron Hellier interviewed by Christopher Smith, 21 January 2011.
48. Quoting Herbert Bennett, 'Herbert Bennett's War', 2 July 1943, in Taylor, *Bletchley and District at War*, pp. 44–45. It is necessary to note that the diary is in the form of edited excerpts and thus it is unclear whether the relative lack of material relating to Bletchley Park is due to absence in the original diary or down to editorial decision.
49. Ron Hellier interviewed by Christopher Smith, 21 January 2011.
50. No relationship to Robert Baden-Powell, founder of the Scout Movement (1907).
51. Baden Powell, 'Patterned Socks', in Cook, *Bletchley Voices*, p. 95.
52. Baden Powell, 'Very Nice People', in Cook, *Bletchley Voices*, p. 94.
53. Hill, *Bletchley Park People*, p. 108.
54. Gwen Blane, 'Outside the Gates', in Cook, *Bletchley Voices*, p. 95.
55. Martin Blane, 'Holiday Camp', in Cook, *Bletchley Voices*, p. 94.
56. Taylor, *Bletchley and District at War*, pp. 65–69. Whether the absence of reference to Bletchley Park was down to absence in memory, a lack of interest on the part of the children at the time, or due to editorial decision is unclear.
57. Ron Hellier interviewed by Christopher Smith, 21 January 2011.
58. Buckinghamshire County Council, 'Buckinghamshire in World War Two', http://www.buckscc.gov.uk/assets/content/bcc/docs/archives/WW2_Evacuation.pdf (accessed 16 January 2012), p. 1.
59. Calder, *The People's War*, p. 35.
60. Taylor, *Bletchley and District*, p. 12.

218  Notes

61. Johnson and Gallehawk, *Figuring it Out*, p. 3.
62. The Milton Keynes Heritage Association compiled a lengthy list of extracts from local newspapers, including the 26 articles referenced here. See Milton Keynes Heritage Association, 'Extracts from the Bletchley Gazette and North Bucks Times During the War Years 1939–1945', http://www.mkheritage.co.uk/bfss/docs/WWIInewspapers.html (accessed 23 March 2012).
63. Milton Keynes Heritage Association, 'Extracts from the Bletchley Gazette and North Bucks Times During the War Years 1939–1945'.
64. Milton Keynes Heritage Association, 'Extracts from the Bletchley Gazette and North Bucks Times During the War Years 1939–1945'.
65. Quoted in Taylor, *Bletchley and District*, p. 66.
66. Quoting Bennett, 'Herbert Bennett's War', 17 November 1949, in Taylor, *Bletchley and District at War*, p. 39.
67. Ron Hellier interviewed by Christopher Smith, 21 January 2011. Interestingly, Ron did not recall any of those evacuees individually, despite attending school with some of them and, in his words, 'cannot have made any hard and fast friends' among them.
68. Such as Woburn Abbey, which in addition to housing members of the WRNS working at Bletchley Park also housed US military personnel. Furthermore, a number of airbases were located within 15 miles of Bletchley Park, all within the circumference of Bletchley Park's billeting range, including bases at Finmere, Wing, Cranfield, Cheddington and Little Horwood. For a full list of UK airbases, by county, during the Second World War see The Wartime Memories Project, 'Airfields', http://www.wartimememoriesproject.com/ww2/airfields/index.php (accessed 23 March 2012).
69. Dennis Comerford quoted in Cook, *Bletchley Voices*, p. 101.
70. History of the Research and Development Section of S.O.E., (no date) HS7/27, TNA, pp. 3–4.
71. Taylor, *Bletchley Park's Secret Sisters*, pp. 1–4.
72. Andrew, *Secret Service*, p. 665.
73. Taylor, *Bletchley Park's Secret Sisters*, pp. 7–27.
74. Taylor, *Bletchley Park's Secret Sisters*, pp. 7–41.
75. Ian McLaine, *Ministry of Morale: Home Front Morale and the Ministry of Information in World War II* (London, 1979), p. 74.
76. McLaine, *Ministry of Morale*, p. 75.
77. Calder, *Myth of the Blitz*, p. 110.
78. Smith, *Station X*, pp. 127–129. See also J. C. Masterman, *The Double-Cross System in the War of 1939 to 1945* (London, 1972).
79. Smith, *Station X*, p. 129.
80. Quoted in McLaine, *Ministry of Morale*, p. 82.
81. Quoted in McLaine, *Ministry of Morale*, p. 82.
82. Normal Longmate, *How We Lived Then: A History of Everyday Life during the Second World War* (London, 1971, 2002), pp. 95–96.
83. Longmate, *How We Lived Then*, p. 96.
84. McLaine, *Ministry of Morale*, p. 83.
85. The National Archives, 'The Art of War: Propaganda: Home Front: "Keep mum – she's not so dumb"', http://www.nationalarchives.gov.uk/theartofwar/prop/home_front/INF3_0229.htm (accessed 29 March 2012).
86. Calder, *The People's War*, p. 136.

87. The head of SIS, Gen. Stuart Menzies, when proposing the construction of the Bletchley Park assembly hall cited the screening of this film in particular as a an example for building a facility that could hold several hundred employees. Menzies to Herbert Brittain, 15 October 1942, HW 64/47, TNA. For a synopsis and production and cast details, see Internet Movie Database, 'Next of Kin (1942)', http://imdb.com/title/tt0035121/ (accessed 29 March 2012).
88. Philip M. Taylor, *British Propaganda in the Twentieth Century: Selling Democracy* (Edinburgh, 1999), p. 180.
89. Nicholas, *Echo of War*, p. 71.
90. Nicholas, *Echo of War*, p. 99.
91. Thirsk, *Bletchley Park*, p. 55.
92. McLaine, *Ministry of Morale*, p. 225.

## Conclusion

1. Johnson and Gallehawk, *Figuring it Out*, p. 14.
2. Johnson and Gallehawk, *Figuring it Out*, p. 127.
3. Johnson and Gallehawk, *Figuring it Out*, p. 119.
4. Johnson and Gallehawk, *Figuring it Out*, p. 14.
5. Johnson and Gallehawk, *Figuring it Out*, pp. 119, 127.
6. Watkins, *Cracking the Luftwaffe Codes*, p. 165.
7. Aldrich, *GCHQ*, p. 68.
8. Briggs, *Secret Days*, pp. 162–181.
9. Smith, *Station X*, p. 64.
10. Johnson and Gallehawk, *Figuring it Out*, p. 20.
11. Agar, *Government Machine*, p. 392.
12. Agar, *Government Machine*, p. 414.
13. David Edgerton, *Britain's War Machine: Weapons, Resources and Experts in the Second World War* (London, 2011), p. 89.
14. Birch, *The Official History of Sigint*, vol. 1:1, p. 20.
15. Grey and Sturdy, 'A Chaos that Worked: Organizing Bletchley Park'.
16. Agar, *Government Machine*, p, 412.
17. Johnson and Gallehawk, *Figuring it Out*, p. 126.
18. Grey, *Decoding Organization*, pp. 235, 70.
19. Summerfield, *Reconstructing Women's Wartime Lives*, p. 7.
20. Smith, 'The Effect of the War on the Status of Women', in Smith, *War and Social Change*, pp. 208–229.
21. Smith, 'The Effect of the War on the Status of Women', in Smith, *War and Social Change*, pp. 216–217.
22. Smith, 'The Effect of the War on the Status of Women', in Smith, *War and Social Change*, 212–217.
23. AD(Mech) [Gordon Welchman] to Director [Edward Travis], 10 July 1944, HW 62/6, TNA. This document was circulated at the highest levels of the agency and bore the mark of GC&CS's Director General and head of the Secret Intelligence Service, Sir Stuart Menzies.

# Bibliography

## Primary sources

### Manuscript sources

*Imperial War Museum Archive, Documents Department, London*
Documents 660, 91/4/1, The Papers of Mrs M. W. Ackroyd.
Misc. 190, Item 2827, Eric Rhodes Papers.

*Bletchley Park Trust Archive: Bletchley*
Whitchurch, D. (ed.), *Other People's Stories*, vols. 1–6, 2000–2002.

*Centre For Buckinghamshire Studies: Aylesbury*
DC 14/1/15–20, Minute Books of the Bletchley Urban District Council: 1938–44.

*The National Archives, Kew*
Records of the Special Operations Executive:
HS 27/7, SOE Research and Development section 1938–1945.
Records created or inherited by Government Communications Headquarters (GCHQ):
HW 14/1, Directorate: Second World War Policy Papers.
HW 14/16, Directorate: Second World War Policy Papers.
HW 43/1–3, *The History of British SIGINT 1914–1945*, vols I–III.
HW 50/50, Post-war Memorandum by Nigel de Grey.
HW 62/8 GCCS Miscellaneous Papers: Breaches of Security 1943–1945.
HW 64/15, Library Stock.
HW 64/16, Security circulars.
HW 64/17, Religious Matters.
HW 64/26, Call-up deferments and exemptions for Bletchley Park staff.
HW 64/27, Medical services.
HW 64/34, Aliens working at Bletchley Park and aliens staying with staff.
HW 64/35, Accidents involving Bletchley Park staff.
HW 64/44, Billeting at GC&CS.
HW 64/47, Assembly Hall at Bletchley Park.
HW 64/56, Catering arrangements at Bletchley Park.
HW 64/61, Various financial matters.
HW 64/62, Welfare.
HW 64/67, Staff matters at Bletchley Park including recruitment, pay and leave.
HW 64/70, Staffing and conditions of work at Bletchley Park.
HW 64/71, Security officers' reports.
HW 64/72, Bletchley Park administrative returns.
HW 64/73, Civil service recruitment for Bletchley Park.

HW 64/75, Women's Committee.
HW 72/1, Correspondence between GC&CS, Foreign Office and the Civil Service Commission concerning the recruitment of Junior and Senior Assistants, 1927–1939.
HW 72/9, Correspondence with universities on Junior Assistant recruitment for GC&CS, 1932–1939.
HW 72/10, Papers on various staff matters including transport, washing facilities, accommodation and air raid precautions (ARP).

### Newspapers

*North Bucks Times and County Observer* (Milton Keynes Library).
*The Bucks Standard* (Milton Keynes Library).

### Contemporary printed sources

Birch, F., *The Official History of Sigint: 1919–1945*, 2 vols, J. Jackson (ed.) (Milton Keynes, 2004–2007).
Denniston, A. G., 'The Government Code and Cypher School Between the Wars', in Andrew, C. (ed.), *Codebreaking and Signals Intelligence* (London, 1986), pp. 48–70.
Glass, F., and Marsden-Smedley, P. (eds), *Articles of War: The Spectator Book of World War II* (London, 1989).
Jackson, J. (ed.), *The Secret War of Hut 3: The First Full Story of How Intelligence from Enigma Signals Decoded at Bletchley Park Was Used During World War Two* (Milton Keynes, 2002).
Johnson, K. and Gallehawk, J. (eds), *Figuring it Out at Bletchley Park 1939–1945* (2007).
Mass-Observation, *War Factory: A Report* (London, 1943).
Orwell, S., and Angus, I. (eds), *As I Please: The Collected Essays, Journalism and Letters of George Orwell*, Volume 3, 1943–45 (Boston, 1968, 2000), pp. 40–43.

### Oral history interviews

*Bletchley Park Trust Archive: Bletchley*
Bletchley Park Veterans Tape Interviews Collection.

*Imperial War Museum Archive, Sound Archive, London*
10595/3, Mrs Mary Z. Pain.

*Conducted by Christopher Smith*
Ruth Bourne, 8 May 2010.
Ron Hellier, 21 January 2011.
Barbara Moor, 30 April 2010.
Gwendoline Page, 29 April 2010.
James Thirsk, 28 April 2010.
Joan Thirsk, 28 April 2010.
Alice Wolynskyj, 27 April 2010.

## On-line primary sources

BBC WW2 People's Stories: An [Online] Archive of World War Two Memories – Written by the Public, Gathered by the BBC: http://www.bbc.co.uk/
Davies, J., 'A W.R.N.S. Life Codebreaking At Stanmore', ID: A5496302.
Ettridge, J., 'Hut 6, Bletchley Park', Article ID: a4163942.
Pulley, A. S., 'W.R.N.S. Breaking the Enigma Code. Bletchley Park', Article ID: A5804499.
Ward, A., 'Life in the Army – Chapter 28', Article ID: A4769364.

## Other

A Vision of Britain Through Time, 'Bletchley UD, 1931 Census of England and Wales, Occupational Tables, Table 17: "Occupations (condensed list) of Males and Females, showing also the total Operatives and the Total Out of Work"', http://www.visionofbritain.org.uk
Milton Keynes Heritage Association, 'Extracts from the Bletchley Gazette and North Bucks Times During the War Years 1939–1945', http://www.mkheritage.co.uk/
The Wartime Memories Project, 'Airfields', http://www.wartimememoriesproject.com/

## Other primary source material

Bletchley Park Trust, *History of Bletchley Park Huts & Blocks 1939–1945*, Bletchley Park Trust Report No. 18, revised by Bonsall, A. (Bletchley, 2009).
England, L., 'Report on Cinema Queue', 24 May 1940, reprinted in Richards, J., and Sheridan, D. (eds), *Mass-Observation at the Movies* (London, 1987), pp. 187–190.
Alice Wolynskyj, unpublished personal recollections provided to Christopher Smith, 27 April 2010.

## Memoirs and works of memory

Adelson, R., 'Interview with Peter Calvocoressi', *The Historian*, 55(2) (Winter, 1993), pp. 235–252.
Briggs, A., *Secret Days: Code-Breaking in Bletchley Park* (London, 2011).
Bertrand, G., *Enigma ou la plus grande énigme de la guerre 1939–1945 (Enigma or the Greatest Enigma of the War of 1939–1945)* (Paris, 1973).
Cairncross, J., *The Enigma Spy: An Autobiography – The Story of the Man Who Changed the Course of World War Two* (London, 1997).
Calvocoressi, P., *Top Secret Ultra: The Full Story of Ultra and its Impact on World War II* (London, 1980, 1981).
Cook, R. (ed.), *Bletchley Voices: Recollections of Local People* (Chalford Oral History Series) (Stroud, 1998).
Croft, J., 'Reminiscences of GCHQ and GCB 1942–45', *Intelligence and National Security*, 13(4) (Winter, 1998), pp. 133–143.
Hinsley, F. H., and Stripp, A. (eds), *Codebreakers: The Inside Story of Bletchley Park* (Oxford, 1993, 1994).
Hogarth, J., *An Extraordinary Mixture: Bletchley Park in Wartime* (Glasgow, 2008).
Lewis-Smith, A., *Off Duty! Bletchley Park Outstation – Gayhurst Manor WW2* (Newport, 2006).

Luke, D. G., *My Road to Bletchley Park: Britain's Best Kept Secret WWII Communications Centre* (Bodmin, 1998).
Marks, L., *Between Silk and Cyanide: A Code Maker's War 1941–45* (Stroud, 2008).
Montagu, E., *Beyond Top Secret U* (London, 1977).
Muggeridge, M., *Chronicles of Wasted Time, Volume Two: The Informal Grove* (London, 1973).
Nash, J., and Esdaile, K., *Bucks Shell Guide, With Notes on Monuments* (London, 1939).
Nicholson, M. (ed.), *What Did You Do In The War, Mummy?* (Bridgend, 1995).
Page, P. (ed.), *They Listened in Secret: More Memories of the Wrens* (Wymondham, 2003).
Page, G. (ed.), *We Kept the Secret: Now it Can be Told – Some Memories of Pembroke V Wrens* (Wymondham, 2002).
Skillen, H. (ed.), *The Enigma Symposium*, 7 vols. (Pinner, 1992–2000).
Smith, M., and Erskine, R. (eds), *Action This Day* (London, 2001), pp. 77–93.
Watkins, G., *Cracking the Luftwaffe Codes: The Secrets of Bletchley Park* (London, 2006).
Welchman, G., *The Hut Six Story: Breaking the Enigma Codes* (London, 1986).
Young, I., *Enigma Variations: Love, War and Bletchley Park* (Edinburgh, 1990).

## Secondary sources

### Books

Addison, P., *The Road to 1945: British Politics and the Second World War* (London, 1975).
Agar, J., *The Government Machine: A Revolutionary History of the Computer* (London, 2003).
Agar, J., *Turing and the Universal Machine: The Making of the Modern Computer* (Duxford, 2001).
Aldrich, R., *GCHQ: The Uncensored Story of Britain's Most Secret Intelligence Agency* (London, 2010).
Andrew, C., *Secret Service: The Making of the British Intelligence Community* (Sevenoaks, 1985, 1986).
Barnett, C., *The Audit of War: The Illusion and Reality of Britain as a Great Nation* (London, 1986).
Barnett, C., *The Collapse of British Power* (Stroud, 1972).
Batey, M., *Dilly: The Man Who Broke Enigmas* (London, 2009).
Bennett, R., *Behind the Battle: Intelligence in the War with Germany, 1939–1945*, revised edition (London, 1999).
Bennett, R. (ed.), *Intelligence Investigations: How Ultra Changed History – Collected Papers of Ralph Bennett* (London, 1996).
Bingham, A., *Gender, Modernity, and the Popular Press in Inter-War Britain* (Oxford, 2004).
Brown, A. C., *Bodyguard of Lies* (London, 1977).
Budiansky, S., *Battle of Wits: The Complete Story of Codebreaking in World War II* (London, 2000).
Calder, A., *The Myth of the Blitz* (London, 1991).

## Bibliography

Calder, A., *The People's War* (London, 1969, 1992).
Campbell-Kelly, M., *ICL: A Business and Technical History* (Oxford, 1989).
Cannadine, D., *Aspects of Aristocracy: Grandeur and Decline in Modern Britain* (London, 1994).
Clayton, A., *The Enemy is Listening: The Story of the Y Service* (London, 1988).
Collier, B., *Hidden Weapons: Allied Secret or Undercover Services in World War II* (Barnsley, 1982, 2006).
Conant, J., *The Irregulars: Roald Dahl and the British Spy Ring in Wartime Washington* (New York, NY, 2008).
Cook, M. (ed.), *A Gay History of Britain: Love and Sex Between Men Since the Middle Ages* (Oxford, 2007).
Cook, R., *Bletchley: Past & Present* (Stroud, 2004).
Copeland, J. B. (ed.), *Colossus: The Secrets of Bletchley Park's Codebreaking Computers* (Oxford, 2006).
Costello, J. *Mask of Treachery* (London, 1988).
DeBruce, J., and Burke, C. *The Secret in Building 26: The Untold Story of America's Ultra War Against the U-boat Enigma Codes* (New York, NY, 2004).
DeGroot, G., and Peniston-Bird, C. (eds), *A Soldier and a Woman: Sexual Integration in the Military* (Harlow, 2000).
Denniston, R., *Thirty Secret Years: A. G. Dennison's Work in Signals Intelligence 1914–1944* (Trowbridge, 2007).
Dunlop, T., *The Bletchley Girls: War, Secrecy, Love and Loss: The Women of Bletchley Park Tell Their Story* (London, 2015).
Drabble, M., *Angus Wilson: A Biography* (London, 1995).
Edgerton, D., *Britain's War Machine: Weapons, Resources and Experts in the Second World War* (London, 2011, 2012).
Edgerton, D., *Warfare State: Britain, 1920–1970* (Cambridge, 2006).
Enever, T., *Britain's Best Kept Secret: Ultra's Base at Bletchley Park* (Stroud, 1994).
Erskine, R., and Smith, M. (eds), *Action This Day* (London, 2001).
Field, G. G., *Blood Sweat and Toil: Remaking the British Working Class, 1939–1945* (Oxford, 2011).
Fisher, I., *Old Bletchley Remembered* (Milton Keynes, 1979).
Fussell, P., *Wartime: Understanding and Behaviour in the Second World War* (Oxford, 1990).
Freedman, M., *Unravelling Enigma: Winning the Code War at Station X* (Barnsley, 2000).
Gannon, P., *Colossus: Bletchley Park's Greatest Secret* (London, 2007).
Garlinski, J. *The Enigma War: The Inside Story of the German Enigma Codes and How the Allies Broke Them* (New York, 1979).
Godson, R. (ed.), *Comparing Foreign Intelligence: the US, the USSR, the UK and the Third World* (London, 1988).
Grey, C., *Decoding Organization: Bletchley Park, Codebreaking and Organization Studies* (Cambridge, 2012).
Harper, S., *Capturing Enigma: How HMS Petard Seized the German Naval Codes* (Stroud, 1999).
Harris, R., *Enigma* (London, 1995).
Haufler, H., *Codebreakers' Victory: How the Allied Cryptographers Won World War II* (London, 2003).
Hickling, P. (ed.), *No Better Place: A Celebration of Parkstone Golf Club 1909–2009* (Parkstone, 2009).

Hill, M., *Bletchley Park People: Churchill's Geese That Never Cackled* (Stroud, 2004).
Hinsley, F. H., Thomas, E. E., Ransom, C. F. G., and Knight, R. C., *British Intelligence in the Second World War*, 5 vols. (London, 1979–1990).
Hodges, A., *Alan Turing: The Enigma* (London, 1983).
Hooper, D., *Official Secret: The Use and Abuse of the Act* (London, 1988).
Hornby, W., *Factories and Plant* (London, 1958).
Howarth, T. E. B., *Cambridge Between Two Wars* (London, 1978).
Hylton, S., *Careless Talk: The Hidden History of the Home Front 1939–45* (Stroud, 2010).
Inman, P., *Labour in the Munitions Industries* (London, 1957).
Jeffrey, K., *MI6: The History of the Secret Intelligence Service 1909–1949* (London, 2010).
Johnson, B., *The Secret War* (London, 1978).
Kahn, D., 'Enigma Uncracked', in Robert Cowley (ed.), *More What If? Eminent Historians Imagine What Might Have Been* (London, 2003).
Kahn, D., *Seizing the Enigma: The Race to Break the German U-Boat Codes, 1939–1943* (London, 1996).
Kahn, D., *The Codebreakers*, abridged version (London, 1974).
Kennedy, P., *The Realities Behind Diplomacy* (London, 1981).
Keren, M., and Herwig, H. R. (eds), *War Memory and Popular Culture: Essays on Modes of Remembrance and Commemoration* (Jefferson, NC, 2009).
Knightley, P., *The Second Oldest Profession* (New York, 1988).
Kozaczuk, W., *Bitwa o tajemnice: Służby wywiadowcze Polski i Rzeszy Niemieckiej 1922–1939 (Secret Battle: The Intelligence Services of Poland and the German Reich, 1922–1939)* (Warsaw, 1967)
Langhorne, R. (ed.), *Diplomacy and Intelligence During the Second World War* (Cambridge, 1985).
Lewin, R., *Ultra Goes to War: The Secret Story* (London, 1978, 1980).
Longmate, N., *How We Lived Then: A History of Everyday Life during the Second World War* (London, 1971, 2002).
Low, D. C., *The History of Bletchley Park and the Mansion* (Great Missenden, 1965).
Macksey, K., *The Searchers: Radio Intercept in Two World Wars* (London, 2003).
Mallmann-Showell, J. P., *Enigma U-Boats: Breaking the Code*, rev. edn (Hersham, 2009).
Mandler, P., *The English National Character: The History of an Idea from Edmund Burke to Tony Blair* (London, 2006).
Marwick, A., *Britain in the Century of Total War* (London, 1968, 1970).
Marwick, A., *The Nature of History*, third edition (London, 1989).
Marwick, A. (ed.), *Total War and Social Change* (London, 1988).
Marwick, A., *War and Social Change in the Twentieth Century: A Comparative Study of Britain, France, Germany, Russia and United States* (Basingstoke, 1974).
Masterman, J. C., *The Double-Cross System in the War of 1939 to 1945* (London, 1972).
McKay, R., *The Test of War: Inside Britain 1939–1945* (London, 1999).
McKay, S., *The Secret Life of Bletchley Park: The WWII Codebreaking Centre and the Men and Women Who Worked There* (London, 2010).
McKibbin, R., *Classes and Cultures: England 1918–1951* (Oxford, 1998).
McLaine, I., *Ministry of Morale: Home Front Morale and the Ministry of Information in World War II* (London, 1979).

Moran, J., *On Roads: A Hidden History* (London, 2009).
Murphy, S., *Cryptography: A Very Short Introduction* (Oxford, 2002).
Nicholas, S., *Echo of War: Home Front Propaganda and the Wartime BBC, 1939–45* (Manchester, 1996).
Nicholls, J., *England Needs You: The Story of Beaumanor Y Station World War II* (2000).
Nicholson, V., *Millions Like Us: Women's Lives in War and Peace 1939–1949* (London, 2011).
Norman, B., *Secret Warfare: The Battle of Codes and Cyphers* (Newton Abbot, 1989).
Oakley, B., *The Bletchley Park War: Some of the Outstanding Individuals – Edition 2.2* (Bletchley, 2006).
Parker, H. D. M., *Manpower: A Study of War-time Policy and Administration* (London, 1957).
Paterson, M., *Voices of the Code Breakers: Personal Accounts of the Secret Heroes of World War II* (Cincinnati, OH, 2008).
Pelling, H., *Britain and the Second World War* (London, 1970).
Perks, R., and Thompson, A. (eds), *The Oral History Reader*, second edition (London, 2006).
Ratcliff, R., *Delusions of Intelligence: Enigma, Ultra, and the End of Secure Ciphers* (Cambridge, 2006).
Scott, J. D., and Hughes, R., *The Administration of War Production* (London, 1955).
Sebag-Montefiore, H., *Enigma: The Battle for the Code* (London, 2000).
Sexton, D. J. *Signals Intelligence in World War II: A Research Guide* (Westport, CT, 1996).
Singh, S., *The Code Book: The Secret History of Codes and Code-Breaking* (London, 2000).
Smith, B. F., *The Shadow Warriors: OSS and the Origins of the CIA*. (New York, 1983).
Smith, B. F., *The Ultra-Magic Deals: And the Most Secret Special Relationship, 1940–1946* (Novato, CA, 1992).
Smith, H. L. (ed.), *War and Social Change: British Society in the Second World War* (Manchester, 1986).
Smith, M., *Station X: The Codebreakers of Bletchley Park* (London, 2004).
Smith, M., *The Debs of Bletchley Park: And Other Stories* (London, 2015).
Stafford, D., *Churchill & Secret Service* (London, 1997).
Summerfield, P., *Reconstructing Women's Wartime Lives: Discourse and Subjectivity in Oral Histories of the Second World War* (Manchester, 1998).
Summerfield, P., *Women Workers in the Second World War: Production and Patriarchy in Conflict* (London, 1984).
Summerfield, P., and Peniston-Bird, C., *Contesting Home Defence: Men, Women and the Home Guard in the Second World War* (Manchester, 2007).
Taylor, J., *Bletchley and District at War: People and Places* (Copt Hewick, 2009).
Taylor, J., *Bletchley Park's Secret Sisters: Psychological Warfare in World War II* (Dunstable, 2005).
Taylor, P. M., *British Propaganda in the Twentieth Century: Selling Democracy* (Edinburgh, 1999).
Thirsk, J., *Bletchley Park: An Inmate's Story* (London, 2008).
Thompson, P., *The Voice of the Past*, third edition (Oxford, 2000).
Titmuss, R., *Problems of Social Policy* (London, 1950).

Tosh, J., *The Pursuit of History: Aims, Methods and New Directions in the Study of Modern History*, second edition (London, 1991).
Trevor-Roper, H., *The Philby Affair: Espionage, Treason and Secret Services* (London, 1968).
Vincent, D., *The Culture of Secrecy: Britain 1932–1998* (Oxford, 1998).
Wark, W., *The Ultimate Enemy: British Intelligence and Nazi Germany 1933–1939* (Oxford, 1986).
West, N., *GCHQ: The Secret Wireless War 1900–86* (London, 1986).
Winterbotham, F. W., *The Ultra Secret: The Inside Story of Operation Ultra, Bletchley Park and Enigma* (London, 1974, 2000).
Zweiniger-Bargielowska, I., *Austerity in Britain: Rationing, Controls and Consumption 1939–1945* (Oxford, 2000).

## Journal articles

Dawson, S. T., 'Busy and Bored: The Politics of Work and Leisure for Women Workers in the Second World War British Government Hostels', *Twentieth Century British History*, 21(1) (January 2010), pp. 29–49.
Deavors, C. A., 'The Black Chamber: A Column – How the British Broke Enigma', *Cryptologia* 4(3) (1980), pp. 129–132.
Gazeley, I., 'Women's pay in British industry during the Second World War', *Economic History Review*, (61)3 (August 2008), pp. 651–671.
Grey, C., and Sturdy, A., 'A Chaos that Worked: Organizing Bletchley Park', i*Public Policy and Administration*, 25(1) (2010), pp. 47–66.
Grey, C., and Sturdy, A., 'The 1942 Reorganization of Government Code & Cypher School', *Cryptologia*, 32(4) (2008), pp. 311–333.
Kruh, L., and Deavours, C. A., 'The Type-x Cryptograph', *Cryptologia*, 7(3) (April 1983), pp. 145–166.
Monckton, L., 'Bletchley Park, Buckinghamshire: The Architecture of the Government Code and Cypher School', *Post-Medieval Archaeology*, 40(2) (2006), pp. 291–300.
Morrison, K. A., '"A Maudlin and Monstrous Pile": The Mansion at Bletchley Park, Buckinghamshire', *Transactions of the Ancient Monuments Society*, 53, (2009), pp. 81–100.
Price, T. J., 'Spy Stories, Espionage and the Public in the Twentieth Century', *Journal of Popular Culture*, 30(3) (Winter, 1996), pp. 81–89.
Smith, C., 'How I Learned to Stop Worrying and Love the Bombe: Machine Research and Development and Bletchley Park', *History of Science*, 52(2) (June 2014), pp. 200–222.
Smith, C., 'Operating Secret Machines: Military Women and the Intelligence Production Line, 1939–1945', *Women's History Magazine*, 76 (Autumn, 2014), pp. 30–36.

## Unpublished secondary sources

Burman, A., 'Gendering Decryption – Decrypting Gender: The Gender Discourse of Labour at Bletchley Park 1939–1945' (Unpublished Master's Dissertation: University of Uppsala, 2013).
Comer, T., Public Lecture, 'The Development of GCHQ and What it Cost' (Department of International Politics, Aberystwyth University, 7 March 2011).

De Witte, M., 'The Ultra Secret: Security of the British Codebreaking Operations in World War II' (Unpublished Master's Dissertation: Université Denis Diderot Paris 7, 2009).
Vigurs, E. K., 'The Women Agents of the Special Operations Executive F Section – Wartime Realities and Post War Representations (Unpublished Doctoral Dissertation: University of Leeds, 2011).

## Online secondary sources

### Newspaper articles

Gray, P., 'The Time 100: Alan Turing', *Time*, 29 March 1999, http://www.time.com/
Kirsch, J., 'BOOK REVIEW – A Techno-Thriller Zeroes in on Nazis – SEIZING THE ENIGMA: The Race to Break the German U-Boat Codes, 1939–1943 \07 by David Kahn', *Los Angeles Times*, 5 June 1991, http://articles.latimes.com/
Macintyre, B., 'The Genius Britain Betrayed', *The Times*, 14 July 2006, http://www.timesonline.co.uk/

### Oxford DNB

Batey, M., 'Knox, (Alfred) Dillwyn (1884–1943)', rev. *Oxford Dictionary of National Biography* (Oxford, 2004); online edn, Oct 2006, http://www.oxforddnb.com/
Carlyle, E. I., 'Ewing, Sir (James) Alfred (1855–1935)', rev. *Oxford Dictionary of National Biography* (Oxford, 2004); online edn, Oct 2006, http://www.oxforddnb.com/
Cecil, R., 'Maclean, Donald Duart (1913–1983)', rev. *Oxford Dictionary of National Biography* (Oxford, 2004); online edn, Jan 2011, http://www.oxforddnb.com/
Denniston, R., 'Welchman, (William) Gordon (1906–1985)', rev. *Oxford Dictionary of National Biography*, http://www.oxforddnb.com/view/article/31817
Heneage, S., 'Robinson, William Heath (1872–1944)', *Oxford Dictionary of National Biography* (Oxford, 2004); online edn, Jan 2011, http://www.oxforddnb.com/
Kerr, S., 'Burgess, Guy Francis de Moncy (1911–1963)', *Oxford Dictionary of National Biography* (Oxford, 2004); online edn, Jan 2011, http://www.oxforddnb.com
Langhorne, R., 'Hinsley, Sir (Francis) Harry (1918–1998)', rev. *Oxford Dictionary of National Biography*, http://www.oxforddnb.com/
Nicoll, D. R., 'Jones, Sir Eric Malcolm (1907–1986)', rev. *Oxford Dictionary of National Biography*, http://www.oxforddnb.com/
Nicoll, D. R., 'Travis, Sir Edward Wilfrid Harry (1888–1956)', rev. *Oxford Dictionary of National Biography,* http://www.oxforddnb.com/
Nicoll, D. R. 'Tiltman, John Hessell (1894–1982)', rev. *Oxford Dictionary of National Biography*, http://www.oxforddnb.com/

### Other

Davis Archive of Female Mathematicians, Turnbull WWW Server: School of Mathematical and Computational Sciences University of St Andrews, http://www-groups.dcs.st-and.ac.uk/
Grey, C., and Sturdy, A., 'The 1942 Reorganization of Government Code & Cypher School', paper presented to the Oxford Intelligence Group, Nuffield College Oxford, 7 June 2007, http://www.nuffield.ox.ac.uk/

Hinsley, F. H., 'The Influence of ULTRA in the Second World War', paper given to the Cambridge University Security Group Seminar, 19 October 1993, revised 26 November 1996, www.cl.cam.ac.uk

Helgason, G., 'Ships Hit by U-Boats in WW2: Ship Losses by Month', http://www.uboat.net/

McGowan, A., 'Codebreakers at Bletchley: Scottish Players at Bletchley', in *Scottish Chess*, 198 (June 2005), http://www.chessscotland.com/

Nicholas, S., 'The Good Servant: The Origins and Development of BBC Listener Research 1936–1950' (2006), http://www.britishonlinearchives.co.uk/

Ward, A., 'Is Your Oral History Legal and Ethical?' *Oral History Society*, http://www.ohs.org.uk/

# Index

accommodation, 95, 100–5, 143, 146, 166
  national problem of, 16
  quality of, 121–4, 138–9
Adcock, Sir Frank E., 46
Admiralty, 6, 16, 18, 21, 75
Adstock, *see* outstations
Agar, Jon, 12, 161–5
Air Ministry, 16, 18, 22, 142
  intervenes in the management of Hut 3, 33
Aitken, James Macrae, 128
alcohol, 127, 131, 136, 138, 144, 149
  public houses, 131, 141, 144
Alexander, Hugh, 29, 47, 128
  head of Hut 8, 32, 38
  on management, 74
Allen, Joan, 84–5
Americans, 132, 146–7
  at Bletchley Park, *see* Bletchley Park, Americans at
Andrew, Christopher, 49, 50, 54
Aspley Guise, 121, 146
atomic bombs, 2
ATS (Auxiliary Territorial Service), 59, 60, 109
Austin, Monica, 151

Baker, Bob, 90
Barker, Jean, Baroness Trumpington, 3
Batey, Keith, 132–3
Batey, Mavis, 49, 68, 73, 132–3
Battle of the Atlantic, 9, 75
BBC (British Broadcasting Corporation), 155–6
Beaumanor, 72
Bedford, 103, 106, 125
Bennett, Herbert, 148, 151
Birch, Francis (Frank), 64, 85, 97
  on Alan Turing, 32
  on development of GC&CS, 39
  and (German) Naval Section, 21, 32, 35

on Hut 6, 28
internal historian of GC&CS, 20
on recruitment, 47, 48
Blane, Gwen, 149
Blane, Martin, 150
Bletchley, 1, 18, 100–3, 130–1, 140–1
  food at, 120–1
  impact of Bletchley Park on, 141–52, 157, 171
  town-gown divide, 131
  Urban District Council, 100–1, 103, 140, 143
Bletchley Park
  acquired for GC&CS, 8, 17–18
  amenities at, 102, 122, 166
  Americans at, 3, 30, 31
  assembly hall, 128–9, 145
  bombed, 148
  communication links of, 18, 140–2
  coverage by local press, 142–3, 148
  Elmer's School, 26, 103, 143
  estate and buildings, 1–2, 15–16, 18, 19, 26–30, 143, 160
  GC&CS departs, 158–9
  local interest in, 145–50, 156–7, 171–2
  mansion, 1, 18, 26–8, 57, 107, 114, 126
  sunray clinic, 28, 116
  *see also* secrecy; security
Bletchley Park Trust, 13, 42
Blocks, 28–32
  C Block, 83
  E Block, 87–9
  'blue-collar', 80
  *compare* 'white-collar'
Blunt, Anthony, 54
Bomba, 8, 23, 165
Bombe machines, 23–4, 27, 30, 73, 160, 165, 166
  maintenance, 55
  operation of, 76–8, 97–8
  operators, *see* WRNS, Bombe operators
Bourne, Ruth, 60

## 232 Index

Bradshaw, Commander Alan, 52, 86, 96, 111, 116, 134
Brassey, Thomas, 140
Briggs, Asa, Baron Briggs, 3, 43, 74, 75, 125, 131
Brister, B., 134
British Tabulating Machine Company, 23, 83, 84, 163
British Telecom, 159
Brittain, Sir Herbert, 128
*Bucks Standard, The*, 142–3
Budiansky, Stephen, 36
Bundy, William (Bill), 31
Bunn, Assistant Resident Engineer, 95

Cairncross, John, 43, 56, 81–2
 Soviet spy, 82, 94, 95, 170
Calder, Angus, 115, 154
Calvocoressi, Peter, 3, 8, 10, 43, 161
 on Bombe operators, 54–5
 on staff backgrounds, 41–2, 53
Cambridge Five, 54
 *see also* Cairncross, John; Philby, Kim
Cambridge, University of, 43–6, 51, 90
Campbell, Marjory, 130
Campbell, Sir Edward, 142
Cannon, Mavis, 133
catering, 107–15, 119–20, 138
 cafeteria, 107–8
 caterers supplied by SIS, 56
 crises in, 111–15
 crockery, 112–13
 mechanisation of, 114
 mess committee, 111
 number of meals provided, 107–10
 quality of, 119–20
 and rationing, 113–14, 138
 subscriptions unpaid, 108–10
 tea, 113–15
chess, 47, 49, 56, 128
*CHESS* (magazine), 128
Chester, Margaret, 90
Chicheley Hall, 141, 153
Chicksands, 115
Churchill, Sir Winston, 36, 99, 130, 155, 164
Civil Aviation Authority, 159
Clarke, Joan, 90
Clarke, William F. (Nobby), 21, 35

Clothier, Reverend Harry L., 146
Coles, Phyllis, 33, 83
collegiate
 collegiality in cryptanalysis, 74–5, 166–7
 collegiality in translation and analysis, 82
 culture at GC&CS, 34–9, 40–54
Collins, Joan, 132
Colossus Machines, 2, 24, 30, 79–80
 destroyed after the war, 79
 *see also* fish; WRNS
Comerford, Dennis, 152
Cook, Matt, 90
Cook, Robert, 142
Cooper, Josh, 22, 75
Cooper, Sir Stanford, 60
Crawley, Mr, 111
crime, 95–6, 144–5
Croft, John, 120, 130
crossword puzzles, 56, 58
cryptanalysis, 5, 70, 81
 crib, 25, 73–4
 during the First World War, 5–6
 GC&CS and, 6–8, 20–6, 34–8, 63, 72–6, 159, 161
 gender imbalance in, 67
 skills required in, 48–50, 72–6
 working conditions, 74–5
 *see also* collegiate; Enigma; recruitment
Curzon, George, Lord Curzon of Kedleston, 21

Dakin, Alec, 47, 81
Dalley, Miss M., 134
Davis, Jenny, 78
de Grey, Nigel, 19, 78, 94, 147
DeGroot, Gerard, 59, 135
Denniston, Commander Alastair, 22, 51, 100, 105, 111, 112
 on catering problems, 112–13
 and Diplomatic and Commercial sections, 25
 leadership of GC&CS, 6, 17, 42
 on Malcolm Saunders, 31
 replacement of, 20, 34–8, 167
 role in recruitment, 45–7, 50–1, 53, 62–3

Douglas, June, 92, 123, 132
Dukes, Sir Paul, 53–4
Dunlop, Tessa, 10
Dunstable, 125

Eastcote, *see* outstations
Edgerton, David, 44, 164
Edinburgh, University of, 44, 47
Egan, Miss, 51
Enigma, 21, 22–4, 25, 34, 50, 164
  British assessment of, 7–8, 24, 28
  British regularly read, 8–9
  cryptanalysis of, 23–4, 72–6
  development of, 7
  *Enigma* (novel), 120
  flaws in, 73–4
  GC&CS initially fails to break, 7, 23
  Poles break, 7–8
  Shark, 75
  specifications of, 7–8
  ubiquity of, 25
Evacuation
  to Bletchley, 100–1, 103–4, 150–2
  in Britain, 103–4, 150–2
  of GC&CS, 16–17, 141
  of institutions, 16–17, 152–4
Ewing, Sir Alfred, 45–6
Eytan, Walter, 47

factory, 69, 137, 149
  Act, 77
  GC&CS and factory methods, 33, 83, 88, 165, 167
  GC&CS as an 'information factory', 5, 15, 38, 105, 112, 158
  GC&CS as a 'production line', 12, 15, 34, 81, 96–7, 161–2, 163
  work, 11
  of GC&CS similar to, 71, 80
Farrow, Bess, 59
Faulkner, Captain Hubert, 27
Faunch, Mavis, 92, 125
Fenny Stratford, 125, 131, 140–1
Fifth Column, 155–6
Fish, 24, 30
  General Report on Tunny, 59
  Tunny machines, 24, 28
  *see also* Colossus
Flowers, Tommy, 79

Foreign Office
  Electra House, 153
  Political Intelligence Department, 153
  recruitment for GC&CS, 51, 53, 55
  relationship with GC&CS, 18, 19, 21
Fougasse (Cyril Kenneth Bird), 155
France
  cryptanalysts, 8, 23
Freeborn, Frederic, 33, 84–5
  sons of, 33
Froxfield Lodge, 153

Gallehawk, John, 61
Gallilee, Mimi, 57, 127
Gannon, Paul, 80
Gawcott, 153
Gayhurst Manor, *see* outstations
GC&CS (Government Code and Cypher School)
  ad hoc development of, 5, 15–16, 20, 36, 104–5, 111, 112–17, 118, 159–68, 172–3
  amateurism at, 1, 2, 15, 31–9, 53–4, 159
  clerical work at, 17–18, 55, 62–3, 70–1
  disputes within, 31–9
  expands operations, 17–20, 34–8
  founded, 5–6
  hierarchy within, 17, 31–8, 75, 84, 120, 161, 166–7
  'Chiefs' and 'Indians' model, 41–2
  third tier, 54–5
  mandate of, 6
  mechanisation of, 12, 23–4, 26, 64–5, 71–2, 73, 79, 114, 159–68
  organisation of, 17–20, 31–8
  post-war, 158–9
  professionalisation of, 4–5, 31–9, 96, 99, 112, 159–68
  reorganisation of, 19, 34–9, 63, 167
  staff numbers, 3, 17–18, 59, 61–5
  *see also* Bletchley Park; outstations; recruitment; secrecy; sections; security
GCHQ (Government Communications Headquarters), 158

gender, 4, 10, 11–14
  and GC&CS, 41, 50–3, 55, 57–60, 133, 163, 168–71
General Post Office, 55, 79, 86, 163
Germany
  *Abwehr*, 23, 154–5
  interwar status of, 6
  *Luftwaffe*, 20, 22, 37, 72, 148
  Operation Sea Lion, 8
  *Wehrmacht*, 72
  *see also* Enigma
Gibbons, Ron, 83
Glasgow, University of, 43
Golombek, Harry, 47, 128
Graham, Lady Jean, 105
Great Brickhill, 123
Grey, Christopher, 13, 31, 35, 53, 58, 88, 165, 167

Hankey, Maurice, 1st Baron Hankey, 56
Hanslope Park, 141
Harding, Ann, 122
Harris, Robert, 120
Harrison, Colonel L. W., 136, 138
Hayward, Gil, 47
health, 52, 78–9, 82, 86–9, 120, 136
  medical facilities at GC&CS, 28, 115–16
  Ministry of, 136
Hellier, Ron, 141, 144, 145, 148, 150, 151
Hill, Marion, 84, 134, 149
Hinsley, Lady Hilary, 133
Hinsley, Sir Harry, 46, 132, 133
  official historian of British wartime intelligence, 2, 9
Hodges, Andrew, 49
Hogarth, James, 58
Hollerith, Hermann, 29
Hollerith machines, *see* tabulated index
Holliday, Mrs L.P., 123
Home Guard, 145
Huts, 26–30
  Hut 1, 115
  Hut 2, 126
  Hut 3, 22, 31, 32–3, 37–9, 41–2, 43, 82, 95
  Hut 4, 81–2, 133, 161

Hut 6, 22, 32, 33, 44, 72, 73, 90, 133
Hut 8, 32, 33, 72, 73–5, 133, 161

*Imitation Game, The*, 70
Italy, 21

Japan, 6, 21
  Imperial Japanese Navy, 20
Jenkins, Roy, Baron Jenkins of Hillhead, 3–4
Johnson, Kerry, 61
Joint Management Committee, 111
Jones, Mr., 101
Jones, Nurse A. M. C., 116
Jones, Sir Eric Malcolm, 43, 47–8
  and Hut 3, 22, 31, 32–3, 37–8, 167

Knightley, Phillip, 54
Knox, Dillwyn, 23, 24, 49, 68, 74, 133, 161
  dispute with Denniston, 34–5
  education, 49
  illness, 36

Lacoste, Gerald, 155
Lancaster, Sheila, 131–2
Lawn, Oliver, 127, 132, 133
Lawn, Sheila, 127, 132
Lawry, Beryl, 123, 127
leave, 125–6
  *see also* recreation
Letchworth, 23
Lewis-Smith, Anne, 124, 135
linguists, *see* translators
London, 125, 132
  Diplomatic and Commercial sections return to, 25, 34, 100
  GC&CS evacuates from, *see* evacuation, of GC&CS
  GC&CS retains offices in, 17
  SIS returns to, 27
  University of, 43–5, 46
Lorenz machines, *see* Fish
Low, D.C., 143
*Luftwaffe*, *see* Germany, *Luftwaffe*
Luke, Doreen, 128

McKay, Sinclair, 127, 130, 132, 134–5
McKibbin, Ross, 130

McLaine, Ian, 155
McPearson, Irene, 123
McVittie, George, 29
Mahon, A. Patrick, 29
Manchester University, 3
Mandler, Peter, 54
Marconi, Guglielmo, 5
Marr, Joan, 132
Martin, Margaret, 84
Marwick, Arthur, 11
Marylands, 153
Mass Observation, 106
  *War Factory*, 137
Meade, Mrs, 115–16
Melrose, Captain (later Major), 28, 88
Menzies, Sir Stuart, 37, 111, 128
Meteorological Office, 25
MI1B (Military Intelligence 1B), 6, 40, 162
MI5, *see* Security Service
MI6, *see* Secret Intelligence Service
Millward, William, 56
Milner-Barry, Sir Stuart, 22, 28, 47, 128
Ministry of Aircraft Production, 101
Ministry of Economic Warfare, 42
Ministry of Food, 113
Ministry of Information, 155
Ministry of Labour and National Service, 12, 52, 69, 103–4
Montagu, Ewan, 10, 147
Moor, Barbara, 60
morale, 107, 112, 118–19, 128–9
  in Britain, 154–5
  of cryptanalysts, 32, 74–5
  of junior staff, 77, 78, 87–9, 97–8
Morton, Rosemary, 81–2
Muggeridge, Malcolm, 129
Munro, Wendy, 127, 130

NAAFI, 27
Naval Intelligence Division 25, *see* Room 40
Newman, Max, 3, 24
Newport Pagnell, 153
Nicholas, Siân, 156
*North Bucks Times and County Observer*, 142, 151
Noskwith, Rolf, 74–5
Nuremberg Trials, 3

outstations, 3, 17, 18, 24, 30, 102, 124, 160
Eastcote, 158
staff numbers at, 159
Stanmore, 78, 146–7
Wavendon, 77
Oxford, University of, 42–5, 47, 50, 90, 128

Page, Gwendoline, 60
Pain, Mary, 68, 85–7, 89
Paris, University of, 43
Parker, H.M.D., 104
pay, 65–6, 84, 108–9, 138
  and gender discrepancy, 52–3
  in the inter-war period, 46
  of women in the WAAF and WRNS, 66
Payne, Diana, 76, 77, 78–9
Peacock, G.E., 101
Perkins, N. Anthony, 128
Persival, Elizabeth Laura, 123–4, 130–1
Philby, Kim, 54
phoney war, 21
Pidgeon, Geoffrey, 139
Plumb, Sir John H., 3
Poland
  cryptanalytic work of, 7–8, 23
Powell, Baden, 149
Price, Thomas J., 54
propaganda, 93, 129, 153, 155–6
*Punch*, 155
Putt, Gorley, 132–3

radio, 5, 155–6
  volume of Axis radio traffic, 62
Rae, Mary, 97–8
RAF (Royal Air Force), 37, 124, 149
  *see also* WAAF
Ratcliff, R.A., 12–13, 25–6, 91
recreation, 137–8, 145
  Bletchley Park Recreational Club, 27, 126–8
  cinema, 128–9, 131, 137, 155
  dancing, 127, 129, 131–2, 133, 144, 146
  highbrow, 127, 137
  music, 127, 129, 137, 145
  sport, 54, 127–8, 129–30
  theatre, 125, 127, 130

recruitment
 and academic disciplines, 48–50
 and 'character', 53–4
 civil service as a source of, 53, 55, 56
 of cryptanalysts and translators,
   40–54
 and education, 41–54, 57–8, 59–60,
   159, 168–71
 interviews, 46, 55–6, 57
 in the interwar period, 17–19, 45–7,
   49–50, 51
 of junior staff, 54–60
 of managers, 41–3, 45–50
 and social class, 41, 53–4, 55, 57–60
 vetting, 46–7
 of women, 50–3, 55, 57–60, 66–9,
   96–7
Rejewski, Marion, 8
Ridley, Captain W.H.W., 111, 113
Robb, Nesca, 52
'Robinson' machine, 79
romance, 132–6
Room 40, 35, 40, 162
 connections to Oxbridge, 45–6, 159
 view of mathematicians, 49
Rowsbotham, Lady, 105
Royal Corps of Signals, 55, 75
Royal Navy, 9, 60, 124
 *see also* WRNS
Różycki, Jerzy, 8
Russell, Herbrand, Duke of Bedford,
   102, 141, 153
Russell, Mary, Duchess of Bedford, 153

Saunders, Malcolm, 22, 31, 32, 37–8,
   167
Scherbius, Arthur, 7
secrecy
 at Bletchley Park, 2–3, 128, 141–3,
   145–8
 of GC&CS, 2–3, 10, 78–9, 156
 impact on staff of, 94
 Official Secrets Acts, 91, 92–3
 in recruitment practises, 59
 and social class and gender, 4, 53–4,
   77–8
 Ultra, 8, 10, 13, 22, 53, 91–5, 143
 *see also* security; Ultra intelligence
sections, 19–29
 Air Section, 41–2

Communications Section, 71–2
Cypher Office, 30, 86, 87–90
Diplomatic and Commercial
   sections, 100
Italian sections, 21, 29
Japanese sections, 26, 29, 30
Naval Section, 35, 144
Tabulating Section, 33, 82–5
Transport Section, 105–7, 144, 166
*see also* Bletchley Park; Blocks;
   GC&CS; Huts
security
 breaches, 92–5, 145–8, 156
 of British ciphers, 6
 compartmentalisation of
   knowledge, 19–20, 33, 77–8,
   92, 162
 guards, 91–2
 importance of trust in, 4, 12, 42, 47,
   77–9, 93, 170
 measures, 22, 93–5
 officers, 94
 passes, 92
 passwords, 91
Security Service (MI5), 54, 154
sexuality
 contraception, 135
 homosexuality, 89–90, 122
 and moral panic, 135–6
 pregnancy, 134
 premarital intercourse, 134–6
shift system, 52, 59, 76, 108, 124
 and catering arrangements, 108
 changed to accommodate romance,
   133
 and exhaustion, 82, 86
 and health, 78–9, 88, 116
 and recreation, 125–6
 visibility to local residents, 144–5
Siemens & Halske T52, *see* Fish
Siemens T42, *see* Fish
Signals Intelligence, 2
Sinclair, Admiral Sir Hugh, 17, 45, 107
SIS (Secret Intelligence Service, MI6),
   9, 17, 18, 37, 152
 acquires Bletchley Park, 26
 departs Bletchley Park, 27, 126
 place on the Bletchley Park Joint
   Management Committee, 111
 qualities in good agents, 53–4

SIS (Secret Intelligence Service, MI6)
– *Continued*
  radio communications, 27, 153
  role in distribution of Ultra, 22–3
  supplies staff and resources to GC&CS, 56–7, 91, 105
Skalak, Lieutenant, 146–7
Smith, Don, 55–5
Smith, Michael, 10
social class, 4, 10, 11–14, 130
  GC&CS and, 80, 84–5, 127, 168–71
  recruitment and, *see* recruitment, and social class
SOE (Special Operations Executive), 18, 152–3
Political Warfare Executive, 153
Sorbonne, the, 43
Sou, Dianne, 105
Soviet Union, 6, 7, 54
  infiltrates Bletchley Park, *see* Cairncross, John, Soviet spy
Spain, 21
*Spectator, The*, 52, 136
Staniford, Ron, 148
Stanmore, *see* outstations
Steeple Claydon, 102, 103, 106
Stephenson, Robert, 140
Stratford-upon-Avon, 125
Sturgeon, *see* Fish
suicide, 75, 90
Summerfield, Penny, 11–12, 68, 78, 80, 87
Supermarine, 16
Swatton, H.L., 55–6, 86

tabulated index, 15, 26, 29, 33, 82–3, 84, 160
  working conditions of operators, 83–4
  *see also* sections, Tabulating Section
Taylor, John, A., 148, 150, 151
Taylor, Telford, 3
teleprinter, 18, 24, 28, 30, 71, 73, 79, 81, 133, 160
  operators of, *see* WAAF, teleprinter operators
Tester, Ralf, 24
Thirsk, James (Jimmy), 56, 72, 104
  on accommodation, 121, 123–4
  on 'careless talk', 145, 156
  on catering, 120
  on leisure, 125
  marriage of, 132
Thirsk, Joan, 44, 60, 132
Thomas, Edward, 82
Thompson, Jean, 79
Thrasher, *see* Fish
Tiltman, Brigadier John, 21–2, 24, 36, 46
Titmuss, Richard, 11
tradesmen, 57, 144
traffic analysis, 72, 161
translators
  number of, 63
  recruitment of, *see* recruitment, of cryptanalysts and translators
  skills required, 81–2
  translation and analysis, 4, 20–3, 27–9, 161
  working conditions of, 80–2
transportation, 4, 144, 148, 165–6
  accidents, 115
  car pool, 100
  dispatch riders, 71, 105, 144
  driver numbers, 56, 105–6, 158
  hitchhiking, 125–6, 171
  importance to Bletchley, 18, 140–1, 156
  national problem of, 106–7
Travis, Commander Sir Edward, 116
  appointment as head of GC&CS, 20, 25, 34, 38, 167
  background of, 42–3
  and Hut 3 crisis, 37
  on letter to Churchill, 36
  on security breaches, 92
  on staff welfare, 136–7
Treasury, 18, 62, 63
Tunny, *see* Fish
Turing, Alan, 3, 23, 32, 70, 120, 163, 167
  recruitment of, 49
  replacement as leader of Hut, 8, 29, 32, 38, 167
  sexuality, 90
Twinn, Peter, 49
Type-x, 23, 30, 33, 68, 72, 160
  maintenance, 55, 56
  operators, 28, 85–9, 97, 166
  poor operating conditions of, 85–9

U-boats, 9, 23, 26, 82
  ciphers, 9
Ultra intelligence, 2, 8
  Boniface, 22
  initially under valued, 8, 159
  revealed to the public, 9–10, 13, 70
  secrecy of, *see* secrecy, Ultra
  significance of, 2–3, 8–9
uniform (military), 75, 77, 78, 80, 136, 147, 166
  common in Bletchley, 152
University of Poznań, 7

Valentine, Jean, 120
Vickers, 16
Vincent, E.R.P., 49
Vivian, Colonel Valentine, 94
Vivian, M.P., 122–3, 124

WAAF (Women's Auxiliary Air Force), 55, 58, 59, 68, 95, 109
  numbers employed by GC&CS, 64–5
  teleprinter operators, 55, 58, 71, 81
  Type-x operators, *see* Type-x, operators
War Office, 6, 16–17, 18, 21–2, 40, 142
  dispute with GC&CS, 36–7
Watkins, Gwen, 120
Watkins, Vernon, 3
Watson, Bob, 57, 144
Wavendon House, *see* outstations
Wavendon Towers, 154
Welchman, Gordon, 28, 32, 75–6, 86, 120–1, 167
  background of, 49
  Bombe machine improved by, 23, 163
  founder of Hut, 6, 22
  managerial techniques of, 33, 74
  on mechanisation, 173
Whaddon Hall, 27, 141, 153
White, Alfred, 88–9
'white-collar', 60, 80, 84, 137
  *compare* 'blue-collar'
Whiteley, John, 142
Wilkinson, Lancelot Patrick, 46
Wilson, Angus, 3, 75, 90, 149
Winterbotham, Frederick, 9–10, 22, 54, 70, 143

wireless telegraphy (W/T), 5
Witherbird, Ann, 105–6, 132
Witherbird, Arthur, 132
Woburn, 141
Woburn Abbey, 104, 124, 132, 141, 153, 154
  *see also* accommodation
Wolverton, 131
Wolynskyj, Alice, 60, 131
women
  and education in Britain, 51
  and GC&CS, 3–4, 11, 33, 44, 46, 55, 163
  under represented in senior roles, 50–1
  machine operators, 76–80, 84–5
  *see also* tabulated index, working conditions of operators; Type-x, operators; WAAF, teleprinter operators; WRNS, Colossus operators
  and MI1B, 6
  number employed by GC&CS, 62–5
  role in British war effort, 11–14, 67–9, 169–70
  *see also* ATS; pay; recruitment; WAAF; WRNS
WRNS (Women's Royal Naval Service), 55, 102, 109, 146–7
  Bombe operators, 54, 55, 58–9, 60, 64, 78
  Colossus operators, 33, 59, 79–80, 97, 169
  numbers of wrens employed by GC&CS, 64–5
  paternalism, 131
  promotion prospects at Bletchley Park, 59
  wrens working conditions, 77–80
  *see also* pay; recruitment; women
Wylie, Shaun, 75

Y Service, 5, 17, 18, 29, 37, 64, 71–2, 75, 105, 139, 144, 161
Young, Irene, 10, 44, 47, 119, 121

Zimmerman Telegram, 6
Zweiniger-Bargielowska, Ina, 138
Zygalski, Henryk, 8